VIETNAM STUDIES

RIVERINE OPERATIONS 1966-1969

Major General William B. Fulton

DEPARTMENT OF THE ARMY

WASHINGTON, D.C., 1985

Vietnam Studies Riverine Operations 1966 – 1969
By Major General William B. Fulton, Lt. General U.S. Army (Ret).

Reprinted by the Mobile Riverine Force Association
with Acclaim Press

In Dedication and Honor to all that served In-Country Vietnam, and who have sacrificed so much for their country and fellow Vietnam Veterans.
Especially all those who fought on the Rivers and Canals, Jungles and Rice Paddies of Vietnam.
Praise is hardly enough.

Remembering Vietnam
Over 2.6 Million Served
Over 58.000 Gave Their Lives
They Fought For Freedom
They Fought With Honor
In The End They Fought For One Another.

AP™

Acclaim Press
P.O. Box 238
Morley, MO 63767
(573) 262-2121

Library of Congress Control No.: 72600370
ISBN: 0-9773198-4-9

Third Printing: 2006
First Printing: 1973

Printed in the United States of America

Foreword

The United States Army has met an unusually complex challenge in Southeast Asia. In conjunction with the other services, the Army has fought in support of a national policy of assisting an emerging nation to develop governmental processes of its own choosing, free of outside coercion. In addition to the usual problems of waging armed conflict, the assignment in Southeast Asia has required superimposing the immensely sophisticated tasks of a modern army upon an underdeveloped environment and adapting them to demands covering a wide spectrum. These involved helping to fulfill the basic needs of an agrarian population, dealing with the frustrations of antiguerrilla operations, and conducting conventional campaigns against well-trained and determined regular units.

As this assignment nears an end, the U.S. Army must prepare for other challenges that may lie ahead. While cognizant that history never repeats itself exactly and that no army ever profited from trying to meet a new challenge in terms of the old one, the Army nevertheless stands to benefit immensely from a study of its experience, its shortcomings no less than its achievements.

Aware that some years must elapse before the official histories will provide a detailed and objective analysis of the experience in Southeast Asia, we have sought a forum whereby some of the more salient aspects of that experience can be made available now. At the request of the Chief of Staff, a representative group of senior officers who served in important posts in Vietnam and who still carry a heavy burden of day-to-day responsibilities has prepared a series of monographs. These studies should be of great value in helping the Army develop future operational concepts while at the same time contributing to the historical record and providing the American public with an interim report on the performance of men and officers who have responded, as others have through our history, to exacting and trying demands.

All monographs in the series are based primarily on official records, with additional material from published and unpublished secondary works, from debriefing reports and interviews with key participants, and from the personal experience of the author. To facilitate security clearance, annotation and detailed bibliography have been omitted from the published version; a fully documented account with bibliography is filed with the Office of the Chief of Military History.

The author of this monograph, Major General William B. Fulton, was intimately involved in the early development of the riverine warfare concept as commander of the 2d Brigade, 9th Infantry Division, which arrived in Vietnam in January 1967 and immediately began combat operations in the Mekong Delta. In March the brigade moved into Dong Tam, the base created by dredging sand from the bottom of an arm of the Mekong River. In early June the brigade teamed with Navy Task Force 117 to form the Mobile Riverine Force. During World War II General Fulton fought in Italy and during the Korean War served on the staff of Army Forces Far East Advance. He is presently the Director of Doctrine Evaluation and Command Systems in the Office of the Assistant Chief of Staff for Force Development and is also Systems Manager for Surveillance, Target Acquisition, and Night Observation Systems.

Washington, D.C.
15 August 1972

VERNE L. BOWERS
Major General, USA
The Adjutant General

Preface

This monograph describes U.S. Army Riverine planning and operations in the Republic of Vietnam during the years 1966 through 1969. Since the personal experience of the author was with preparations for riverine operations and the initial operations themselves, emphasis has been placed on these activities through early 1968. In summarizing operations conducted in the balance of the three-year period, particular attention has been called to significant trends or changes in riverine operations in Vietnam, a co-operative enterprise of the U.S. Army and the U.S. Navy.

Looking back from the vantage point of early 1972, this study attempts to reconstruct the events and describe the situation as it was from 1966 through 1969, using official records, reports, and personal interviews.

The author is indebted especially to the officers of the 9th Infantry Division who helped in the research and writing of this monograph. Major Johnnie H. Corns was initially the intelligence officer and later the operations officer of the 2d Brigade during 1966 and 1967. His research, writing, and continuous editing have been indispensable in preparation of this study. Colonel Lucien E. Bolduc, Jr., commanded the 3d Battalion, 47th Infantry, and was later operations officer of the 9th Infantry Division during preparations for and initial conduct of riverine operations. His contributions in preparing the 2d Brigade of the Old Reliables for these operations and in preparing this manuscript are fully appreciated. Colonel Thomas C. Loper, 9th Infantry Division Engineer in 1967 and 1968, contributed both in the enactment and the recording of the riverine story. The author also wishes to acknowledge the typing assistance of Miss Ann M. Faherty and Miss Judith A. Secondo, who patiently saw the manuscript through several drafts.

Washington, D.C.
15 August 1972

WILLIAM B. FULTON
Major General, U.S. Army

We started on the project in December 2005. In January 2006, we lost the author of the book, Lt. General William B. Fulton. General Fulton was a dedicated member of the Mobile Riverine Force Association—a Soldier's Soldier who fought with honor, pride and distinction in three wars. He was truly an Officer and a Gentleman. We, the association, hope you enjoy reading the *Vietnam Studies Riverine Operations 1966-1969* and while doing so remember all our Brothers we lost in Vietnam and those who we've lost in past and recent years. Like General Fulton, they are all America's heroes and will be missed by all. The world is a better place because of heroes such as these Men of Vietnam. They will never be forgotten. To all our Army and Navy brothers, God bless each and every one of you, and thank you for your service (Keep marching—Keep marching).

Albert B. Moore, President MRFA
Roy Moseman, Vice President MRFA

Lt. General William B. Fulton

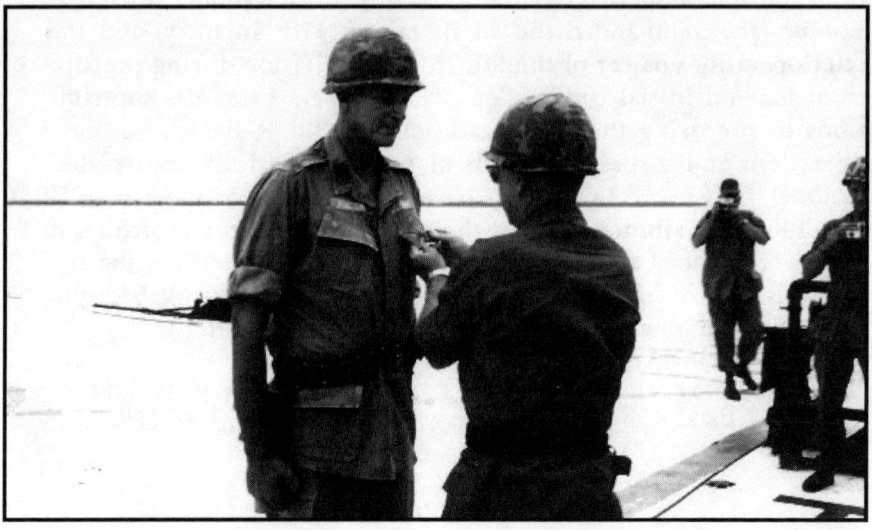

Brig. General Fulton being awarded a medal on board the USS Benewah APB-35, *September 1967.*

Contents

Charts

Diagrams

Tables

Maps

Illustrations

Page

All illustrations are from Department of Defense files.

RIVERINE OPERATIONS, 1966-1969

CHAPTER I

Background

During 1965 and 1966 when the possibility of creating a U.S. riverine force for operations in the Mekong Delta was being discussed, there were three basic considerations that weighed heavily in favor of the force: a tradition of past American success in riverine operations, particularly Union operations in the Mississippi basin during the Civil War; the success more recently achieved by the French in riverine operations during the Indochina War under conditions that appeared to have changed little during the years that had intervened; and, most important, a situation in the Mekong Delta that seemed ripe for exploitation by a riverine force.

Previous American Experience

American forces conducted riverine operations as early as the Revolutionary War and made use of them frequently during the century that followed. In each case, the operations were part of a larger land campaign. While they were not always tactically successful, they usually made a substantial contribution to the success of the campaign.

In 1775, on the heels of the battles of Lexington and Concord, both the Americans and British sought to gain control of the strategic Hudson River-Lake Champlain-St. Lawrence River waterway system connecting New York and the British centers in Canada. Forces under Colonels Benedict Arnold and Ethan Allan seized the British forts at Ticonderoga and Crown Point; Arnold then armed a captured schooner and pressed north along Lake Champlain to attack the British base at St. Johns on the Richelieu River above the lake. In a daring surprise attack, he captured or destroyed a large number of boats and considerable amounts of supplies and equipment before returning to Lake Champlain. By means of this lake and river operation, Arnold effectually blunted the British ability to counterattack.

Pressing their advantage, the Americans then undertook an invasion of Canada, with one line of advance up the lake and river chain. Their attack on Quebec was repulsed, and by the spring of 1776 the British, heavily reinforced from the home country, regained the offensive. The British began to assemble a fleet at St. Johns. Some of the larger vessels were actually built in England, knocked down for shipment across the ocean, and reassembled at St. Johns. Spurred on by Benedict Arnold, the Americans sought to keep pace with the British at their own Skenesborough shipyard, near the southern end of Lake Champlain. On 11 October 1776 the Americans, with a fleet of fifteen boats hastily constructed of green timber and manned by a scratch force of backwoodsmen and recruits from the seacoast—"the flotsam of the waterfront and the jetsam from the taverns"—engaged the formidable British force of twenty-nine vessels at Valcour Island, just north of Ticonderoga. The poorly organized and ill-equipped American force lost its ships one by one, and the Americans were forced to retire to Crown Point. The British tenaciously pursued and drove Arnold's force out of Crown Point into Ticonderoga at the southern tip of the lake. Although Arnold had lost the engagement, his small flotilla delayed the British advance until the following year, when Major General John Burgoyne attempted a thrust southward to cut the colonies in two and was defeated at Saratoga.

Some thirty-five years later in the War of 1812, U.S. forces again fought the British on American waterways. In 1813 Commodore Oliver H. Perry assembled a fleet on Lake Erie to counter the British threat from Canada, and by defeating the British fleet in a series of engagements gained control of the Great Lakes, permitting a subsequent American advance into Canada. During the next year the British made three major attempts to exploit inland waterways: one from Chesapeake Bay against Washington, a second overland from Canada toward New York, and a third from the Gulf of Mexico against New Orleans. Each British effort was met by an opposing American riverine force. In August 1814 British forces pushing up the Chesapeake were met by a force under Commodore Joshua Barney. After several engagements in which Barney's initiative and dogged persistence frustrated the British advance, the British disembarked at Benedict, Maryland, and then marched the thirty-one miles to Washington, where they burned the public buildings. The British drive down Lake Champlain was blocked in September 1814 by American Commodore Thomas Macdonough in the river battle of Plattsburg.

A few months later, in December 1814, the British moved against New Orleans, connected to the Gulf of Mexico by the lakes and bayous of the Mississippi Delta. While the British assembled forces off the coast, American Commodore Daniel T. Patterson prepared his river forces to oppose the attack. He placed obstructions in the waterways leading directly to the city, and with five gunboats and two tenders met the advancing British forces on Lake Borgne. Outgunned and outmaneuvered, Patterson was thoroughly beaten. Despite his defeat he continued with the remnants of his shallow-water navy to oppose the British advance with skill and energy, thus gaining enough time to permit General Andrew Jackson to ready the defenses of the city. Then Patterson, with the *Carolina* and the *Louisiana,* his two largest ships, deployed on the river, joined forces with Jackson in a defense that resulted in ultimate defeat of the British.

From 1835 to 1842 Army and Navy forces fought in the Florida Everglades against the Creeks and the Seminoles in a particularly frustrating and indecisive campaign. To navigate the inlets along the coast as well as the waterway mazes of the swamps, a mosquito fleet of some 150 craft—schooners, flat-bottomed boats, bateaux, and canoes—was assembled and manned by soldiers, sailors, and marines. Operating in conjunction with Army Colonel William J. Worth, Navy Lieutenant John T. McLaughlin transported men, equipment, and supplies, patrolled waterways, and conducted raids. Because of its mobility and striking power, the riverine force, well adapted to conditions in the Everglades, was able to reduce the Indian threat.

A few years later during the War with Mexico, 1846–1848, the American Navy conducted two river raids which, although not particularly decisive in themselves, made a strong impression on one of the younger participants, Lieutenant David Dixon Porter, who was to use the experience in another war. The raids were conducted some seventy-five miles up the Tabasco River against San Juan Bautista, an enemy crossing point and operating base. Commodore Matthew C. Perry utilized steamers to tow two sailing schooners and smaller craft up the winding river against a strong current. On his first raid he bombarded the city without debarking any troops. On his second, he landed a force of 2,500 sailors and marines, which had been formed into infantry and artillery divisions, and assaulted the city from the shore, supported by fire from the force afloat that included four steam warships, six schooners, some "bomb rigs" that mounted mortars, and a number of ships' boats. While Perry was ashore leading his men, the ships and boats were left under the command of Lieutenant Porter.

Extensive riverine operations were conducted during the Civil War. Along the coasts of the Confederacy, the Union launched joint Army-Navy expeditions that gradually gained footholds in the vicinity of Mobile, Alabama; Savannah, Georgia; Charleston, South Carolina; and Wilmington, North Carolina. At the same time there was a concerted Army-Navy effort to control the inland waterways of the Mississippi basin and thus cut the Confederacy in two. At the outset, Union Commodore John D. Rodgers assembled a fleet of steam-powered, shallow-draft vessels at Cairo, Illinois, where the Ohio River flows into the Mississippi. The gunboats were well armed and well armored, could carry a dozen large guns—8-inch, 32- and 42-pounders—and ranged up to a 50-foot beam and a length of 175 feet, with ironclad, sloping superstructures. Rodgers used his craft to patrol and gather intelligence of the Confederate forces that lay within striking distance. Relying in part on the intelligence Rodgers obtained, Brigadier General Ulysses S. Grant decided to move against Confederate forces at Belmont, Missouri. Rodgers transported 3,000 of Grant's men and provided fire support for the operation. When substantial Confederate reinforcements arrived unexpectedly to bolster the garrison at Belmont, Grant prudently re-embarked and withdrew, demonstrating that river craft may be as useful in a withdrawal as they are in an advance.

Soon afterward, Commodore Andrew H. Foote, who succeeded Rodgers, and General Grant requested permission to undertake offensive river operations. In January 1862 their plan for a joint Army-Navy operation was approved. In February the combined forces moved up the Ohio River and then the Tennessee River to attack Confederate Fort Henry. The force used regular civilian transports as well as the specialized shallow-water gunboats. Grant landed his men five miles above the fort and advanced overland. The gunboats began the attack alone, firing as they approached the fort. They closed to point-blank range, silenced the Confederate shore batteries, and unexpectedly forced the surrender of the garrison. It was a riverine victory for Union forces, and the news was welcome in Washington, where it contrasted dramatically with disappointing reports from other areas.

The victory at Fort Henry was followed by Navy gunboat raids up the Tennessee River. The raids ranged across the entire state of Tennessee, probed into Mississippi, and even pushed into Alabama as far as Muscle Shoals. At the same time, General Grant and Commodore Foote moved against nearby Confederate Fort Donelson, which lay on the Cumberland River and covered the land routes to Nashville. Grant moved most of his troops directly overland, while Foote descended the Cumberland to the Ohio, then sailed up the Tennessee. The battle began when Foote moved his gunboats against the Confederate shore batteries. Heavy fire from the shore soon forced the gunboats to withdraw; each of the six ships took twenty or more hits and two ships were put out of action. Casualties were high and included Commodore Foote, who was seriously wounded. Later, under renewed Union attack from river and shore, the Confederate garrison surrendered. While Fort Henry was essentially a Navy victory, it was a combination of Army and Navy forces that proved decisive at Fort Donelson.

Shortly thereafter the Union Navy in the Gulf of Mexico moved inland against New Orleans. Forces under Admiral David Glasgow Farragut first crossed the sandbar at the mouth of the Mississippi, then rerigged ships for river operations. Farragut directed a five-day bombardment by a specially prepared mortar flotilla to soften up the Confederate defenses along the river. He assembled his force and in a daring night maneuver ran the gauntlet of forts and Confederate warships that blocked the way. Once he had penetrated the Confederate defenses, he moved on unopposed to his objective. With a force of less than 3,500 men, he succeeded in capturing the South's largest city.

Although he had achieved success, Farragut was nonetheless impressed by some of the difficulties which his deepwater force had encountered on the river. He wrote, "Fighting is nothing to the evils of the river—getting on shore, running afoul of one another, losing anchors, etc."

A few weeks later, in June 1862, Farragut moved up the Mississippi and tried to seize Vicksburg but was repulsed. He succeeded, however, in running by the Confederate fortifications to link up with Navy forces under Captain Charles Henry Davis, who had relieved Commodore Foote. The combined flotillas then operated in support of Grant. Confederate resistance at Vicksburg prevented further passage along the river and delayed Union attempts to split the Confederacy. It was nearly a year before Grant could force the surrender of the city. During Farragut's June operations, Union Navy forces in the vicinity of Vicksburg were under the command of Rear Admiral David Dixon Porter, who had earlier taken part in river warfare in Mexico. Throughout the campaign of the lower Mississippi, the Confederates skillfully used water mines—torpedoes, as they were called—to counter the riverine threat. Some forty Union craft fell victim to these torpedoes. Confederate snipers and shore batteries as well as such navigational difficulties as shallow water and tree stumps also helped to frustrate Union attempts on Vicksburg.

In the end, Navy forces from the north succeeded in running the gauntlet at Vicksburg. Grant's brilliant maneuvering first to the south and then to the east of the fortress defeated the Confederate forces that might have come to the relief of Vicksburg, permitting Grant to bring about its surrender. The fall of Vicksburg split the Confederacy in two: Union control of the Mississippi, the Ohio, the Cumberland, and the Tennessee proved decisive in the final Union victory.

For many years after the Civil War the United States had little occasion to engage in riverine warfare. Perhaps the most notable U.S. river operation in the early twentieth century was the American Navy's patrol of the Yangtze River after the Boxer Rebellion in China. During the twenties and thirties a flotilla of U.S. Navy gunboats known as the Yangtze Patrol maneuvered along some 1,500 miles of meandering river, faced with occasionally swift currents, and with water levels that were subject to sudden and violent change—up to twenty-four feet in twenty-four hours. In addition to the difficulties of navigating the Yangtze, the patrol had to cope with snipers, ambushes rigged by warlords, and the necessity to conduct rescue missions that sometimes required the use of landing parties. During World War II American forces were used in some operations that might be termed riverine warfare, but it was not until the Vietnam War that the United States organized a complicated river flotilla to fight on inland waterways.

French River Warfare in Indochina, 1945–1954

During the nineteenth century the French had used the waterways of the Mekong and the Red River Deltas in their conquest of Indochina. When French forces returned to Vietnam in 1945 after World War II in an attempt to regain control of the country, they used conventional military tactics at first and such riverine operations as were launched were characterized by improvisation, but in the next nine years the French developed a remarkable riverine force.

In the north, in Tonkin, where most of the fighting occurred, the delta formed by the combined Red, Black, and Clear Rivers, and in the south, in Cochinchina, the delta formed by the Mekong, the Bassac, the Dong Nai, the Saigon, and the Vam Co rivers

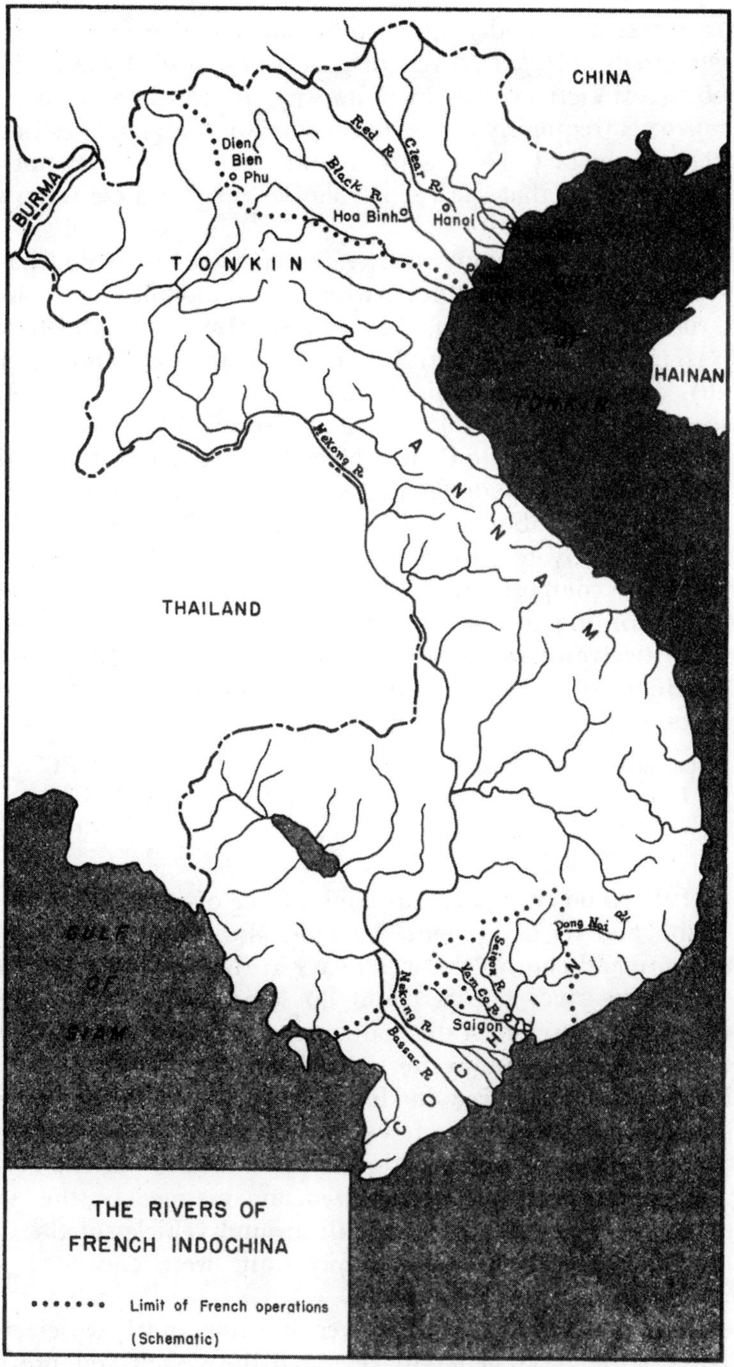
CHINA
Dien Bien Phu
Red R.
Clear R.
Black R.
Hoa Binh
Hanoi
BURMA
TONKIN
HAINAN
Mekong R.
ANNAM
THAILAND
Dong Nai R.
Saigon R.
Vam Co R.
Saigon
Mekong R.
Bassac R.
COCHIN
GULF OF SIAM
THE RIVERS OF FRENCH INDOCHINA
Limit of French operations (Schematic)

MAP 1

offered mazes of meandering streams connected here and there by straight canals. (*Map 1*) Even in peacetime most of the traffic in the north of Vietnam was by waterway. In wartime, with roads and railroads frequently cut by enemy action, the French estimated that 90 percent of traffic was by inland waterway. It was not surprising, therefore, that the French should turn to these waterways for military operations.

The French started out with craft that were available locally—native or left by the Japanese—which they modified with armor and armament. In addition, they received from the British some LCI's (landing craft, infantry) and a few LCA's (landing craft, assault) and LCT's (landing craft, tank). The French Army created a number of river flotillas that were used for transport and river patrols. By 1946 the French Navy had organized river flotillas and in 1947 these were designated *divisions navales d'assaut* (naval assault divisions), abbreviated to Dinassauts. The divisions were organized initially to provide transport with fire support escort. In time their composition changed, and one flotilla differed from another according to the area in which it operated. Each flotilla had from twelve to eighteen craft, ranging from LCVP's (landing craft, vehicle or personnel) to LSSL's (landing ships, support, large), and contained at least these elements:

Command and fire support	1 LCI or LSSL
Transport	1 LCT
Landing and support	2 LCM's and 4 LCVP's
Patrol and Liaison	1 harbor patrol boat

The flotilla could transport and land a force of approximately battalion size and its equipment. It could also support the landing force by fire and control the waterways in the vicinity of the landing area. The river flotilla could do some patrolling, and even some raiding in support of the main operating force ashore. Toward the end of the campaign as the Viet Minh massed their forces, the single river flotilla proved inadequate and the French organized river task forces consisting of several flotillas, reinforced by additional troop transports. In addition to these naval units, the French had other specialized units, organized and manned by the Army for river operations; some were built around vehicles of the Crab and Alligator type and some supply units were equipped with LCM's (landing craft, mechanized).

Command relations between French Army and Navy elements varied, but the Navy generally operated the vessels and provided support to Army operations. In Tonkin the Commander, River

Forces, maintained close liaison with Headquarters, Ground Forces, North Vietnam, and to all intents and purposes the four flotillas in the area operated in support of the Army. In Cochinchina the River Forces Command provided support to the Commanding General, Ground Forces, South Vietnam, as agreed with the Commander, French Naval Forces, Indochina.

These arrangements appeared to the French commanders, even in retrospect, to have been satisfactory, although there seems to have been some Army complaint that there were not enough landing craft, and some Navy complaint that the local Navy commanders had no organic infantry capable of defending Navy bases, either fixed or afloat. The naval command was responsible for all river forces regardless of their parent service. Thus, French Army troops transported by a Dinassaut were under operational control of the French Navy. Co-ordination with the Army was achieved through river posts, which maintained direct liaison with ground force commanders in their areas. A continuing difficulty was the problem of Dinassaut base defense. Generally, each Dinassaut had a small Navy Commando detachment or an Army light support company attached to it. But the Dinassaut did not have regular battalion-strength landing forces permanently assigned; these would have permitted greater autonomy and better control of an area between major operations. The infantry landing forces, when made available by the Army for a particular operation, usually lacked training or experience in river warfare.

A river assault flotilla generally deployed in column. Leading the column was an opening group of minesweepers and a guide for navigation, followed by a fire support ship. Next came the troop transports and, bringing up the rear, the command and support vessels. (*Diagram 1*) When a flotilla was attacked it usually attempted to force passage, using what the French called "the ball of fire," or heaviest possible volume of immediate fire directed at enemy positions on shore. One theory held that when there was reason to suspect an ambush, a direct assault against the enemy was most effective; such improvised assaults, however, were rare. In an assault the opening group consisted of a guide ship and minesweepers. Close behind was the shock group, consisting of a command vessel, one or more fire support ships, and several landing craft carrying the assault troops. The remainder of the force trailed at a distance of 1,000 to 1,500 meters. Upon arrival at the assault site, the shock group would fire a preparation bombardment and the assault troops would then land. Once the landing site was se-

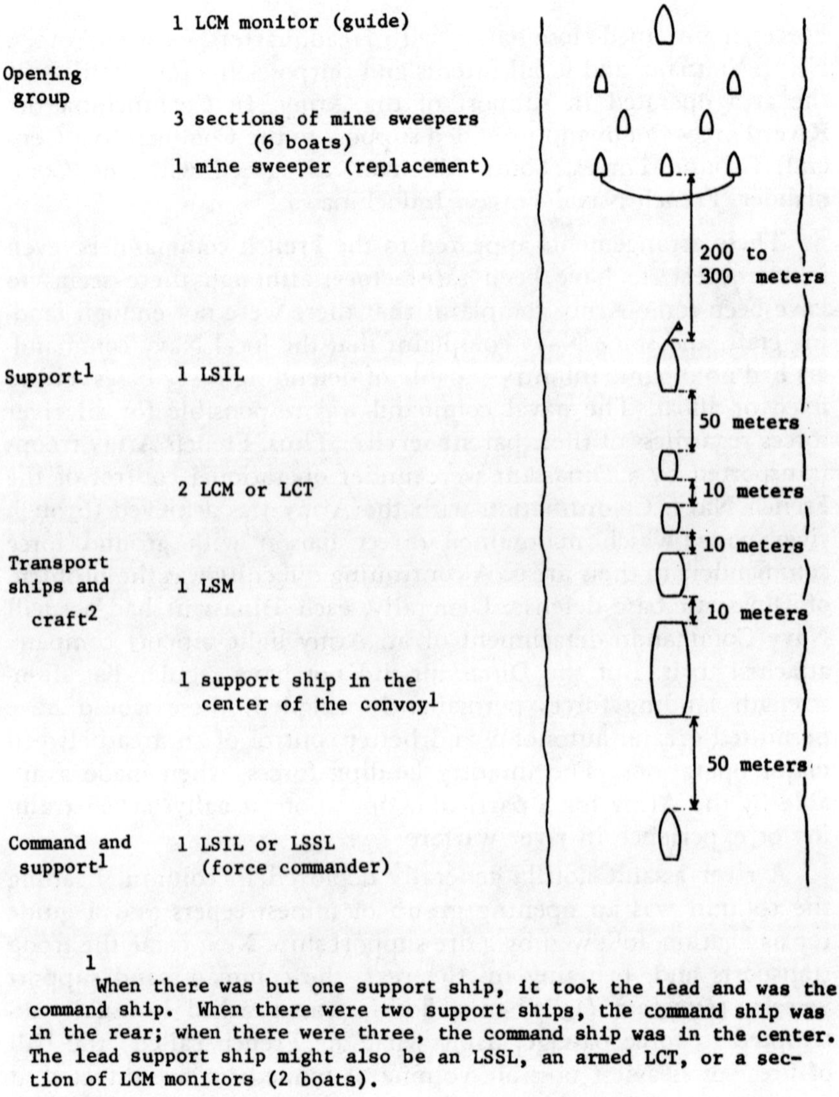

[1] When there was but one support ship, it took the lead and was the command ship. When there were two support ships, the command ship was in the rear; when there were three, the command ship was in the center. The lead support ship might also be an LSSL, an armed LCT, or a section of LCM monitors (2 boats).

[2] Sometimes the transport craft were in two columns, lashed in pairs.

Diagram 1. A typical French river convoy in North Vietnam.

cured, the remainder of the landing force would beach and unload. During the landing and until the river craft were withdrawn, the force afloat provided fire support, protected the flanks of the land-

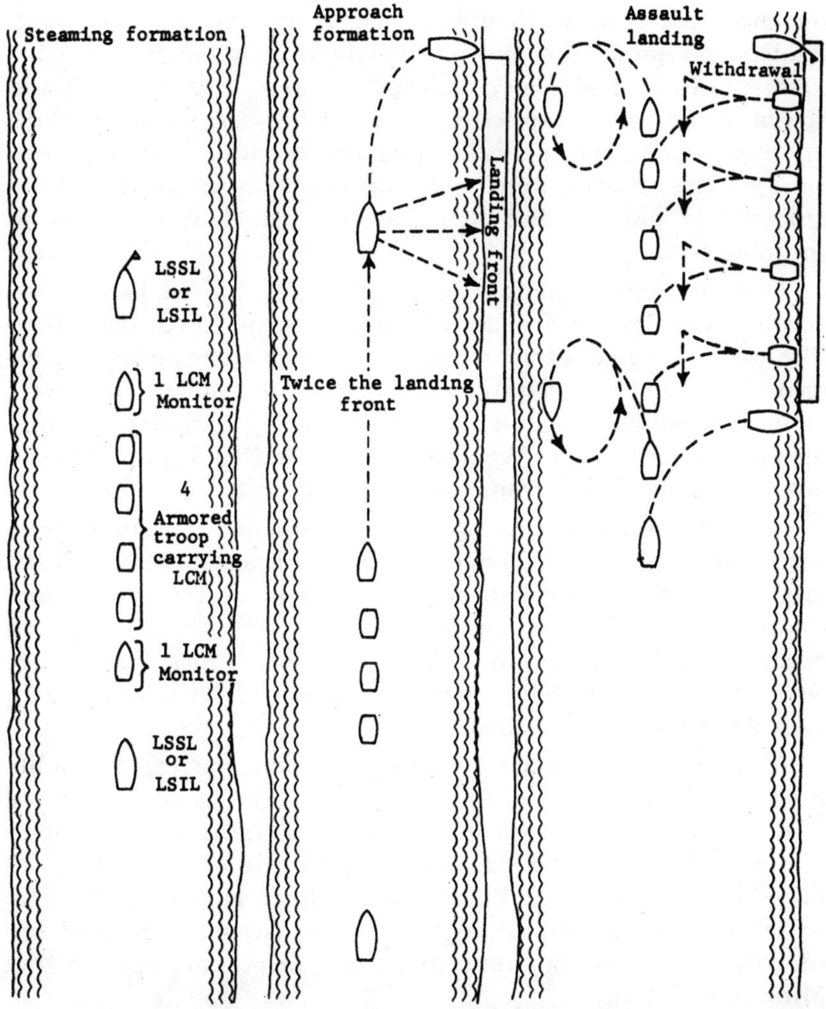

Diagram 2. French assault landing.

ing site, and patrolled in the vicinity to provide additional security. Some craft were used for logistic support, and the larger ships served temporarily as command posts for the ground unit commanders. (*Diagram 2*)

French reports show that during the entire campaign from 1945 through 1954 losses from attack while vessels were at anchor exceeded those suffered while a convoy was under way. Most Viet Minh attacks against French river forces were carefully planned and made use of some combination of swimmers, drifting mines, artillery and mortar fire, and occasionally overland assaults. French countermeasures had spotty success. Nets were used with ebb and flow of the tide to trap mines; security watches were set up; all floating objects were systematically fired upon; patrol craft were sent out; grenade attacks were made at irregular intervals and on unidentified objects; and lights were installed at entrances to anchorages.

Harassing enemy mortar and artillery fire proved particularly effective, causing the French to withdraw some forces that otherwise would have remained on station. French commanders discovered they could not rely on passive measures alone. They were sometimes obliged to shift anchorages during darkness to avoid planned Viet Minh fire. When boats were beached it proved necessary to cover the beach front with a ground unit.

The river assault flotillas were rarely employed in coastal operations, since craft modified for river use were less seaworthy, had less cargo capacity, and had armored superstructures that hindered troop transfers. Troops experienced in riverine assaults required extensive additional training for coastal operations before they were able to master going down cargo nets with their equipment, even when the sea was calm.

The tempo of French riverine operations increased steadily from 1946 until the end of the war in 1954. The Dinassauts played a key role in the battles for the Red River Delta from the summer of 1951 through early 1952. During the battle of Ninh Binh, 29 May–18 June 1951, 100 kilometers south of Hanoi on the Day River, a Dinassaut reinforced the French garrison, provided fire support, cut enemy communications, and helped to force the Viet Minh to withdraw.

During the battle of Hoa Binh, 14 November 1951–24 February 1952, sixty kilometers west of Hanoi on the Black River, two Dinassauts escorted convoys through a sector in which one bank of the river was controlled by the enemy for a distance of about fifty kilometers. As the Viet Minh increased pressure on the lines of communication connecting the garrison at Hoa Binh with the main French forces to the east, the overland routes were severed. The Dinassauts, however, continued to run the gauntlet until 12 January 1952, when an entire river convoy was ambushed and took heavy losses. Finally, when the decision was made to evacuate Hoa Binh—Operation Armaranth—the Dinassauts supported the operation by reopening the Black River corridor, ferrying retreating troops and refugees, then fighting their way out along the river toward Hanoi. Later, two Dinassauts played a key role in the offensive phase of Operation Lorraine, 29 October–8 November 1952, northwest of Hanoi on the Clear and Red Rivers.

By the end of the war, French riverine forces were fully committed and were taking heavy casualties. In over a dozen ambushes fourteen naval craft were sunk or damaged, with nearly 100 men killed or wounded. (*Table 1*)

TABLE 1—VIET MINH RIVER AMBUSHES, 5 JANUARY–16 FEBRUARY 1954

Date	Waterway	Group or Type of Craft	Enemy Weapons	Comments
5 January...	Song Thai Binh	*Dinassaut* 4	Mine	LSIL sunk; Navy, 10 killed or missing, including 2 officers; Army, 40 wounded
13 January..	Red River	*Dinassaut* 12	Automatic weapons	....
14 January..	Bamboo Canal	*Dinassaut* 4, *Javeline*	Mine	....
15 January..	Nam Dinh Giang	LCT 9.063, barge convoy, and LCM	Bazooka, automatic weapons	1 barge sunk; Navy, 4 wounded; Army, 1 killed
20 January..	Song Thai Binh	Platoon river patrol boat	Bazooka, automatic weapons	1 launch sunk; 2 killed, 3 Army wounded
22 January..	Song Thai Dinh	*Dinassaut* 1	Bazooka, automatic weapons	Detected by Morane observation plane, neutralized by artillery fire
1 February..	Red River	LCI with LCM	Mines	LCI damaged
1 February..	Van Uc Canal	Platoon river patrol boat	Mine	....
2 February..	Day River	*Pertuisane*, LCM, river patrol boat	Bazooka, automatic weapons	River patrol boat burned, LSSL *Pertuisane* damaged; 4 Navy killed or missing, 2 wounded
4 February..	Upper Red River	LCM and *Mytho Dinassaut* 12	Bazooka, automatic weapons	1 *Mytho* sunk, 1 Navy wounded
5 February..	Song Thai Binh	*Dinassaut* 1	Mine, bazooka, automatic weapons	....

TABLE 1—VIET MINH RIVER AMBUSHES, 5 JANUARY–16 FEBRUARY 1954—Continued

Date	Waterway	Group or Type of Craft	Enemy Weapons	Comments
9 February . .	Nam Dinh Giane	*Dinassaut* 3	Bazooka, automatic weapons	LSSL *Arquebuse* and 2 LCM's damaged; 3 Navy killed, including 2 officers; 15 Navy wounded
14 February . .	Middle Red River (Hung Yen)	*Dinassaut* 12	Bazooka, automatic weapons	LCT 9047 damaged; Army, 1 killed, 1 wounded; Navy, 4 killed
16 February . .	Nam Dinh Giang	*Dinassaut* 13	Bazooka, automatic weapons	LCT 9033 damaged, 1 boat sunk, 1 LCM damaged; 1 killed, 7 seriously wounded

After the war the French analyzed their experience with river warfare in Vietnam. French matériel, they concluded, was generally adequate, although increased armament might have improved performance. Operational techniques were generally adequate, but French riverine forces proved highly vulnerable in base defense and susceptible to water mines. Command relationships were satisfactory but effectiveness of the forces would have been greatly improved by permanently marrying Army assault forces to Navy lift capacity. In short, there was a need to organize an amphibious force made up of permanently assigned Army and Navy elements.

It was the observation of the French that the enemy, the Viet Minh, were remarkable infantrymen, but they made no attempt to launch armed water craft against French river forces. Rather, Viet Minh action was in the main restricted to the banks of the waterways, from which the enemy tried to intercept French movements by means of ambush, fixed obstacles, or use of remotely controlled floating mines. Enjoying excellent intelligence and the support of the population, the Viet Minh proved meticulous in their planning and masterful in the use of terrain and camouflage. Because of their excellent fire discipline, they usually enjoyed the advantage of surprise. The French thought that the Viet Minh tended to disperse their weapons too much along the banks rather than mass them, thus reducing the effectiveness of the surprise and firepower they could bring to bear against individual elements of the French floating force.

The French operated in both the Red River and Mekong Deltas, and their experience was to prove applicable in some part for U.S. river forces operating more than a decade later in the Mekong Delta.

The Mekong Delta

The Mekong Delta extends from Saigon south and west to the Gulf of Thailand and the border with Cambodia. With an area of about 40,000 square kilometers and an estimated eight million inhabitants, it constitutes about one-fourth of the total land area of South Vietnam, and contains about one-half of the country's population. (*Map 2*) The delta is generally a flat alluvial plain created by the Mekong River and its distributaries. Much of the land surface is covered by rice paddies, making the area one of the world's most productive in rice growing. It is by far the most important region in South Vietnam.

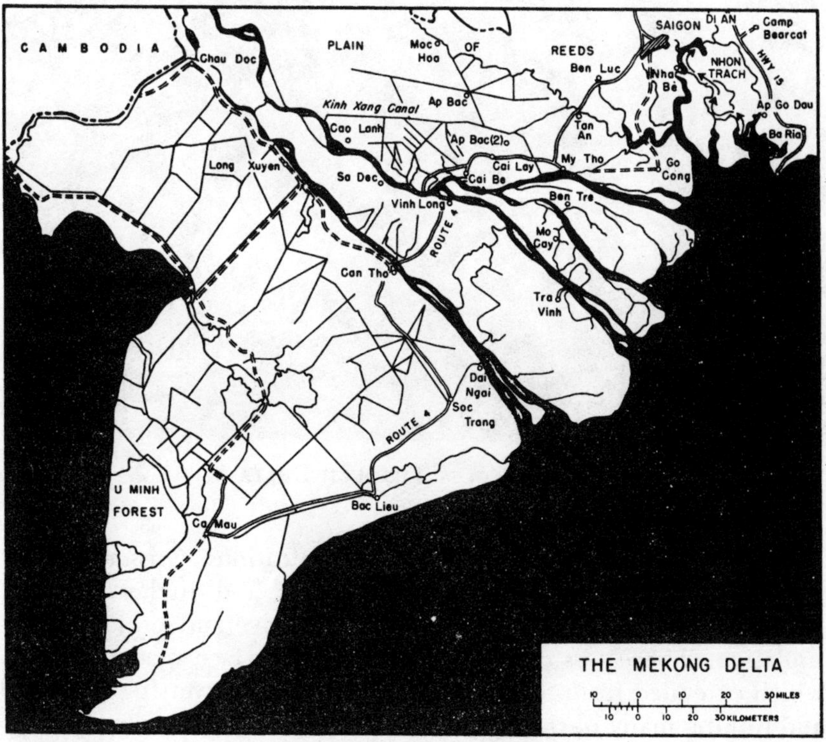

Soldier Struggles Through Delta Mud

The delta had poor overland communications. Crisscrossed by a complex network of rivers, canals, streams, and ditches, the low, poorly drained surface was subject to extensive and prolonged inundation. There was only one major hard surface road, Route 4, which extended from Saigon south to Ca Mau, traversing the delta and linking many of the larger towns. Secondary roads were poorly surfaced, and by the mid-1960's had deteriorated because of lack of maintenance and enemy action. The waterway system made frequent bridging necessary; bridge capacities were mainly in the 10- to 20-ton range. In short, the roadnet was of limited use for military operations.

Any movement off the roads was limited. It was best during the dry season—November to March—when paddies were dry and would support light tracked vehicles and artillery pieces; it was poorest during the wet season—May to October—when paddies were inundated. It was restricted all year round by the network of rivers, canals, streams and ditches. There were many swamps, marshes, and forests, generally bordering the seacoast.

In comparison with most of the other areas of Vietnam, the Mekong Delta was good for air operations, since landing zones were abundant and weather seldom prevented helicopter operations. Once troops debarked from helicopters, however, their movement was sharply restricted by ditches and waterways.

In sharp contrast to the limited overland transportation, the delta had a highly developed inland waterway system. There is evidence that the inhabitants began to improve natural drainage as early as 800 A.D., and succeeding generations have continued the work. As a result, the 2,400 kilometers of navigable natural waterways were supplemented by about 4,000 kilometers of land-cut canals of varying width and depth, and in good to poor condition.

The wet season, the time of the southwest monsoon, permits deliberate flooding of rice paddies, but also causes some unavoidable flooding as rivers overflow their banks. Waterways grow wider, sharply curtailing cross-country traffic and limiting the amount of firm ground suitable for placing artillery. Off-road movement of troops and vehicles can cause damage to crops and drainage systems, and was therefore unpopular with the farmers. Further, the high humidity and extensive flooding aggravated the foot problems of the soldier, who got his feet wet from frequent water crossings. One-third of the delta is marsh, forest, or swamp forest. In the north lies the Plain of Reeds, a flat, grassy basin with almost no trees. During the wet season it is generally inundated to a depth of two to three meters; during the dry season, much of the plain dries out to the extent that large grass fires are frequent. There are relatively few points in the delta that lie more than a few hundred meters from a navigable waterway; even the marshes, swamps, and forests can be reached by water. In short, the delta is well suited to riverine operations.

Military operations on the waterways of the Mekong Delta had to be governed by the life of the delta. By any standard, the delta is densely populated; it has an average of about 200 inhabitants per square kilometer, about the same density as Massachusetts. The people are concentrated along the waterways that constitute their principal transportation routes. Transportation, essential to the people and to the national economy, felt the impact of military operations, and the U.S. commander was obliged to maneuver his forces so as to interfere as little as possible with the normal flow of civilian transport.

Where people lived there were trees and bushes cultivated for their fruit, shade, or decoration. Since these offered protection to an enemy seeking concealment, military engagements often took place in populated areas. Thus a commander was faced with the task of inflicting damage on an armed enemy, and at the same time trying to avoid damage to the unarmed local inhabitants. High population density makes it difficult to conceal military activity from observation; weaknesses may be noted and word passed to the enemy, moves may be telegraphed before they can achieve their purpose.

Seacoasts of the delta have extensive mangrove swamps, including the Rung Sat southeast of Saigon, and the U Minh Forest along the west coast; vegetation on the tidal mudflats is dense, root structure is high and tangled, and covering is thick, making access difficult and cross-country movement arduous. The paddy land is interspersed with thickets of trees and bushes in patterns that vary: in one area vegetation is clustered polka-dot style about scattered dwellings; a few kilometers away, it is in continuous strips along waterways. There are large cultivated plantations—rows of palm trees grown on embankments which alternate with wide drainage ditches. In the wide-ranging operations characteristic of riverine warfare, it was necessary to adapt tactics to the lay of the land.

Riverine operations in the delta also had to deal with the strong influence of sea tides along the inland waterways throughout the region. Tidal fluctuations range up to about four meters. The twice daily tidal flow influences the velocity of currents, and has an important bearing on the feasibility of navigation in many waterways. Variations in sea tides, together with the complex nature of the interconnecting waterways, make tidal effects exceptionally difficult to predict with confidence. As a consequence, planning for water operations involves a good deal of guesswork, for the time required to travel from one point to another cannot be predicted.

The condition of the inland waterways added obstacles to military movement. By 1960 many canals had deteriorated from neglect; of some 1,500 surveyed that year, nearly half required "restoration," and could carry traffic only at full tide. Some waterways had been deliberately obstructed by the enemy. In the smaller streams there were many fishtraps that restricted passage. Bridges are always to be dealt with in waterborne movement, since frequently there is not enough clearance to permit passage of vessels. This problem is further complicated by variation in water levels due to tidal fluctuations, which may permit passage for short periods twice a day only.

Finally, it was difficult to base troops in the Mekong Delta since firm ground was limited. Military needs for land bases tended to conflict with the needs of the population, so that a floating base offered a clear advantage.

Enemy Forces

As elsewhere in Vietnam, the enemy had in 1966 and early 1967 both a political and a military organization in the delta. In mid-1966 estimated strength of the Viet Cong in the IV Corps Tactical Zone, which corresponds roughly to the delta, was 82,545 men. Of these, 19,270 were combat troops; 1,290 were support troops; 50,765 were local part-time guerrillas; and 11,220 were working as political cadre. At the time, no North Vietnam Army forces were reported in the IV Corps Tactical Zone. In the summer of 1966 the office of the assistant chief of staff for intelligence estimated that organized military forces in the IV Corps Tactical Zone consisted of three regimental headquarters, 28 battalions (8 of which were in the regiments), 69 separate companies, and 11 separate platoons—an estimate that agreed closely with that of U.S. Military Assistance Command, Vietnam. (*Map 3*)

It was believed that Viet Cong logistics depended on support from the population, on captures from Republic of Vietnam units, and on supplies furnished by the Democratic Republic of Vietnam —primarily weapons and ammunition—infiltrated by sea, or by land from Cambodia. The base area was believed to be fundamental to the Viet Cong logistical system. Base areas such as the Plain of Reeds, the U Minh Forest, and the Cam Son Secret Zone west of My Tho served as sites for political, military, logistical, and training installations, and were supplemented by "combat villages" on South Vietnamese territory, organized and controlled by the Viet Cong. Cambodia provided a rear service area for 10,000 or

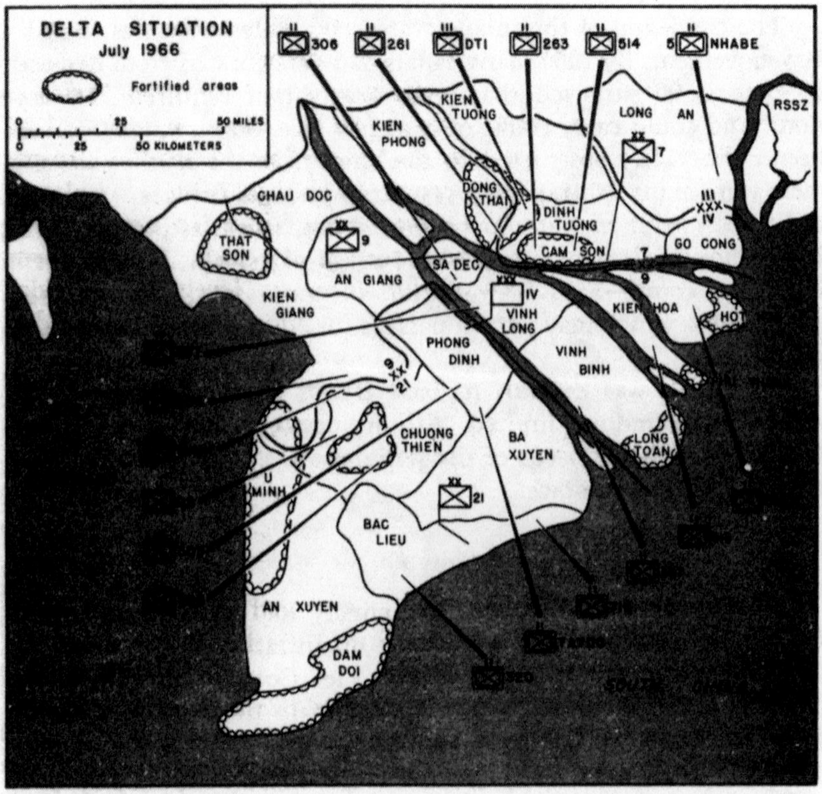

MAP 3

more main and local Viet Cong forces in Vietnamese provinces that offered free access to Cambodian territory.

Viet Cong forces in the delta were as well armed as those elsewhere in Vietnam. The new family of 7.62-mm. weapons manufactured by the Chinese Communists were first captured in the delta on 11 December 1964 by Republic of Vietnam armed forces. The capture included copies of the AK47, the SKS carbine, the RPD light machine gun, and a quantity of M43 intermediate 7.62-mm. cartridges of Soviet design. During the same month, the Vietnam Army also captured the first RPG2 antitank grenade launcher, capable of penetrating six to seven inches of armor at ranges of 100 to 200 meters—a potent weapon for use against riverine craft.

Viet Cong communications equipment, while not abundant, appeared adequate. The enemy was able to interfere with and intrude on voice circuits of U.S. and South Vietnam forces, blanking out transmissions and employing tactical deception.

Viet Cong methods of operation in the delta were not substantially different from those employed by the enemy in other regions. In 1966 it was reported that Viet Cong activities had been primarily small unit operations—harassment, terrorism, and sabotage, with the delta accounting for approximately one-third of all Viet Cong initiated incidents in South Vietnam. The enemy, however, was also able to mount battalion-size attacks. Several times the Viet Cong demonstrated a willingness and an ability to slug it out with government forces. In January 1963 at Ap Bac a Viet Cong force engaged a superior Army of Vietnam force that was attempting to surround the Viet Cong by using heliborne assault in conjunction with conventional ground movement. Five helicopters were destroyed and nine damaged as the Viet Cong inflicted heavy casualties and withdrew. In December 1964 the Viet Cong 9th Division with two regiments seized the Catholic village of Binh Gia. During the next four days the enemy ambushed and virtually destroyed the Vietnamese 33d Ranger Battalion and 4th Marine Battalion and inflicted heavy casualties on armored and mechanized relief forces.

Republic of Vietnam Forces

In 1966 most of the Mekong Delta was included in the IV Corps Tactical Zone, although Gia Dinh Province, Long An Province, and the Rung Sat Special Zone in the north were part of the III Corps Tactical Zone. The IV Corps Tactical Zone was in turn subdivided into three division tactical areas. In the north the 7th Division had its headquarters at My Tho; in the center was the 9th Division with headquarters at Sa Dec; and in the south was the 21st Division with headquarters at Bac Lieu. In 1966 Army of Vietnam assigned strength in IV Corps Zone averaged 40,000. In addition to the three divisions, there were five Ranger battalions and three armored cavalry squadrons.

South Vietnam paramilitary forces included Regional Forces, Popular Forces, Civilian Irregular Defense Group (CIDG) troops, and National Police. In 1966 Regional and Popular Forces manned outposts and watchtowers scattered throughout the delta. Poorly supported and highly vulnerable to Viet Cong attack, both these forces had high desertion rates. The Civilian Irregular Defense Group troops were employed generally along the Cambodian border as part of an effort to seal the frontier against Viet Cong and North Vietnamese movements of men, equipment, and supplies. The National Police were organized after the manner of the French *gendarmerie,* and exercised similar functions.

Vietnam naval forces attached to the Vietnamese 4th Naval Zone in the delta included six river assault groups, which had evolved directly from the French Dinassauts, and eleven coastal groups known collectively as the Junk Fleet. The assault groups were under the operational control of the IV Corps commander with the primary mission of supporting Vietnam Army riverine operations. Each group could lift a Vietnamese infantry battalion, giving the IV Corps Zone the capability of a six-battalion lift. The river assault groups were in 1966 being used in their primary role only 10 percent of the time. Vietnam Army division commanders apparently preferred airmobile operations to riverine operations, hence the river assault groups were employed in support of small unit operations by Regional or Popular Forces under the control of province chiefs. Often they were used simply as escort for commercial craft.

U.S. Forces

The American military first entered the Mekong Delta in 1957 when U.S. Navy advisers replaced French advisers. By early 1966 the American advisory effort had permeated the Republic of Vietnam military structure. Advisers included nearly 700 officers and over 2,000 enlisted men from the U.S. Army, Navy, and Air Force. American Army advisers were present at corps, division, and sector (province) level, and with the IV Corps Tactical Zone Area Logistics Command. The U.S. Navy Advisory Group, Vietnam, provided advisers to the Vietnamese Navy's six river assault groups and eleven coastal groups.

In 1965 the U.S. Army 13th Combat Aviation Battalion had been sent to the delta to support Republic of Vietnam operations, and by August of that year the battalion had four assault helicopter companies and one reconnaissance airplane company. By mid-1966, U.S. naval forces included Task Force 115, with the code name MARKET TIME, and Task Force 116, known as GAME WARDEN. MARKET TIME had the mission of patrolling coastal areas to prevent resupply of Viet Cong and North Vietnam forces by sea. GAME WARDEN had the mission of interdicting enemy lines of communications and assisting government forces in repelling enemy attacks on river outposts of the Regional and Popular Forces.

The Situation in 1966

In April 1964 the American Ambassador, Henry Cabot Lodge, Jr., had remarked: " . . . I would not be surprised to see the

Mekong Delta totally cleared of Communist forces by the end of 1965." In the summer of 1966, however, the Military Assistance Command, Vietnam, reported that about one-third of all Viet Cong actions against the government in South Vietnam occurred in the IV Corps Tactical Zone, and estimated that the Viet Cong controlled 24.6 percent of the population of IV Corps.

Government influence varied widely from province to province. An Giang Province was considered "pacified," while in An Xuyen Province it was estimated that government forces controlled as little as 4 percent of the land. In many areas government forces claimed control by day, but acknowledged that the "night belongs to the Viet Cong." With few exceptions, the large towns served as either province or district capitals and in 1966 were largely under government control. All, however, were occasionally subject to terrorist incidents, mortar or rocket attacks, or assaults upon outlying guard posts. The Viet Cong was, furthermore, choking off the flow of rice to market: in 1963 rice arriving at the market in Saigon reached a high of about four million metric tons; in 1966 amounts declined to about three million tons, making importation of rice necessary. Far from being "totally cleared of Communist forces," in 1966 the delta was more than ever under Viet Cong control and something different was going to have to be done to change the situation. The introduction of additional forces might help, but such forces would require bases, which were difficult to provide. It was against this background that the basic decisions for the creation of an American riverine force were made in late 1965 and early 1966.

CHAPTER II

The Concept of a Riverine Force

In July 1965 the staff of the United States Military Assistance Command, Vietnam (MACV), was drafting the campaign plan for 1966, the purpose of which was to help the government of South Vietnam establish control over the people. The staff concluded that it was possible to secure government control over the I, II, and III Corps Tactical Zones, a conclusion largely based on the presence of American and other Free World Military Assistance Forces in these corps areas. In the IV Corps Tactical Zone, however, where there were no U.S. ground forces to bolster the efforts of the Vietnam armed forces, the staff questioned whether the objective of the campaign plan could be attained. The armed forces of Vietnam were considered capable of maintaining their position in the IV Corps, but not of reducing Communist control over significant portions of the population and terrain in the Mekong Delta. While additional American and other Free World Military Assistance Forces were planned for the other corps areas, none were planned for the IV Corps area. In the opinion of the staff, there could be no substantial progress in the IV Corps Tactical Zone unless U.S. ground forces were introduced.

As a preliminary step in studying the possibility of sending U.S. forces into the delta, Brigadier General William E. DePuy, J-3 (assistant chief of staff for military operations) of the MACV staff, directed his planners to survey the delta for land suitable for basing ground troops. A team dispatched to examine My Tho, Vinh Long, Sa Dec, and Can Tho concluded that all land suitable for large tactical units was either heavily populated or occupied by Republic of Vietnam armed forces. If U.S. units were based in the delta, they would have to share already crowded areas or displace a portion of the population. Since neither of these courses was acceptable, the planning staff then searched for other means of basing troops. Obtaining river sand as fill material and building up an area to accommodate a division base was considered. U.S. Military Assistance Command engineers estimated that with the dredge equipment at hand seventeen and a half dredge-years would be necessary to fill an area large enough to base a division. Since adequate dredge equipment was not available in Southeast Asia, immediate steps were taken to procure additional dredges from the United States, but these were not expected to arrive until late 1966. Although not entirely satisfied with this solution, the planning staff believed the building of a base area by dredging operations to be a sound choice.

In addition to a land base, other means of operating in the delta were needed, and the planning staff turned to the experience of the French in Indochina for answers. The French had used small landing craft extensively to exploit the net of waterways from land bases. The American staff planned to use not only small craft but also a group of larger landing craft that would house and support a riverine force. These ships, the planners believed, might also be able to move along the coastline and major rivers and serve as mobile bases. It was known that during World War II the Navy had converted LST's (landing ships, tank) into barracks ships, and the planners believed that such ships could provide a base for a brigade force afloat. As the concept of an American river flotilla took form, the planners concluded that the LST barracks ships could be altered to furnish a helicopter flight deck and that barges could be provided on which helicopters would be able to land for maintainance. The ships could also be equipped with weapons for defense.

In their initial survey to find anchorage sites in the delta, the planners of the Military Assistance Command suggested seven that might serve. An LST could resupply the river force by traveling from Vung Tau across a stretch of the South China Sea into the selected anchorage sites on the Mekong and Bassac Rivers.

Captain David F. Welch of the U.S. Navy, who headed the Plans and Requirements Division of J-3, the Operations Directorate, U.S. Military Assistance Command, Vietnam, believed that the afloat force concept merited full study and suggested that a task force be set up under a U.S. Navy commander. He discussed the matter with Rear Admiral Norvell G. Ward, Commander, U.S. Naval Forces, Vietnam, who agreed that the idea had possibilities and that some naval ships could be made available.

In early December of 1965, during the monthly Commander's Meeting of the Military Assistance Command, Vietnam, General DePuy briefed General William C. Westmoreland and his commanders on the concept of a Mekong Delta riverine force that would employ an Army brigade with a comparable Navy organiza-

LST WITH ARMORED TROOP CARRIERS AND MONITORS

tion, and that would operate from various anchorages within the delta. The plan called for the development of two land bases, one for an infantry division headquarters and one brigade, and another for one brigade to be located in the northern part of the delta, probably in Long An Province. A third brigade would be based on the water. With the use of a mobile floating base, the mingling of U.S. troops with the Vietnamese population could be reduced—a prime consideration in view of the reluctance of the Vietnamese to accept U.S. ground forces within the delta. General Westmoreland declared the idea of a floating base "most imaginative," and directed that a team be sent to brief Headquarters, Pacific Command, and solicit its support.

When General Westmoreland had accepted the idea, reconnaissance was conducted to find a land base for a division headquarters and one brigade. General DePuy and Colonel Sidney B. Berry, Jr., Senior Advisor, 7th Division, Army of Vietnam, selected a base site approximately eight kilometers west of the town of My Tho, where the Kinh Xang Canal enters the My Tho branch of the Mekong River. According to French hydrographic maps, adequate sand deposits for fill material existed nearby. A request was then sent to the Joint Chiefs of Staff in Washington for an additional infantry division to employ in the IV Corps area. For planning purposes the unit was designated Z Division.

During the latter part of December a MACV team headed by General DePuy met with the Pacific Command staff and outlined a general plan for the riverine force. After a period of discussion, the Pacific Command staff accepted the feasibility of the proposal. In the discussion the concept that the river force operating within the Mekong Delta would be a joint Army-Navy task force was emphasized. It was felt that barracks ships, then in storage, could be utilized to house part of the force, and that these barracks ships could be supported by small landing craft, patrol boats, and helicopters. Such support would enable the river force to conduct operations within a defined radius of the floating base. In addition, the mobility of the small craft would help to protect the floating base.

Upon acceptance by the Commander in Chief, Pacific, of the feasibility of a riverine force, the Joint Chiefs of Staff tentatively approved the employment of an Army division in the Mekong Delta to put the plan in operation. The force was to be provided barracks ships and LCM-8's. The matter of land bases was left unanswered in the joint staff action of the Commander in Chief, Pacific.

In Washington the Vice Chief of Naval Operations, Admiral Horacio Rivero, Jr., supported the concept of a riverine force and approved a proposal to send a planning group to Saigon to work with the MACV staff. The group was asked to develop a complete plan and to specify the means to support it. Headed by Captain David Bill, U.S. Navy, Office of the Chief of Naval Operations, and consisting of representatives of the Bureau of Ships, the Marine Corps, and the Amphibious Command, Pacific, the planning group arrived in Vietnam in January of 1966. Together the MACV staff and the Navy group studied in detail the experience of the French and Vietnamese with river assault forces in order to establish a similar American force, but one with greater capabilities. Under the leadership of Captain Welsh and Captain Bill, requirements were drawn up for self-propelled barracks ships (APB's), LST's, large covered lighters (YFNB's), large harbor tugs (YTB's), landing craft repair ships (ARL's), and a mine countermeasures support ship (MCS); all were to carry appropriate armament for the area of operations. The LCM-6 would be used instead of the LCM-8, which was in limited supply.

In a message of 19 February, the Commander in Chief, Pacific,

SELF-PROPELLED BARRACKS SHIP WITH AMMI BARGE MOORED ALONGSIDE

requested that the Commander, U.S. Military Assistance Command, Vietnam, develop and submit a detailed plan of operations and logistical support for the employment of a Mekong Delta Mobile Afloat Force. The plan was to cover force composition and phasing, tasks to be executed, methods of execution, navigable areas, operating areas, afloat force locations, afloat force base, provisions for U.S. Air Force, Navy gunfire, and helicopter support, and command relationships. The Commander in Chief, Pacific, Admiral Ulysses S. Grant Sharp, Jr., also asked for amplification of the logistics involved: depots and ports from which support would be provided, additional facilities required at the logistic support base, requirements for additional lighterage, and specification of other resources needed to support operations. Representatives of Admiral Sharp would meet with the MACV staff to "assist in the development of the foregoing and to facilitate subsequent evaluation and review." The MACV-Navy group continued to plan, following the guidance of the Commander in Chief, Pacific.

The planning culminated in a MACV study, Mekong Delta Mobile Afloat Force Concept and Requirements, dated 7 March 1966, which was forwarded on 15 March 1966 to the Commander in Chief, Pacific, for approval. The study articulated fully for the first time the concept for the Army-Navy force afloat. It later proved to be a far-sighted and comprehensive blueprint for the preparation of both Army and Navy components and the conduct of operations. Most of the planned features of the force as stated in this document later materialized in the operational force.

The study recommended that the force contain a U.S. Army reinforced brigade consisting of three infantry battalions, an artillery battalion, and other combat and combat service support. The force would be based aboard U.S. Navy ships that would include 5 self-propelled barracks ships, 2 LST's, 2 large harbor tugs, and 2 landing craft repair ships. In addition, two U.S. Navy river assault groups would provide tactical water mobility. Each assault group would be capable of lifting the combat elements of one reinforced infantry battalion. A small salvage craft would be necessary to recover damaged ships or craft. The reinforced brigade would be organized under the current standard ROAD (Reorganization Objective Army Divisions) tables of organization and equipment, with limited augmentation. Certain equipment specified in the tables, such as tents, mess facilities, 106-mm. recoilless rifles, anti-tank wire-guided missiles, and all wheeled vehicles except artillery prime movers were to be deleted from the force requirements. The number of 90-mm. recoilless rifles in each rifle company was to be reduced from six to three to improve the mobility of the weapons squads. The 4.2-inch mortars would accompany the force and be moved by water or air to field positions as necessary. Radios would be either ship-mounted or man-portable. Coxswains of plastic assault boats were to be designated in the proposed tables and trained upon arrival in Vietnam. Enough troops from each of the units afloat would be left at a land base to maintain equipment left in storage. The plan provided for an augmentation of three counter-mortar radar sections, each manned by nine men, to operate and maintain ship-mounted countermortar radars. A mobile Army surgical hospital team, U.S. Air Force tactical air control parties which included forward air controllers, Vietnam Army liaison troops, and additional ANPRC–25 radios were to be furnished from sources outside the parent division of the brigade.

Each river assault group, later designated river assault squadron, was to consist of the following: 52 LCM–6's to serve as armored troop carriers, 5 LCM–6's to serve as command and communication boats, 10 LCM–6's to serve as monitors, 32 assault support patrol boats, and 2 LCM–6's to serve as refuelers. A salvage force would include: 2 2,000-ton heavy lift craft, 2 YTB's for salvage, 2 LCU's

ARMORED TROOP CARRIER

(landing craft, utility), and 3 100-ton floating dry docks. The Mobile Afloat Force concept stated the specific tasks the force was to accomplish: secure U.S. base areas and lines of communication required for U.S. operations; conduct offensive operations against Viet Cong forces and base areas that posed a threat both to the national and to the IV Corps Tactical Zone priority areas for rural construction in co-ordination with Republic of Vietnam armed forces and other U.S. forces; isolate the most heavily populated and key food-producing areas from Viet Cong base areas; interdict Viet Cong supply routes; and in co-ordination with the Vietnam armed forces provide reserve and reaction forces in the IV Corps Tactical Zone.

Because the Viet Cong forces were dispersed throughout the Mekong Delta, the river force would be required to operate in many locations. Initial operations would be conducted in the provinces to the north of the Mekong River—Go Cong, Dinh Tuong, Kien Phong, Kien Tuong, and as far north as the Plain of Reeds. (*See Map 5.*) Once the Viet Cong main force units were neutralized in these areas, with the U.S. Navy GAME WARDEN forces con-

COMMAND AND COMMUNICATIONS BOAT

trolling Viet Cong cross-river movements, the center of gravity of U.S. operations would shift south into the provinces between the Mekong and the Bassac and eventually south of the Bassac River.

It was decided to use a brigade for initial operations because the experience of U.S. forces in Vietnam indicated that the brigade was the smallest U.S. unit that could be safely and economically kept in the delta. It was large enough to defend its base against heavy enemy attack and at the same time to have forces available for offensive operations.

The formal plan of the Military Assistance Command required the construction of a land base by dredging. Since land reclamation would be expensive and time-consuming, however, the plan also recommended the creation of a water base as well in order to use American forces most effectively. The plan indicated that the land base near My Tho could be made available at the end of 1966 or in early 1967.

Criteria for the selection of anchorages for the floating base were established. The base was to be reasonably near an airfield;

be within or contiguous to a relatively secure area; have access to a land line of communications; have enough room to anchor the entire force; and have a river bank that would permit debarking of artillery to provide fire support to the force. Sites that met most of the above criteria were found in the vicinity of My Tho, Vinh Long, Cao Lanh, Tra Vinh, Can Tho, Long Xuyen, and Dai Ngai, which was in the vicinity of Soc Trang.

Recognizing that the My Tho land base would not be large enough to accommodate a division headquarters until early in 1968, the plan called for the Z Division to go initially to Ba Ria, which lies north of Vung Tau. The division base was to include a division headquarters, a support command, one brigade, and a storage area for the heavy equipment and rolling stock of the two brigades sent into the delta—one to be land-based near My Tho rather than in Long An Province, and a second to be the Army component of the Mobile Afloat Force. Vung Tau was to be the port for staging and resupplying the Mobile Afloat Force. Minimum security measures would be needed for the force when it was at Vung Tau and when it was traveling from there to the Mekong River. During navigation of the major rivers, however, continuous security measures would be necessary. Such movements were to be considered ventures through hostile territory and were to be handled much the same way as running a tactical land convoy.

The plan provided for continuous air cover, both by fixed-wing tactical aircraft and armed helicopters. Advance, flank, and rear security on the rivers was to be provided by U.S. Navy river assault groups. GAME WARDEN forces would provide intelligence to assist in reconnoitering the route. The mine countermeasures were to be chain drags pulled along either side of the channel to cut command detonation wires of river mines, and mine-hunting sonar. Canals terminating in the main river might harbor hostile boats and were therefore to be reconnoitered by both boat and air. Armed helicopters, in conjunction with the Navy assault groups, were to cover the banks of the rivers and search out possible ambush sites. The major ships were to be at a condition of highest watertight integrity during transit, and fixed weapons were to be manned to counter enemy attack. Major ships of the force were to be moved in daylight hours.

At the anchorage of the afloat base, an area security plan would be in effect, with Army security forces on shore and reinforced by artillery. Outposts including foot and boat patrols would be used. The barracks ships would be moored near the center of the river and their countermortar radars could provide coverage of the surrounding area. All weapons would be manned, with an Army-Navy reaction force standing by while the ships were at anchor.

The plan recognized three principal enemy threats. The first was infiltration by small mortar or recoilless rifle teams which would attempt to penetrate the infantry perimeter ashore. These teams would probably fire several rounds quickly and then withdraw rapidly. The second threat was that of a large-scale, overt attack. The third and possibly the most critical threat to the floating base would come from the water—floating mines, swimmer saboteurs, and suicide boats. Measures to counter the threats were left to the commanders immediately concerned.

The Mobile Afloat Force concept provided for a variety of tactical operations. The force would remain in an enemy base area as long as operations could be profitably conducted—about four to six weeks. Ground operations would last four to five days, after which troops would be allowed a rest of two or three days to dry out and to repair equipment. It was believed that the force could conduct four operations a month. A brigade would be deployed in the delta for as long as six months, with the possibility of rotation with either the brigade at My Tho or that at Ba Ria. The force would obtain intelligence and develop plans prior to its arrival in a base area, and operations would commence as soon as the floating base arrived at its anchorage. The brigade would rely heavily on local Vietnamese intelligence organizations.

To acquire knowledge of the area in which the force was operating, elements of the brigade, embarked in Navy assault group boats, helicopters, and plastic assault boats, would be employed to gather data on stream and canal depths, height of banks, areas for beaching, possible artillery positions, helicopter landing zones, the local population, and the enemy.

Full-scale operations would be conducted by deploying the force into the combat area by water, land, and air. Security for the floating base would require from a company to as much as a battalion in the immediate base area. Operations could range up to fifty kilometers from the floating base and, in exceptional cases, beyond. Security measures similar to those for relocation of the major ships would be taken for the movement of the assault craft formations during operations. Tactical air and armed helicopters were to fly cover, and artillery would displace by echelon as required to provide continuous fire support. The assault support patrol boats were to furnish forward, flank, and rear security, and to sweep for shore-

ASSAULT SUPPORT PATROL BOAT. *A high-speed armored boat used for waterway interdiction, surveillance, escort, mine-sweeping, and fire support.*

commanded mines. Preparatory fire could be delivered by the armament of the Navy assault groups, by artillery, and by air. Landing of the force would be in accordance with the tactical plan and the armored troop carriers would then withdraw to rendezvous points or return to the afloat base for resupply. At least one armored troop carrier would be designated as a floating aid station located at a prearranged point in the operational area of the battalion that it was supporting. Some elements of the force could deploy by water or air beyond the immediate landing areas to cut off withdrawing enemy troops and some could be held afloat as a reserve. The river force would prevent the enemy from withdrawing across the major rivers. Assault support patrol boats and monitors not required to protect the troop carriers would be used to provide flank and rear security, close-in fire support, and forward command post protection.

Command and control would be exercised through the use of command and communications boats, which were to provide space and communications for battalion and brigade command groups. Command helicopters could also be used to control operations.

MONITOR

Helicopters would be used to deploy a portion of the ground force, to position artillery, and to deliver reserves for the purpose of blocking the enemy or exploiting success. Armed helicopters would be employed for escort and fire support. Large Viet Cong forces encountered in these operations were to be neutralized or destroyed by fire and land maneuver. Should no large enemy force be encountered, the Mobile Afloat Force would be redeployed to another area of operations or the area would be systematically searched and enemy resources captured or destroyed. It was estimated that a battalion could conduct an operation throughout an area of forty square kilometers in four to six days. After troops had closed in on the final objective they would be met and withdrawn by the Navy assault group boats or possibly by helicopters. The withdrawal phase was considered critical because of the possibility of ambush and mines. Alternate routes and decoys would be used, but the basic concept for withdrawal would be the same as that of the movement to contact. Mine-clearing devices and air cover would be used. *(Diagram 3)*

All available means of fire support would be employed by the force, using the air and ground operations system common throughout Vietnam. Sorties would be allocated upon planned requests; emergency requests would be honored in accordance with priorities. The Direct Air Support Center at IV Corps Tactical Zone headquarters in Can Tho would be responsible for the allocation of

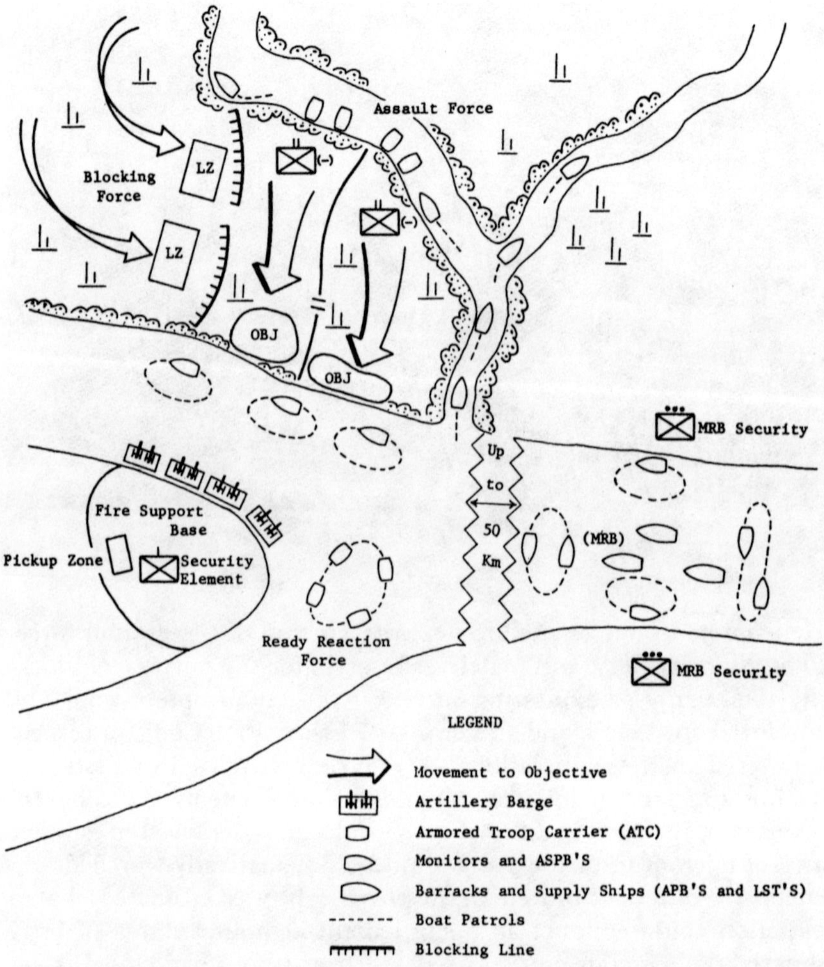

Diagram 3. Riverine operation and base defense.

tactical air support with airborne forward air controllers utilized to the maximum. Artillery support would be furnished in the traditional manner, providing fire support to all echelons of the force. Gunfire support would also be supplied by assault support patrol boats and monitors. Army helicopter gunships would be requested and allocated by the division in the same manner as for other divisional brigades.

The Vung Tau Area Support Command would provide common items of supply and logistic support peculiar to the Army; the Navy would furnish items peculiar to the Navy. A small Navy support facility at Vung Tau would probably be necessary. Two LST's from Vung Tau would take care of all resupply except Class III. Each would be capable of carrying ten days' dry cargo for all elements of the force. One LST would remain on station with the force for seven days as a floating supply point. At the end of the seven days, the LST on station would be relieved by the second ship carrying ten days of supply, and would return to Vung Tau for replenishment.

Self-propelled barracks ships would be stocked with thirty days of frozen and chilled components of Class I and thirty days of dry components prior to deployment. Resupply of Class I would be scheduled to draw on the initial provisioning to a fifteen-day level by the time an APB returned to Vung Tau. The Navy would be responsible for operating all messes aboard ships, utilizing both Army and Navy mess personnel.

Resupply of petroleum products would be accomplished by having the craft of the Navy assault groups refuel from the APB's and the supply LST. The supply LST would refuel the APB's and other ships of the flotilla as required. Gasoline for the assault boats and vehicles would be supplied from two LCM-6 tankers, each with a capacity of 10,000 gallons. The LST would be refilled by commercial barge at ten-day intervals. Fuel for helicopter companies would be provided to the base by commercial contractor. U.S. Army, Vietnam, would supply what the commercial contractors could not.

The LST supply ships would carry that portion of the Class V basic load not carried on the APB's and ATC's. Army Class V carried aboard an APB would be limited to that portion of the basic load carried by the individual soldier and ten days' supply for Army weapons mounted on the ship. A normal allowance would be carried for the Navy weapons. The Army element of the force would prepare loading plans for that portion of the basic load to be carried on the ATC's. An operating allowance of Class V would be carried on the Navy assault group craft for all mounted weapons, with a ten-day resupply for these weapons on the supply ship.

Resupply of forces operating away from the Mobile Afloat Force anchorage would be tailored to the specific operation and would vary with the size of the force, duration of the operation, and distance from the anchorage. Resupply would be accomplished primarily by ATC and helicopter. Airlift and other means of transportation could be called upon to augment the capacity of the organic force for resupply as warranted by the area and nature of operations. Matériel to be evacuated to Vung Tau or to the division base at Ba Ria would be carried by the resupply ships on their return to Vung Tau. Aircraft would be used for evacuation and for the replacement of urgently needed matériel between supply ship turnarounds. The Army and Navy components would retain maintenance responsibility for organic matériel, including parts supply for service-peculiar items. Each component would provide repair stores and load lists accordingly.

Army responsibility for maintenance would be limited to organizational maintenance of all matériel and direct support maintenance of weapons, vehicles, signal equipment, and assault boats and motors. Shops on the APB's would be used by unit armorers and maintenance men to perform organizational maintenance. Billeting space for a maintenance detachment of one officer, three warrant officers, and twenty-seven enlisted men, and shop space of approximately 1,500 square feet would be required on the ARL's to meet the Army direct support requirements.

All Navy ships and smaller craft were to arrive in Vietnam in operational condition. Maximum operational time would be available prior to regular overhaul. Two ARL's constituted the major repair and maintenance assets for the force and would normally remain with the force to function as advanced tenders. ARL shop spaces and equipment would be designed for a broad range of repair and maintenance of all craft and ships of the force and for overhaul of all assault craft. In addition, shop spaces were to be manned by the Army to provide for repair and maintenance of Army equipment.

Medical care would remain a service responsibility aboard ship. The Army would provide medical service for all elements of the force when they were away from the flotilla on an operation. Two medical evacuation helicopters would be stationed at the airfield closest to the area of operations to evacuate patients from battalion aid stations located on ATC's or from the battlefield to a mobile Army surgical hospital or an APB. Further evacuation to hospitals in the Saigon or Vung Tau area would be by helicopter or fixed-wing aircraft. Hospitalization would be in the Saigon, Bien Hoa, and Vung Tau areas. A mobile Army surgical hospital located at the land base near My Tho, in conjunction with the brigade to be based there, and a surgical team located on an APB, would provide surgery and medical treatment necessary to prepare critically injured or ill patients for evacuation to hospitals. A helicopter pad, sixteen-bed dispensary, and surgical suites with equipment necessary for one surgical team would be provided on each APB.

Communications would be provided by the permanently installed Army and Navy radio equipment aboard each ship and assault craft. This equipment would provide command, tactical, and logistical communication links to higher and subordinate headquarters. Tactical communications ashore would be by man-packed radios and by airborne relay when required.

General command arrangements had been set forth previously by General Westmoreland. The plan indicated that they would be further developed by study. The command relationships of the force were to be a major topic of discussion for many months after the publication of the Mobile Afloat Force concept.

CHAPTER III

Riverine Preparations in the United States and in Vietnam

During the final preparation of the Mobile Afloat Force plan in South Vietnam, the 9th Infantry Division was activated at Fort Riley, Kansas, on 1 February 1966 under the command of Major General George S. Eckhardt. This was the one infantry division to be organized in the United States during the fighting in Vietnam—the so-called Z Division that had been scheduled for operations in the Mekong Delta. It was probably no coincidence that the division had been designated the 9th U.S. Infantry; General Westmoreland had seen extensive service with the 9th in World War II, having commanded the 60th Infantry and having served as chief of staff of the division during operations in both France and Germany.

Because of a shortage of men and equipment the activation order provided for incremental formation of the division. Division base elements such as the headquarters and headquarters company, division support command, and brigade headquarters and headquarters companies were activated first. Activation of the battalions of each brigade was phased, commencing in April for the 1st Brigade, May for the 2d Brigade, and June for the 3d Brigade. The artillery and separate units were scheduled for activation during April and May. Some of the division's officers who had been previously assigned to the Department of the Army staff had learned that the 9th Infantry Division was scheduled to operate in the southern portion of the III Corps Tactical Zone and the northern portion of the IV Corps Tactical Zone and that it was to provide a floating brigade. This information was not discussed officially but was known to the brigade commanders and the division artillery commander.

The division was organized as a standard infantry division composed of nine infantry battalions of which one was initially mechanized. It had a cavalry squadron and the normal artillery and supporting units. The division training program was limited to eight weeks for basic combat training, eight weeks for advanced individual training, and eight weeks for both basic and advanced unit training—a total of twenty-four weeks. This compression of training time eliminated four weeks from each of the unit training periods and the four weeks usually allowed for field training exercises and division maneuvers—a total of twelve weeks from the normal Army training time for a division. Although it was not generally known in the division, the division training period as established in Army training programs had been reduced in order to conclude at the time of the beginning of the Vietnam dry season in December 1966 when the MACV plan called for the introduction of U.S. ground forces into the Mekong Delta.

The normal Army training programs were followed for the basic combat and advanced individual training. General Eckhardt, perceiving that the existing training programs had limitations for combat in Vietnam, by means of a personal letter gave his brigade commanders the latitude to make innovations and to modify training in order to prepare their men for the physical conditions and the tactics of the enemy in Vietnam. The training given by the brigade commanders was based on lessons learned and standing operating procedures of United States units then fighting in Vietnam. Although aware of possible employment of his unit in the Mekong Delta, each of the brigade commanders required the training he deemed advisable to prepare his unit for operations in any part of Vietnam. Although the brigade afloat had not been designated, Colonel William B. Fulton, Commanding Officer, 2d Brigade, felt that the mission could ultimately be assigned to his brigade. Because the training period was short, however, he elected to adhere to normal basic training in counterinsurgency for his units.

Colonel Fulton established a training course for the brigade and battalion commanders and their staffs that was designed to develop proficiency in command and staff actions for land operations in Vietnam. The class was held every ten days in a map exercise room with a sand table and map boards depicting selected areas of Vietnam. The sessions lasted approximately five hours. Three days before the class a brigade operations order was issued to the battalion commanders, requesting each battalion to prepare plans and orders in accordance with the brigade tactical concept. At the start of the session the brigade staff outlined the situation. Each battalion commander was then required to furnish a copy of his orders and to explain why he deployed his units as he did. There was a general critique, after which a new situation was assigned for study. Each commander and his staff, which included representatives of artillery, engineer, aviation, and other supporting elements, then prepared the next set of orders. These in turn were presented to the group for analysis and critique.

The commanders and staff studied various forms of land movement by wheeled and tracked vehicles on roads and cross-country. Next, air movement was considered, including troop lift and logistics computations, various formations, and the selection of landing and pickup zones. This in turn was followed by a study of water movement by small craft.

In conjunction with command and staff training, the brigade was developing a standing operating procedure, which was reviewed at sessions of the command and staff course. The course began in May when the brigade was activated and was separate from the Army training programs being undertaken by the units. Officer and noncommissioned officer classes in the subject matter covered in the Army training programs were conducted at the battalion level.

Following the map exercises on movement, a series of exercises was conducted involving the organization and security of the base area and patrolling outside of the base in the brigade tactical area of responsibility. Subsequently, exercises were conducted combining both air and ground movement in search and destroy operations.

The brigade patterned its standing operating procedure and its methods of tactical operations primarily after those of the 1st Infantry Division. At the time that the command and staff training course was in full swing, several unit commanders from the 1st Infantry Division were returning from Vietnam to Fort Riley and Junction City, Kansas, where they had left their families when they departed with the 1st Division in 1965. Extensive interviews were conducted by the brigade commander and staff, who incorporated the information obtained into the standing operating procedures and the command and staff course.

The command and staff course did not specifically deal with riverine operations. Some of the map exercises were plotted in the northern delta immediately adjacent to the Saigon area and Di An where the 1st Division was operating, and one problem explored water movement. Too little was known about riverine operations to incorporate them fully into training. Furthermore, Colonel Fulton felt that the basic operational essentials should be mastered first; riverine operations could be studied after unit training was completed.

Review of the Mobile Afloat Force Concept

On receipt of the MACV Mobile Afloat Force concept in mid-March 1966, the Commander in Chief, Pacific, Admiral Sharp, requested that it be reviewed by the Commander in Chief, Pacific Fleet, Admiral Roy L. Johnson. The latter generally concurred in the plan but pointed out that while the Mobile Afloat Force concept provided for maintaining a brigade in the delta for up to six months, it might be necessary to rotate the APB's for maintenance and upkeep every two to three months.

Admiral Sharp had questioned the command arrangements. Under the Mobile Afloat Force plan it had been recommended that the Navy commander be charged with the security of the mobile base, while the Army brigade commander would provide support. Admiral Johnson, on the other hand, believed that the Army commander should be responsible for base security with the Navy commander providing supporting fire and protection against waterborne threat. He also questioned whether the Mobile Afloat Force could search junks effectively and protect naval craft against water mines and ambushes. He expressed concern that hydrographic charts of the delta waterways were incomplete, and that river assault craft were not properly designed and were, furthermore, too noisy.

Except for operational control, the Navy units were under the control of the Commander in Chief, Pacific Fleet. The Commander, Amphibious Force, Pacific, and Commander, Service Force, Pacific, had specific responsibilities and part of the subsequent success of the force stemmed from the professional manner in which the Navy fulfilled its obligations. In the case of logistics, support was given not only by units in Vietnam such as the harbor clearance units of Service Force, Pacific, but also by other units of the logistic support system, afloat and ashore, as set forth in the support plan of the Service Force. Each of the commanders concerned felt personal responsibility for the performance of those of his units that would be operating under Military Assistance Command, Vietnam.

As staffing of the Mobile Afloat Force proceeded, General Westmoreland continued to call attention to the need for beginning immediately U.S. operations in the Mekong Delta. In a message to Admiral Sharp on 11 May, with respect to intensification of the efforts of Vietnam armed forces and early initiation of U.S. operations in the Mekong Delta, he stated that "enemy access to Delta resources must be terminated without delay."

The planned deployment into the delta had appeared in MACV Planning Directive 3–66 published 21 April 1966. The directive had emphasized widening the range of operations in the northern coastal areas of South Vietnam and close-in clearing and securing operations around Saigon. It did not provide for any major American effort in the delta during the rainy season of May–November 1966, but the possibility of short operations by units such as the Special Landing Force was cited. These operations were to have as their target the mangrove swamps along the coastal areas in the southern III Corps and northern IV Corps Tactical Zones. Plans for the operations were based on the success of operation JACKSTAY in the Rung Sat Special Zone in 1966.

General Westmoreland expected to send forces in late 1966 and early 1967 from the III Corps Tactical Zone to the Plain of Reeds and other northern delta areas. The planning provided for the Commanding General, II Field Force, Vietnam, Lieutenant General Jonathan O. Seaman, to assume command of U.S. tactical operations in the IV Corps Tactical Zone, co-ordinating operations with the Commanding General, IV Corps, through the American senior adviser who was to be a brigadier general. (Colonel William D. Desobry, Senior Advisor, IV Corps Tactical Zone, was promoted to brigadier general in August of 1966.)

On 29 May 1966 General Westmoreland was briefed on the deployment of the 9th Infantry Division to the IV Corps Tactical Zone. He approved the plan and ordered his staff to discuss with General Seaman an alternate location for the 9th Division base. General Westmoreland directed that the Mobile Afloat Force plan to locate a division headquarters and one brigade at Ba Ria be reconsidered. He called attention to his previous decision that the 9th Division would be placed under General Seaman to facilitate tactical operations along the III and IV Corps border and that the Commanding General, 9th Division, would not become the senior adviser to the IV Corps Tactical Zone. General Westmoreland pointed out further that the introduction of a division force into IV Corps would require discussion with General Cao Van Vien, chairman of the Joint General Staff of the Republic of Vietnam.

On 9 June General Westmoreland suggested that the delta might well be a source of stabilization of the Vietnamese economy. The delta could produce enough rice for the entire country if it were kept under government control; other areas of the country would then be free to industrialize. The delta was also the source of nearly 50 percent of the country's manpower. It therefore followed that development of the region had to be accelerated; sending in a U.S. division would aid in this acceleration.

On 10 June General Westmoreland discussed with General Vien and Lieutenant General Dang Van Quang, Commanding General, IV Corps Tactical Zone, the possible introduction of U.S. forces into the IV Corps Tactical Zone. On 13 June the matter came up for discussion in the Mission Council meeting. General Quang, who had made a statement to the press some weeks earlier against the stationing of U.S. troops in IV Corps, but in the meantime had apparently had a change of heart, now expressed in the meeting a desire that a U.S. brigade be stationed in IV Corps. General Westmoreland told the council that a final decision on the matter of basing American troops in IV Corps would be made in October. Dredges had already been ordered, and the proposed site would be ready by December. He further stated that the troops would be located about eight kilometers from My Tho, which would be off limits to U.S. troops, and that travel through My Tho would be sharply restricted. Since the base would be completely self-sufficient, it would be no drain on local resources. When Ambassador Henry Cabot Lodge, Jr., and the political counselor expressed reservations, General Westmoreland agreed with them that it would be preferable to use Vietnamese troops, but pointed out that up to this time Vietnamese troops had not been completely successful in the delta, and important Viet Cong units were still operating there.

The land base had been selected by General Westmoreland himself from four sites submitted by the engineers as suitable for building by dredging. The sites were designated W, X, Y, and Z, and the one near My Tho chosen by General Westmoreland was W. The general's staff immediately referred phonetically to Site W as Base Whisky, the word used in the military phonetic alphabet for the letter W. General Westmoreland felt that the site should be given a significant name in keeping with its role as the first American base camp in the Mekong Delta. He asked the official MACV translator to give him several possible Vietnamese names for the base, such as the translation of "friendship" or "co-operation." The translator's list included the Vietnamese term *Dong Tam,* literally meaning "united hearts and minds." General Westmoreland selected this name for three reasons: first, it signified the bond between the American and Vietnamese peoples with respect to the objectives to be achieved in the delta. Second, it connoted an appro-

LANDING CRAFT REPAIR SHIP WITH ARMORED TROOP CARRIERS

priate objective compatible with the introduction of U.S. forces into the populous delta where their prospective presence had evoked some official concern. Third, Dong Tam was a name which Americans would find easy to pronounce and remember. Having chosen the name of Dong Tam, General Westmoreland asked General Vien, the chairman of the Joint General Staff, his English translation of the name. General Vien confirmed that "united hearts and minds" was the literal translation. Thus the name Base Whisky was changed to Dong Tam, which became a well-known landmark during the subsequent co-operative efforts of American and Vietnamese troops in the delta.

Later in the month, at the Honolulu Requirements Planning Conference, the Mobile Afloat Force was included in requirements for the calendar years 1967 and 1968.

> The Mekong Delta Mobile Afloat Force will provide a means to introduce, employ and sustain substantial U.S. combat power in that vital area. Introduction of the MDMAF [Mekong Delta Mobile Afloat Force] at the earliest practicable date, whether it be an increment of that force or all of it, will provide a capability for more rapid achievement of U.S. objectives in that area.

These requirements as set forth in the conference provided for the arrival of the first component of that force by April 1967 and the second, final component by March 1968.

On 5 July Robert S. McNamara, Secretary of Defense, approved activation and deployment of a Mobile Afloat Force consisting of two river assault groups. At the time of the approval, he reduced the number of self-propelled barracks ships from five to two and eliminated one landing craft repair ship from the force. He was not willing to provide for the total package requested for the Mobile Afloat Force because he felt that the force could be fully tested with the equipment he had approved. Included in the cut was the salvage force, which required two heavy lift craft of 2,000 tons, two YTB's altered for salvage, two LCU's, and three 100-ton floating dry docks. Only one YTB was authorized. Secretary McNamara's decision was to have an appreciable impact on the preparation for and the operations of the Mobile Riverine Force as it was constituted in June of the following year. Subsequently General Westmoreland, through Admiral Sharp, requested reconsideration of the decision to field only two self-propelled barracks ships and two river assault groups; again four river assault groups and at least four barracks ships were requested.

In view of the request, the Joint Chiefs of Staff asked for an evaluation of the planned employment and of the additional effectiveness which these ships and craft would contribute to the force. Such an evaluation already had been completed by the MACV staff in May. The evaluation pointed out the lack of firm ground for stationing major troop elements and noted that "the time-consuming process of dredging" required to base additional units on land justified the additional two barracks ships. Admiral Johnson called attention to the fact that the Mobile Afloat Force concept also provided for a mobile brigade independent of a land base. One brigade of the 9th Division was to be stationed at Dong Tam in early 1967. When barracks ships became available, a reinforced battalion from a brigade in III Corps Tactical Zone would be put afloat.

The two river assault groups approved by Secretary McNamara for fiscal year 1967 would be stationed at Dong Tam. Omission of the repair boat to provide mobile maintenance would preclude the permanent basing of assault groups with the two barracks ships in the first increment of the Mobile Afloat Force. Either assault group would be available on call from a land base to provide lift for a battalion afloat. Some of the boats of an assault group would remain to protect the barracks ships.

Units of the 9th Division not stationed at Dong Tam or aboard APB's would be based in III Corps Tactical Zone north and east of the Rung Sat Special Zone, permitting extensive operations into the special zone and IV Corps by assault group craft. With the arrival of a third assault group, which would include an ARL, one group could be permanently assigned to the forces afloat. This would leave two river assault groups assigned to Dong Tam for lifting battalions of that brigade or the other brigade from the Vung Tau area for operations in the upper delta. When the second increment arrived, at least two river assault groups would be needed for the floating base and one each to support the other two brigades of the 9th Division.

General Westmoreland strongly recommended to Admiral Sharp that the two additional APB's and assault groups be included in the calendar year 1967 force requirements and that they be activated and deployed at the earliest practicable date. Admiral Sharp supported General Westmoreland's position and forwarded it to the Joint Chiefs of Staff on 16 July, with a further justification of the two river assault groups on the grounds that "projection of U.S. combat operations into the Delta is an objective of major importance." Admiral Sharp stated that with three thousand kilometers of navigable waterways, an absence of adequate roads, and a lack of helicopters, the 9th Division, which "will be the principal riverine ground combat force," would require river assault group support. Four groups (two organic to the Mobile Afloat Force and two additional) could lift about half of the riverine ground force at any one time. In addition, river assault group craft would be used in reconnaissance and patrolling missions and resupply operations, would reinforce GAME WARDEN and MARKET TIME operations when necessary, and would support operations to open and secure important water routes.

In August while the question of whether to increase the number of Navy boats was being decided at higher headquarters, in Vietnam Mobile Afloat Force preparations were nearing completion. On 1 August, MACV published Planning Directive 4-66—Operations in the Delta. The directive called for employment of riverine forces "regardless of whether based on land (Dong Tam or elsewhere) or on MDMAF [Mekong Delta Mobile Afloat Force]." Composition of a river assault group was established as 26 armored troop carriers, 16 assault support patrol boats, 5 monitors, 2 command communications boats, and 2 LCM-6 refuelers. This composition was to vary little throughout the entire period of river assault group operations.

The MACV plan would operate in three phases. During the first, the Construction Phase, 1 July 1966–31 January 1967, all actions required to prepare the ground and facilities for occupation of the base would be completed. In the second, the Preparation and Occupation Phase, also to run from 1 July 1966 through 31 January 1967, all actions required to prepare the Army and Navy units to occupy bases, and the actual occupation would be completed. Preparation of the forces would proceed concurrently with base construction. The Improvement and Operations Phase would begin when the Army and Navy units had occupied the bases and were ready to begin combat operations. All actions necessary to conduct and sustain combat operations from the Dong Tam base would be undertaken during this phase and base facilities would be improved and expanded as necessary.

9th Infantry Division Studies the Mobile Afloat Force

In July 1966 the 9th Division at Fort Riley had been furnished copies of the plan and requirements of the Mobile Afloat Force. These were studied by the division staff and, after approximately two weeks, the chief of staff, Colonel Crosby P. Miller, assembled the brigade commanders. In very broad terms, Colonel Miller outlined the intended area of operations for the division and referred to the provision for a brigade afloat. This briefing aroused the curiosity of Colonel Fulton, commander of the 2d Brigade. He requested copies of the complete plan for study by himself and his staff, and the division commander approved. An intensive analysis was then made by the appropriate staff officers and the study was returned to division headquarters.

Exhibiting the foresight that had characterized its planning effort, MACV sent one of the principal planners for the Mobile Afloat Force to the United States on normal rotation and placed him on temporary duty with the 9th Division for a week. This officer, Lieutenant Colonel John E. Murray, Field Artillery, was extremely enthusiastic about the project and was familiar with all aspects of the plan and with the area of intended operations in the delta. Colonel Fulton arranged for Colonel Murray to spend some time with his brigade staff and battalion commanders to discuss all facets of the project. Through questions and answers, a clear understanding of what was intended was conveyed to the brigade officers.

Later in the week, Colonel Murray addressed the division staff and subordinate commanders. He outlined the Mobile Afloat Force plan, discussed the environment, and sketched the nature of intended activity. He also explained that the Marine Corps had developed a basic riverine manual entitled Small Unit Operations in the Riverine Environment. This document was obtained by the 2d Brigade for study from the division G-3 (assistant chief of staff for operations), Lieutenant Colonel Richard E. Zastrow.

In early May the Department of the Army had informed the 9th Division that it would be sent to the Republic of Vietnam, beginning in December. The assistant division commander, Brigadier General Morgan E. Roseborough, headed an advance element that left for South Vietnam in late August to plan deployment of the division.

The Coronado Conference and Doctrine

On the 12th of September, Colonel Fulton was informed by General Eckhardt that a conference would be held on the 17th of September at Coronado Naval Base, California, and was designated the division representative at the conference. The conference had been co-ordinated by Headquarters, U.S. Continental Army Command, to examine the joint training implications which would be imposed on the 9th Division and the Army U.S. training base by participation in the Mobile Afloat Force. General Eckhardt directed Colonel Fulton to prepare a brief of the Army views on the Mobile Afloat Force that would include a plan for logistic support. General Eckhardt further asked that he receive a briefing on the presentation to be made at the conference. It was also decided that the division support commander, Colonel John H. Barner, should accompany Colonel Fulton to Coronado to handle the logistical aspects.

On 19 September, accompanied by Captain Johnnie H. Corns of his staff, Colonel Barner, division G-2 and G-3 representatives, and a representative of the division signal office, Colonel Fulton proceeded to Coronado. The conference was held under the auspices of the Commander, Amphibious Command, Pacific, Vice Admiral Francis J. Blouin. Navy attendees included representatives from the Chief of Naval Operations, Commander in Chief, Pacific Fleet, the Amphibious Training Center, the U.S. Marine Corps, and Commander, Service Force, U.S. Pacific Fleet. The Army delegation also included representatives from Continental Army Command headquarters, U.S. Army Combat Developments Command, Fifth Army headquarters, and Sixth Army headquarters. The commander of River Assault Flotilla One, Captain Wade C. Wells, who was to be the U.S. Navy component commander of the Mobile Afloat Force, his chief of staff, Captain Paul B. Smith, and the rest of his staff attended. The conference was chaired by Rear Admiral Julian T. Burke, who had the additional responsibility of preparing a U.S. Navy doctrinal manual for riverine operations. Presentations were made of the organization and operations of the two components as well as the broad problem of command relationships of the joint force. Afterward several working groups were established to deal with command and control, joint staff arrangements, training, logistics, communications, and medical support.

During the conference Captain Wells informed Colonel Fulton that the River Assault Flotilla One chief of staff and representatives of N-1, N-2, N-3, and N-4 staff sections, as well as a communications officer, were going to Vietnam as an advance party in early October. Upon learning that the 9th Division had an advanced planning element at Headquarters, U.S. Army, Vietnam, Captain Wells agreed that the two advance elements should be the basis for co-ordination in Vietnam. Captain Wells and Colonel Fulton also made informal arrangements to co-ordinate mutual problems that might arise between the time of the conference and the departure of the 2d Brigade for Vietnam, which was tentatively scheduled for early January 1967. While there were no official provisions for direct communications and co-ordination between the two component commanders of the Mobile Afloat Force, this early meeting proved extremely beneficial in resolving matters that could have impaired the entire undertaking.

Returning to Fort Riley, Kansas, Colonel Fulton and Captain Corns briefed General Eckhardt and his staff on the results of the Coronado conference. General Eckhardt then designated Colonel Fulton as the executive agent for the division on riverine matters, and specified that this responsibility carried with it the designation of commander of the floating brigade and the U.S. Army component for the Mobile Afloat Force. Colonel Fulton still chose not to incorporate riverine operations in his training program because of the great amount of normal training to be accomplished. It was implied, however, at the conference that there would be a training period in Vietnam of approximately two to three months during which the Army and Navy components would be able to train their forces for the joint riverine operations. Nevertheless when Colonel Fulton informed Lieutenant Colonel William B. Cronin, Commanding Officer, 2d Battalion, 47th Infantry, and Lieutenant Colonel Guy I. Tutwiler, Commanding Officer, 4th Battalion, 47th Infantry, of the riverine mission, they decided as part of their normal training programs to incorporate techniques and equipment for crossing small rivers.

While at Coronado, Colonel Fulton explored with the commander of the Amphibious Training School the possibility of conducting a riverine course for his brigade staff, the battalion commanders and their staffs, and the brigade supporting unit commanders. This school was a repository of amphibious doctrine and concepts as well as lessons learned in the MARKET TIME and GAME WARDEN operations, which were, respectively, the U.S. Navy offshore and river operations in South Vietnam. All the U.S. Navy advisers for the Vietnamese river assault groups were trained under Amphibious Training School auspices. The Navy SEAL (sea-air-land) teams, which were rotated in and out of South Vietnam, were also trained there. Many of the school faculty had already completed tours of duty in both the U.S. and Vietnamese navies. The idea of conducting a riverine course was acceptable to the commander of the Amphibious Training School, and plans for instruction were developed through subsequent correspondence between the brigade and the Amphibious School during the period October through December. Also it was agreed that the Amphibious Training School would provide a team at Fort Riley during December 1966 for the purpose of training selected men from brigade and battalion in techniques of waterproofing, small boat loading and handling, and combat offloading from transports. Also included was instruction in water safety techniques that was to prove immensely valuable once operations commenced.

In early October Colonel Fulton was informed that he would accompany the division commander to Vietnam on an orientation visit to reconnoiter the riverine environment and get a preview of the requirements for riverine operations. The division commander and a small staff left on 9 October for a three-week visit to Vietnam. Colonel Fulton's arrival coincided with that of the advance party of the River Assault Flotilla One staff. Colonel Fulton and Captain Smith, chief of staff of the flotilla, were able to visit and analyze the proposed training site in the vicinity of Ap Go Dau, adjacent to the Rung Sat Special Zone, approximately fifteen kilometers south of Bearcat. Bearcat, ten miles south of Long Binh, was to be the 9th Division base instead of Ba Ria, which had been specified in the original Mobile Afloat Force plan. Bearcat was to be expanded into a base capable of accommodating the entire division until the 2d Brigade base at Ap Go Dau could be built. Colonel Fulton and Captain Smith agreed on the site near Ap Go Dau, and plans were developed by Company B, 15th Engineer Battalion, to construct the joint training base. A phased training schedule based on actual combat operations from the new location was also tentatively agreed upon. The shift of the division base from Ba Ria to Bearcat was to have no significant effect on the Mobile Afloat Force plan.

Colonel Fulton also visited the Dong Tam construction site, the 7th Division headquarters of the Army of Vietnam, and General Desobry, senior adviser of IV Corps Tactical Zone at Can Tho. Discussions centered on projected operations of U.S. forces in the Mekong Delta. It was especially fortuitous that Colonel Fulton, General Desobry, and the Senior Advisor, 7th Division, Colonel John E. Lance, Jr., had been on the faculty of the Army War College during the period 1962 to 1965. This professional association proved to be very valuable during the ensuing months as the 2d Brigade planned for and conducted operations in the Mekong Delta.

While at Headquarters, U.S. Army, Vietnam, Colonel Fulton learned that the Army had not completed the preparation of the riverine doctrine, a task assigned to it by MACV Directive 3-66. In discussing the task, Colonel Fulton found that Major John R. Witherell, the U.S. Army Combat Developments Command liaison officer, had developed an active interest in the Mobile Afloat Force plan and had started preparation of a rather detailed manuscript which dealt with organization and tactics of units as envisaged by the Mobile Afloat Force planners. At Colonel Fulton's suggestion Major Witherell agreed to propose to Headquarters, Combat Developments Command, that it undertake the drafting of a test field manual on riverine operations. In making this recommendation, Major Witherell planned to furnish his draft manuscript. The meeting proved to be beneficial since during the Coronado conference the doctrine matter had been explored with both Navy representatives and Major Donald R. Morelli, the Combat Developments Command representative at the conference. It was agreed that if the manual was undertaken, the writing should be done at the Amphibious Training School at Coronado, the best source of information on riverine warfare.

Upon his return to Fort Riley, Colonel Fulton was visited by a representative from Combat Developments Command who had outlined a manual based on Major Witherell's manuscript. Colonel Fulton suggested that this be accepted as the basis for the manual which was to be prepared at Coronado with representatives from the various Army service schools and Combat Developments agencies under the leadership of the Institute of Combined Arms Group, Fort Leavenworth. Colonel Fulton stressed that the manual should be available when the brigade and battalion staffs departed for South Vietnam on 14 January 1967. The need for the manual was quite apparent since the U.S. Marine Corps Fleet Marine Force Manual 8–4, the only doctrinal manual on riverine operations, dealt with only small boat tactics and did not cover joint riverine operations.

Final Decisions on Deployment

Secretary of Defense McNamara during his October visit to South Vietnam was briefed on the Mobile Afloat Force, and the need for two additional river assault squadrons was stressed at that time. The designation river assault group had been changed to river assault squadron in order to avoid confusion with the Vietnamese river assault groups. During this briefing it was emphasized to Mr. McNamara that if the objectives of the MACV campaign plan were to be achieved, U.S. ground operations in the IV Corps area were needed to assist the Republic of Vietnam armed forces. It was further pointed out to Mr. McNamara that roughly 50 percent of the population and 68 percent of the rice-producing area in the Republic of Vietnam were in the Mekong Delta. In this briefing it was explained that the 9th Division, due in Vietnam in December 1966 and January 1967, was to be the principal river ground force, and that the river assault boats needed to provide tactical mobility would conform to standard U.S. Navy organization structure, with two assault squadrons of about fifty boats each under command of River Assault Flotilla One. The Mobile Afloat Force with the two approved river assault squadrons would provide a good start, but there was a need for at least two additional assault squadrons by the end of calendar year 1967 in order to sustain the momentum of the riverine operations. The 9th Division, now planned with seven infantry battalions and two, rather than one, mechanized battalions, would require the support of two river assault squadrons. Two additional battalions from the U.S. 25th Division and the Australian Task Force would bring the total to eleven infantry battalions for riverine operations. No decision was made by Mr. McNamara on the two river assault squadrons during his visit.

On 21 November General Westmoreland suggested to the Mission Council that it was feasible to deploy a battalion to Dong Tam in January 1967, and requested the council's endorsement of this action. Anticipating the council's concurrence, General Westmoreland directed the planning and preparation for deployment of a brigade in February 1967 if it was deemed feasible by II Field Force, Vietnam. By 29 November, Ambassador Lodge had approved this deployment.

On 1 December, Headquarters, Military Assistance Command, Vietnam, published a plan for logistical support for the Mobile Afloat Force. This plan provided for two kinds of support—one for the units based at Dong Tam and one for the units afloat. The land base commander was assigned responsibility for the logistical support for Dong Tam, and the mobile riverine base commander would have responsibility for the mobile riverine base, while service-peculiar supply would be the responsibility of the component commander concerned. Saigon was designated as the primary supply source for the Dong Tam base, with Vung Tau as the alternate, and land lines of communication were to be used wherever possible. The mobile riverine base would be supported by Vung Tau, with Saigon as the alternate.

After evaluating the progress of the base construction at Dong Tam, II Field Force reported on 4 December that it was feasible to support a battalion at Dong Tam in late February 1967. The planning and liaison machinery went into high gear early in December. Elements of the 9th Division would be available for training at the Vung Tau base in early January. The commander of Naval Forces, Vietnam, had shifted all efforts to prepare the base for riverine training when the proposed training site at Ap Go Dau was abandoned in favor of Vung Tau. He recommended liaison between 9th Division and Vietnamese and U.S. agencies. He also asked Admiral Johnson to provide a suitable support ship at Vung Tau about 7 January and at the same time to place aboard it one river assault squadron staff and one river division staff. The commander of River Assault Flotilla One and his staff, less the advance element, were to leave Coronado in mid-February and a second river division was to leave in late February.

General Westmoreland directed the commander of II Field Force to prepare to send an infantry battalion task force from the

9th Division to Dong Tam, to add forces later to increase it to a brigade, and to advise him of the arrival dates. The Commanding General, U.S. Army, Vietnam, was to support the task forces and Senior Advisor, IV Corps Tactical Zone, was directed to plan for the provision of Vietnam Army security forces, co-ordinate Vietnamese and U.S. security arrangements, and prepare the Vietnamese people for the presence of U.S. troops at Dong Tam.

The first elements of the 9th Division landed at Vung Tau on 19 December, and on 20 December General Westmoreland estimated that the battalion task force would move to Dong Tam on 25 January following two engineer companies that were to arrive there on 7 January. He calculated that strength would increase to brigade level in late February or early March.

The Mobile Afloat Force, conceived and approved during 1966, was one of the most important MACV accomplishments of the year. This force was expected to play a major role in the control of the delta, not only in a military sense, but also economically and politically. Further, the entire delta campaign could well be a key to the success of the combined operations of the United States and the Republic of Vietnam.

2d Brigade, 9th Infantry Division, Arrives in Vietnam

Upon completion of training at Fort Riley at the end of November 1966, the 2d brigade began preparation for overseas movement. During this time, selected men from the brigade and battalions were given training by the Marine Training Team from the Naval Amphibious School. On 3 January, the brigade commander and staff, the commander and staff of the 2d Battalion, 4th artillery, the commanders and staffs of the 3d and 4th Battalions, 47th Infantry, and the S–2, 2d Battalion, 47th Infantry, went to Coronado to attend the ten-day riverine course that had been established at the request of the brigade commander. The course provided a great deal of useful information on operations of the Vietnamese river assault groups, U.S. Navy SEAL teams, Viet Cong intelligence operations in the delta, and the riverine environment. The ten days gave the commanders and staffs of the brigade's attached and supporting units the opportunity to concentrate on purely riverine problems for the first time.

When the course ended on 12 January, the Combat Developments Command writing group had completed the first draft of Training Text 31–75, Riverine Operations. Colonel Fulton now learned that although the Navy had provided advice and consultation, it would not formally accept the manual, nor would the commander of River Assault Flotilla One acknowledge the text as a source of doctrine to which he would subscribe. When agreement had been reached in September that a manual would be written, Navy acceptance was tacitly understood, but since it was not forthcoming the question of agreement on joint procedures remained. The brigade commander and his officers, however, considered the training text a sound new source of riverine doctrine and concepts on which subsequent training in Vietnam could be based. Improvement could be made in the text after the experience of actual operations.

The 2d Brigade officers who had attended the Coronado riverine course arrived at Bien Hoa on 15 January and proceeded to Bearcat. Shortly afterward the remainder of the advance party arrived by air from Fort Riley; included were all the squad leaders from the three infantry battalions, two platoon sergeants and two platoon leaders from each of the companies, and all company commanders. The main body was en route by water from San Francisco under the supervision of Lieutenant Colonel Thomas F. O'Connor, the brigade executive officer. The other officer cadre consisted of the company executive officers, two platoon leaders from each company, and the battalion executive officers with small staffs. The purpose of the large brigade advance party was to give most of the tactical unit combat leaders battle experience before the main body arrived at the end of January. To this end the unit advance parties were sent to operate with the U.S. 1st and 25th Divisions for approximately two and one-half weeks.

The main body debarked at Vung Tau on 31 January and 1 February 1967 and reached Bearcat on 1 February. On 7 February the 2d Brigade, with the 2d, 3d, and 4th Battalions, 47th Infantry, and 3d Squadron, 5th Cavalry, commenced a one-week operation in the Nhon Trach District of Bien Hoa Province just north of the Rung Sat Special Zone. The 2d Brigade had an excellent opportunity to shake itself down operationally in a combat environment and to compensate for the lack of a brigade field training exercise which it had been unable to conduct at Fort Riley because of the short training period.

Rung Sat Special Zone Operational Training

During the latter part of January the 3d Battalion, 60th Infantry, an element of the 3d Brigade, 9th U.S. Division, had begun riverine training with the advance River Assault Flotilla One elements that were aboard USS *Whitfield County* (LST 1169), anchored in Vung Tau harbor. The 3d Battalion, 60th Infantry, was to be the first infantry unit sent to Dong Tam and was to arrive there by the end of January. It would be followed in training by the 3d Battalion, 47th Infantry, which was then participating in the 2d Brigade operation in Nhon Trach.

On 10 February, two companies and the staff of the 3d Battalion, 47th Infantry, under Lieutenant Colonel Lucien E. Bolduc, Jr., left for riverine training in the Rung Sat Special Zone. The Navy crews with which the battalion would work had received on-the-job training with the Vietnamese Navy river assault groups in the delta.

On 15 February, as the brigade was returning from the Nhon Trach operation to its base camp at Bearcat, an order was received from II Field Force directing that an entire battalion conduct operations in the Rung Sat Special Zone beginning 16 February. The order was prompted by a Viet Cong attack on a freighter navigating the Long Tau, the main shipping channel connecting Saigon and Vung Tau, on 15 February. It brought to an abrupt halt the organized training for Colonel Bolduc's battalion, which had accomplished only three of the scheduled ten days of training; full-scale combat operations would have to begin. The battalion commander was aboard USS *Whitfield County* with two companies when Colonel Fulton talked to him. Colonel Fulton had already ordered the remaining companies of the 3d Battalion, 47th Infantry, as well as a direct support battery of the 2d Battalion, 4th Artillery, into the northern portion of the Rung Sat Special Zone. Colonel Bolduc's mission was to disrupt enemy activities in the major base areas of the Viet Cong.

The resulting operation initiated on 16 February 1967 and terminated on 20 March was designated RIVER RAIDER I. It was the first joint operation by U.S. Army and U.S. Navy units that were later to constitute the Mobile Riverine Force. The 3d Battalion, 47th Infantry, was supported by River Assault Division 91 of River Assault Squadron 9. (*Chart 1*)

Joint operations centers were maintained twenty-four hours a day both at land bases and aboard the APA *Henrico,* and joint plans were made for each project. River Assault Flotilla One provided rear area support and planning assistance for river squadron operations. Squadron 9's assault division was commanded by Lieutenant Charles H. Sibley, who operated LCM-6's and a command vessel borrowed from the Vietnam Navy since the squadron's boats

CHART 1—RIVER ASSAULT SQUADRON ORGANIZATION

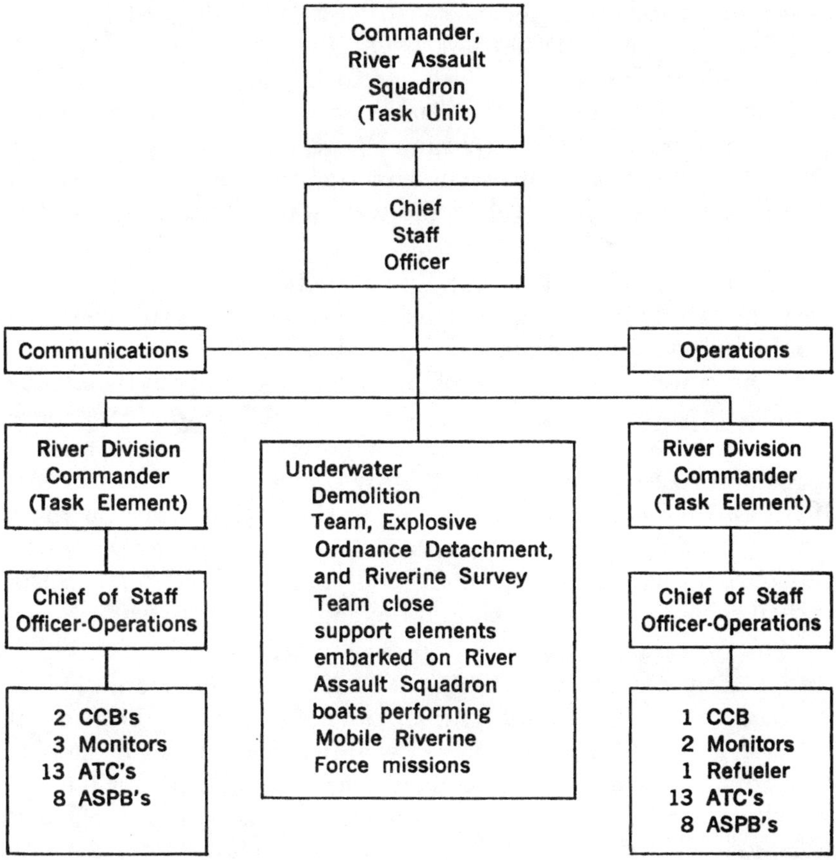

had not yet been delivered. Vietnam River Assault Group 26 provided mine-sweeping support and escorts for movement on narrow and dangerous waterways.

Particularly important was the support provided by the Infantry Advisor, Rung Sat Special Zone, Major McLendon G. Morris, USMC, who joined the battalion command group at the outset of the operation and remained till the battalion's operations were completed. Major Morris furnished liaison to the Senior Advisor, Rung Sat Special Zone, at Nha Be and invaluable advice and assistance. His extensive knowledge of and experience in the zone, his familiarity with complex fire support procedures, and his ability to get support on short notice made a significant contribution to RIVER RAIDER I's success.

During the operation boats of River Assault Division 91 moved troops to and from the barracks ship by ATC at all hours of the day and night, delivering them primarily to friendly ambush sites, sometimes to the battalion land base. They remained in ambush sites at night, and one boat was normally kept within a fifteen-minute standby range of the land base as transportation for the platoon-size ground force. Division 91 was called on a number of times and was twice instrumental in the capture of sampans and documents. Its boats patrolled the waterways and gave great flexibility to the river force.

Use of deception in the conduct of night operations was found very effective in the Rung Sat Special Zone. Usually a rifle company would be positioned around the battalion command post during daylight hours. Under cover of darkness this company would be withdrawn and transported to a new area where it would establish a perimeter, then move out to place ambushes. It would then be in a position to begin search and destroy or strike operations at first light. On one occasion a complete riverine assault, with artillery fire and radio transmissions, was staged as a feint while troops remained quietly aboard landing craft that resumed their patrol stations from which small landings were subsequently made.

For operations on small waterways plastic assault boats and water safety devices were useful. The battalion used one 27-foot engineer boat and several 13-man inflatable rubber rafts to advantage, but they, like the plastic assault boats, offered no protection from small arms fire and their slow speed and the inevitable bunching of troops made them highly vulnerable. Water movement was essential, however, since the Viet Cong moved primarily by sampan; no amount of trudging through mangrove swamps would outmaneuver an enemy who sought to avoid contact.

While salt water damaged clothing, the need for exchange was not much higher than in normal field use. The jungle boot stood up well under protracted use; jungle fatigues were washed overnight aboard the support ship, and a small direct exchange stock was maintained. The principal damage was to weapons and ammunition, which salt water corroded. It was necessary to break down weapons and scrub them with a mixture of cleaning solvent and oil on each return to the ship. The 7.62 metal link belt ammunition was frequently so badly corroded that it had to be discarded.

Only essential equipment was carried, the normal load consisting of seven magazines for the M16 rifle, 200 rounds for the machine gun, and twelve rounds of 40-mm. grenades. Each squad carried 100 feet of nylon rope, a 10-foot rope with snap link per man, and a grappling hook with 50 feet of line—items that were invaluable in water crossing operations as well as in detonating booby traps.

Ambushes were found to be most successful on well-traveled waterways. While airborne infrared devices for detecting people or things by their difference in temperature from the surrounding area proved valuable in the sparsely populated Rung Sat Special Zone, they were later less successful in the heavily populated delta.

The common rule that an ambush should be moved after being tripped did not always apply to water ambush in the Rung Sat Special Zone. On one occasion, an ambush was tripped three times in one night, with the result that seven of the enemy were killed and three sampans and two weapons captured.

Lack of positions suitable for placing artillery and the great distances involved produced a large zone in which the enemy was not subject to friendly fires. The zone was sparsely populated, with friendly civilians concentrated in a few widely dispersed villages separated by areas which the government warned citizens not to enter. Here the U.S. effort was to keep the enemy out of areas where troops had already discovered and destroyed large Viet Cong base camps, factories, munitions, stocks of rice, and other matériel.

As a result of the experiences in RIVER RAIDER I, Colonel Bolduc submitted several suggestions that assisted later operations of the Mobile Riverine Force. He advised that any unit operating in the Rung Sat Special Zone for other than a limited objective should either be a riverine unit or receive riverine training at the outset of the operation. Techniques were relatively simple and easily learned; troops that were well conditioned and adequately commanded could operate in the zone for a long time without suffering adverse effects. The longer the operation, the longer the troops needed to rest and dry out.

Since the enemy scrupulously avoided contact, current tactical intelligence was of paramount importance. Units operating in the Rung Sat therefore had to seek intelligence aggressively from all sources and agencies. Quick translation of enemy documents was also important. In one case the battalion captured at night from a group of five sampans documents and maps showing the location of a Viet Cong regional headquarters and various stops made by the sampan owners along the route they had traveled. One document showed delivery of arms to specified Viet Cong units and compromised an entire Viet Cong signal system. Although the general nature of the contents and their importance was immediately apparent to the battalion commander, he was obliged to send all the documents to the senior adviser of the Rung Sat Special Zone. Although he dispatched them immediately, no translation was received for more than a week—too long a delay to permit timely exploitation. During the last stages of the operation, all documents were quickly translated by the S-2 and an interpreter before being sent to higher headquarters so that information could be acted upon at once.

Airmobility was essential to effective riverine operations; it was necessary to have a command helicopter capable of carrying a commander, a fire support co-ordinator, an S-2 intelligence officer, an S-3, and necessary radio communications. When naval helicopters were used a Navy representative had to be aboard. When not required for direct control of operations, the helicopter was fully utilized for reconnaissance and liaison.

One UH-ID helicopter was placed in direct support of the battalion to permit resupply and emergency lift of widely scattered troops. The battalion could fully utilize five transport helicopters and two armed helicopters on a daily basis for about ten hours. They were needed for airmobile assaults, positioning of ambushes, troop extractions and transfers, ground reconnaissance of beaches and helicopter landing zones, checking sampans, and return to areas previously worked in order to keep the enemy off-balance. In addition, there was a need for night missions using one helicopter with two starlight scopes and two armed helicopters in order to interrupt Viet Cong sampan traffic along the myriad waterways. Finally, airlift was necessary to make use of any substantial finds in the area of operations. Without helicopter transport, it was frequently necessary to destroy captured matériel—munitions, cement, large rice stores—because it could not be moved.

Fire support was diverse and highly effective. Artillery fire support bases were established with as many as three separate artillery batteries (105-mm., towed) employed at the same time from different locations. Naval gunfire was used continuously throughout the operation, including indirect fire of several destroyers and the direct and indirect fire of weapons organic to boats of Division 91, U.S. Navy, and River Assault Group 26, Vietnam Navy. Other fire support was provided by tactical air, and by U.S. Air Force, Army, and Navy fixed-wing and helicopter gunships.

Fire support presented a number of co-ordination and clearance problems. The main shipping channel was patrolled constantly by U.S. Navy river patrol boats and aircraft which, because of daylight

A Wet But Peaceful Landing

traffic in shipping, required close control to prevent damage to U.S. or South Vietnamese forces and equipment. An additional problem was that in some areas clearance from the government of Vietnam was required for each mission. U.S. ground clearance for indirect fire was co-ordinated by the artillery liaison officer. Getting government clearance at first proved to be time-consuming. Requests had to be submitted to the senior adviser of the zone at Nha Be. Any aircraft in the area of operation would cause a cease fire in the entire Rung Sat. A zonal clearance system was worked out by all parties concerned and proved highly successful. It consisted of a circle with a radius of 11.5 kilometers drawn on the fire support map using the fire support base (battery center) as the center. The circle was then subdivided like a pie into eight equal parts or zones and each was numbered from one to eight. Thereafter, to obtain clearance all that was required was to ask permission to fire into the zone in question. Artillery and mortar fire could thus be applied to the zone or zones where it was needed and withheld from the rest of the area.

Troops on combat operations in the Rung Sat Special Zone

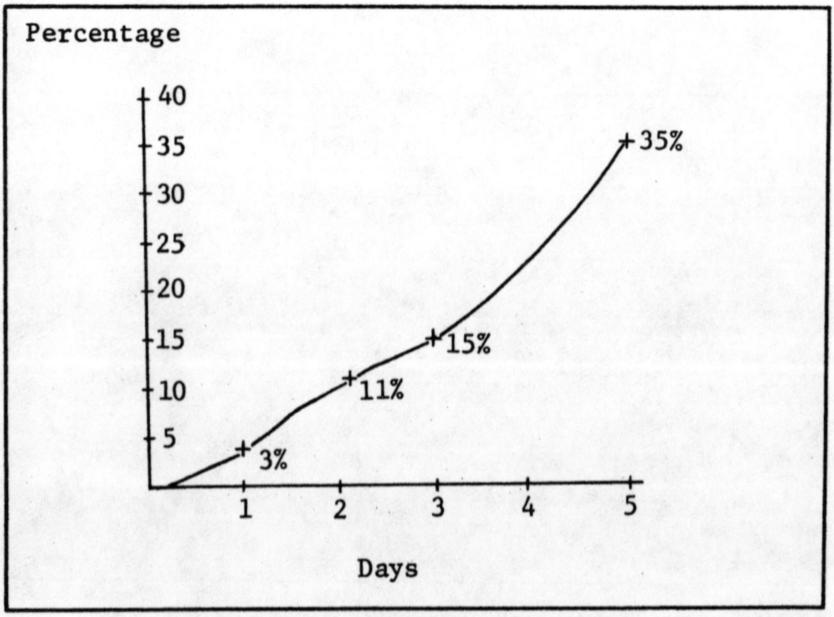

Diagram 4. Foot disease incident rate.

were continually in mud and the salty, dirty water could not be used for bathing. Certain measures were therefore taken to safeguard the health of the troops. Men stayed on combat operations for forty-eight hours at a time and were then sent to the troopship in the Vung Tau area where adequate shower facilities were available and every man had a bunk for the night. All companies received instructions on care of the feet, which included thorough washing, drying, and daily inspection of the feet by medics. The battalion surgeons carried out frequent inspections and all cases of dermatophytosis were treated with fungicidal ointments and powders. (*Diagram 4*)

An experiment to determine the efficiency of a silicone ointment was carried out with seventy-six soldiers who used the ointment daily. During some twenty days, six cases of immersion foot occurred, four of them on men who used the silicone. It was found that the system of rotating troops for a forty-eight-hour drying out period and conducting inspections of feet to insure necessary treatment of conditions as soon as they arose was of far greater benefit than use of the preventive ointment.

Positioning mortars ashore in the Rung Sat was difficult and time-consuming because of lack of firm ground, and was done only in the area of the battalion forward command post, which was seldom moved. For support of wide-ranging operations more mobility than this semipermanent location of the mortars was required. During RIVER RAIDER I, two 81-mm. mortars were installed in the forward portion of an LCM. The mortar boat was nosed into the bank, engines kept running to advance or back in accordance with the tide, and steadied against the current by quartering lines running from the stern forward and outward at an angle of about 30 degrees to the bank on either side of the bow ramp. Most of the mortar crews were used to establish local security on the bank. This arrangement permitted a high degree of mobility, rapid positioning for firing, minimum wasted effort by the gun crews, and an ample supply of ammunition close at hand. The mortar boat was used both day and night throughout the operation, and provided flexible, mobile fire support for all types of maneuver.

The major operational success of RIVER RAIDER I was the capture of substantial stores of water mines and the destruction of facilities for constructing water mines. It is highly probable that these losses suffered by the Viet Cong account in part for the very limited use of water mines against riverine forces during later operations in the northern Mekong Delta as well as in the Rung Sat Special Zone.

After RIVER RAIDER I, the 4th Battalion, 47th Infantry, took up operations in the Rung Sat Special Zone, making use during April and early May of the experiences of the 3d Battalion, 47th Infantry, and improvising other techniques. During this time so-called Ammi barges were obtained from the Navy for use alongside the LST of River Flotilla One. With this type of ponton, rope ladders were not needed and the training time for riverine troops was drastically reduced. The Ammi barges provided as well some much needed space for cleaning and storage of ammunition, crew-served weapons, and individual equipment.

CHAPTER IV

Initial Delta Operations

Movement to Dong Tam

When the 3d Battalion, 60th Infantry, was sent to Dong Tam in January 1967, the Headquarters, 3d Brigade, U.S. 9th Infantry Division, also went to Dong Tam to direct construction of the base and to conduct operations in Dinh Tuong Province. The 5th Battalion, 60th Infantry (Mechanized), was stationed at Tan Hiep, an airstrip about eight kilometers northeast of My Tho along Highway 4. The 3d Brigade conducted the first of a series of operations in late February 1967; these operations were usually limited to one battalion and one or two companies of another battalion because so many troops were needed to protect the construction work at Dong Tam Base.

Implementing earlier planning, General Westmoreland decided to move Headquarters, 2d Brigade, to Dong Tam so that it would become operational at that location on 10 March. The 3d Brigade was moved north to Tan An, the capital of Long An Province, with the mission of conducting a consolidation operation to assist the pacification program in the southern portion of the III Corps Tactical Zone. With the arrival of Headquarters, 2d Brigade, at Dong Tam, the brigade began a demanding 90-day period of performing four separate but related tasks: the defense and construction of the Dong Tam Base; limited offensive operations in Dinh Tuong and Kien Hoa Provinces; operations in the Rung Sat Special Zone to protect the shipping channel; and planning with Task Force 117 to move aboard the Navy ships.

Conducting operations in Dinh Tuong Province was to prove as important in the seasoning of the battalions of 2d Brigade as was the riverine training in the Rung Sat Special Zone. The threat posed to Dong Tam by the Viet Cong 514th Provincial Battalion, the 263d Main Force Battalion, and local force sapper and infantry companies and guerrillas demanded a varied offensive campaign to protect the base as well as to reduce the Viet Cong influence.

Although Dinh Tuong Province was bordered on the south by

the My Tho River, the limited navigability of smaller streams greatly limited boat movement within the province. Most canals were blocked by the debris of destroyed bridges or by earthen dams erected by the Viet Cong to prevent their use by civilians or military forces. Therefore, although the brigade was scheduled for a riverine role, it was to carry on between March and June a variety of operations common to all U.S. infantry units in Vietnam. These included throwing a cordon around hamlets and searching them in the hope of capturing members of the local Viet Cong political organization and guerrilla squads and platoons; brigade and battalion reconnaissance in force operations; and extensive patrolling. Troops moved by helicopter, boat, wheeled and tracked vehicles, or on foot. During the wet season the brigade operated in the Dong Tam area by boat and helicopter chiefly. When aircraft were not available, wheeled vehicles could carry troops on Highway 4 to find the enemy near suspected Viet Cong bases. The troops then moved on foot into the operational areas to the north and south of the road.

During March and April the brigade commander and staff, assisted by the senior U.S. adviser of the 7th Vietnam Army Division, Colonel Lance, assembled good intelligence covering Dinh Tuong and Kien Hoa Provinces. In addition, through the U.S. senior adviser to IV Corps, General Desobry, arrangements were made for periodic briefings of the brigade staff by the G-2, IV Corps advisory staff. This information was used in a series of co-operative operations undertaken by the 2d Brigade with the 7th Vietnam Army Division. These were to provide beneficial combat experience for the brigade before it embarked as the Army component of the Mobile Riverine Force.

The diverse tasks of the brigade seldom permitted more than two infantry battalions to be used in offensive operations. Thus in covering large base areas without exact intelligence of enemy locations, participation of additional forces was co-ordinated with the 7th Vietnam Army Division to search thoroughly and to block escape routes. The Commanding General, 7th Vietnam Army Division, approved of such operations because they permitted him to deploy small forces into Viet Cong base areas, for which he would otherwise have been obliged to use more Vietnamese troops than he could spare from their security missions. Throughout the experience of the Mobile Riverine Force, it was to prove necessary to obtain additional troops, whether they were other U.S. units, Vietnam Army units, or Vietnamese marines, to augment the two battalions routinely operating within the Mobile Riverine Force.

During the period 15 February–10 May, the 2d Brigade, although physically based at Dong Tam, conducted infantry operations with the 3d and 4th Battalions, 47th Infantry, in the Rung Sat Special Zone and southern Bien Hoa Province. While the 3d Battalion, 47th Infantry, was located in the Rung Sat during February and March, the 4th Battalion, 47th Infantry, was used in the southern portion of Bien Hoa Province, south of Bearcat and bordering the Rung Sat. The boats of the Navy's River Assault Squadron 9 supported Army operations in the Rung Sat during this period.

Final Mobile Riverine Force Preparations

At the same time active co-ordination and planning for the Mobile Afloat Force was begun by the 2d Brigade staff with the advance staff of River Assault Flotilla One. General Eckhardt assigned Lieutenant Colonel John R. Witherell, who had been the Combat Developments Command liaison officer to the G–3 Section, U.S. Army, Vietnam, to 2d Brigade. As a major, Colonel Witherell had initiated the first outline draft of the riverine doctrine manual. He was made the deputy for riverine planning for the 2d Brigade, augmenting the brigade staff. At this time, Lieutenant Colonel James S. G. Turner, U.S. Marine Corps, was placed on duty with Headquarters, 9th Division, by the Commandant of the Marine Corps as an observer and liaison officer for riverine operations. At the request of the brigade commander, Colonel Turner was placed on special duty with the brigade staff. Colonels Witherell and Turner proved to be valuable additions because the brigade staff was involved in planning for and conducting daily operations of the two maneuver battalions, including Dong Tam Base defense operations, as well as in formulating plans to establish the brigade at Dong Tam. In the early draft plans prepared by Colonel Witherell, the term Mekong Delta Mobile Afloat Force was dropped and the title Mobile Riverine Force was formally adopted.

As of mid-January, two APB's, *Colleton* and *Benewah,* were scheduled to arrive in Vietnam during May or June 1967. The two ships would provide only 1,600 berthing spaces for Army troops. When troop space for artillery support, base security forces, and the brigade staff was subtracted, there would remain spaces for a combat force of approximately one reinforced battalion. It was considered essential to increase the combat strength of the brigade to at least two battalions. Since only two APB's were available, it

NON-SELF-PROPELLED BARRACKS SHIP

was recommended by the 2d Brigade that a towed barracks ship, an APL, with a berthing capacity for 660 troops be made available. This recommendation was forwarded through division to the commander of II Field Force, who, in turn, requested the commander of the naval force in Vietnam to make the APL available. He proposed that if the APL was diverted, Navy men be provided to operate and maintain only the equipment peculiar to the Navy and that Army troops be required to perform all other support functions such as cleaning, preventive maintenance, messing, laundry service, and security. This proposal was satisfactory to the Army and APL-26 was diverted to Dong Tam in May, along with two sea-going tugs to move the barracks ship. An additional 175 berths were provided by building bunks on the top side of the APL under a canvas canopy.

Frequent co-ordination meetings were held with Captain Wells aboard his flagship at Vung Tau. During the last two weeks of March Colonels Witherell and Turner moved aboard the flagship to participate with the Navy staff in the development of a Mobile Riverine Force standing order. The brigade operations officer, Major Clyde J. Tate, continued to concentrate on the current

ARTILLERY BARGE

brigade operations. Colonel Fulton felt that the Mobile Afloat Force plan had not provided effective artillery support for the Mobile Riverine Force operations. The armored troop carriers were to lift the 105-mm. howitzers and their prime movers. The artillery battalion, after being moved by water, would debark at a suitable place along the river and establish firing positions. Terrain reconnaissance conducted during his October 1966 visit had convinced Colonel Fulton that the off-loading of the prime movers from an ATC as provided for in the plan would greatly restrict operations because of the varying tides of four to thirteen feet and the steepness of the river banks. Consequently, the Commanding Officer, 3d Battalion, 34th Artillery, Lieutenant Colonel Carroll S. Meek, began to experiment with barge-mounted artillery. He placed a 105-mm. howitzer on an Ammi barge, using cleats and segments of telephone poles against which the trails of the howitzer rested. Successful firing demonstrated the feasibility of this method. By use of aiming stakes placed ashore routine fire support could be provided from the barges anchored securely against the river bank.

During these experiments, the Deputy Commanding General,

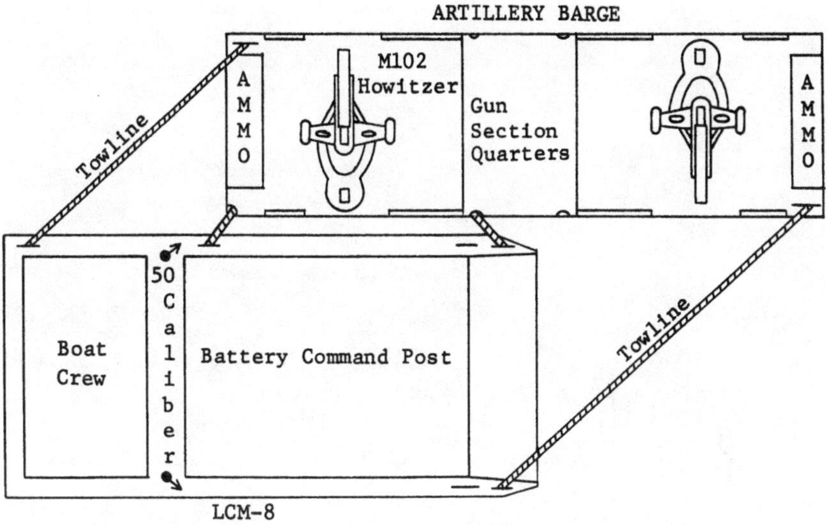

Diagram 5. Artillery barge towing position.

U.S. Army, Vietnam, Lieutenant General Jean E. Engler, placed a liaison officer from the G-4 Section on temporary duty with the brigade. This officer's sole mission was to procure special equipment requested by the brigade, thus eliminating the procedure of requesting items through normal channels and greatly facilitating the acquisition of equipment. After Colonel Meek's initial firing experience with the barge-mounted artillery, the liaison officer was asked to arrange fabrication of an experimental artillery barge. The work was done in a few weeks at Cam Ranh Bay, where small pontons were welded together into an artillery barge. The barge was then towed down the coast and brought up the Mekong River to Dong Tam by a commercial ocean-going tug. Further firing experiments proved the barge unsatisfactory in that the high bow of the ponton was nearly perpendicular to the surface of the water, making it hard to maneuver and tow, especially against the current, tide, or prevailing wind. The barge was redesigned so that it floated lower in the water and had a sloped bow, and the design was forwarded by the G-4 liaison officer to Cam Ranh Bay. As a result of successful experiments with the new design, six barges were fabricated, each barge to accommodate two tubes of 105-mm. howitzer, M102. (*Diagram 5*) Each barge was to be towed by an LCM-8 throughout the areas in which the Navy assault craft supported Army forces. The decision to develop the artillery barges was the most important equipment decision made by the Army for the

Artillery Fires From Barges Anchored on River Bank

Mobile Riverine Force because the barges provided effective artillery support at all times. Had General Engler not had the foresight to furnish liaison and to make special arrangements to obtain unique equipment, the initial effectiveness of the Mobile Riverine Force would have been greatly impaired.

Also during the March-April period, Colonel Fulton decided that there was not enough helicopter landing space aboard the ships of the river force. Each APB had one helicopter landing pad, and the LST could accommodate the landing of one helicopter. Through the same expedited development process used for the artillery barges, a helicopter landing barge was provided that could accommodate three UH-1 helicopters and would have a refueling capacity for the helicopters of 1,500 gallons of JP-4. This barge would be towed by an LCM-8 of the Army transportation boat company.

As more U.S. Navy craft arrived in Vietnam and the initial training was completed, River Assault Flotilla One elements were sent from the Vung Tau-Rung Sat Special Zone training area into Dinh Tuong Province. On 10 April the first river assault division

HELICOPTER BARGE

moved to Dong Tam with 18 ATC's, 1 CCB, and 2 monitors and immediately began waterborne operations with the 3d Battalion, 47th Infantry, which had also left Rung Sat Special Zone for Dong Tam. Although these operations on the Mekong River were small in scale during the month of April, the men soon learned that unlike the rivers of the Rung Sat Special Zone, where obstacles were few, the delta waterways had many man-made obstructions such as low bridges, fish traps, and earthen blocks on canals.

During April a small staff group of River Assault Flotilla One went to Dong Tam to work closely with the 2d Brigade staff in developing the final plans for Mobile Riverine Force operations, which were to begin on 2 June. The first embarkation was to include the brigade headquarters and staff; 3d Battalion, 34th Artillery; Company C, 15th Engineers; and the division support elements. In the final planning phase for this embarkation it was decided that a larger supply LST would be needed to provide an additional 375 U.S. Army berthing spaces. Originally two class 542 LST's were scheduled as the logistics support ships to rotate between Vung Tau and the riverine base. Since the 542 class is much smaller and provides less billeting space, a request was made to River Assault Flotilla One for one of the larger 1152 class LST's. Again, the Navy accommodated the Army request. Acquisition of the larger LST was to prove very advantageous in that the entire brigade aviation section, which included four OH-23 helicopters, and the maintenance section were placed aboard the LST and were operated from the flight deck. Limited air resources were now available for combat operations regardless of the remoteness of the location of the mobile riverine base from 9th Division support.

Both the brigade headquarters and the infantry battalions were internally reorganized so that all equipment not necessary for riverine operations could be left at the Dong Tam base under the control of unit rear detachments. Spaces for jobs not needed by the Riverine Force, such as for drivers and mechanics, were converted to spaces with shipboard and combat duties. The combat support company of each battalion was reconstituted into a reconnaissance and surveillance company. Men assigned to spaces whose function was not required in the Mobile Riverine Force were placed in these two companies and thus two additional rifle platoons were created in each of the two battalions. When these two platoons were added to the reconnaissance platoon normally found in the combat support company, a fourth rifle company for each battalion was organized. This arrangement was to prove most satisfactory because it provided for base defense and other security missions and at the same time left three companies for battalion tactical operations.

2d Brigade Operations

While planning of the riverine organization of the infantry battalions was taking place, in April and May the battalions were actually conducting land operations. The 3d Battalion, 47th Infantry, and 3d Battalion, 60th Infantry, were increasing their proficiency in airmobile operations and learning to work with the officials of Dinh Tuong Province and Army of Vietnam division forces.

On 1 April 2d Brigade forces made a raid into northern Kien Hoa Province on the My Tho River south of Dong Tam, using barge-mounted artillery. During darkness, one battery was moved west on the river from the land base, followed closely by infantry mounted in ATC's. Once opposite a manned station of a Viet Cong communications liaison route, the artillery poured surprise, direct fire into the target area. To protect a Ham Long District company, which had occupied a blocking position south of the target, time

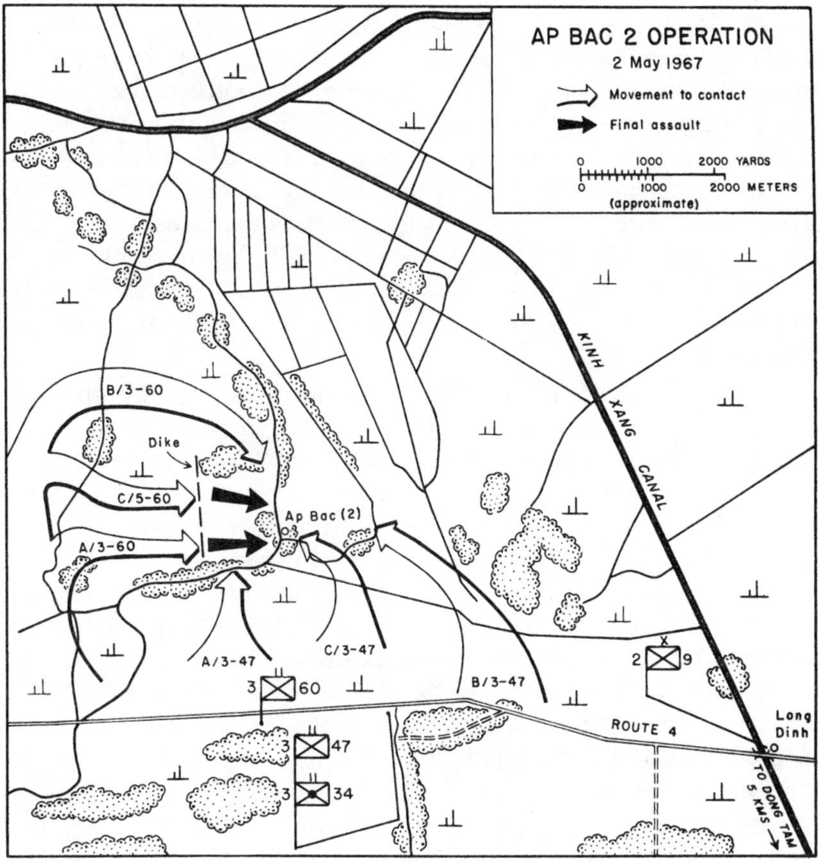

MAP 4

fuzes were used. Immediately after the artillery fire, infantry troops landed and swept through the station. The artillery then anchored against the north bank of the river and prepared to provide indirect fire support. The raiders captured enemy ammunition and a portion of the labor force of the enemy communication-liaison platoon.

On 2 May the 3d Battalion, 47th Infantry, and 3d Battalion, 60th Infantry, participated in the 2d Brigade's heaviest fighting to date. The target of the brigade assault was the 514th Local Force Battalion in the Ap Bac 2 area, which had been identified by the commanding general of the 7th Vietnam Army Division as a normal operating area for the Viet Cong. (*Map 4*) The ground over which the battle would take place was alternately rice paddy and thick patches of vegetation with heavy foliage along the streams and canals. The brigade plan was to conduct an airmobile operation in co-operation with the 7th Vietnam Army Division. On the morning of the operation, however, shortly after the scheduled time for the airlift of the first company, the brigade was notified that no airmobile company was available. The brigade commander decided to send the unit by truck, a move requiring approximately two hours. At the same time the brigade forward command post elements moved north by ATC's on the Kinh Xang Canal to set up a post at Long Binh. The 3d Battalion, 60th Infantry, truck convoy was followed by the 3d Battalion, 47th Infantry, on the same route. The companies of both battalions were off-loaded facing north from Highway 4.

By 0830 both battalions were moving north to their first objectives. Elements of the 3d Battalion, 60th Infantry, on the west met no resistance. Units of the 3d Battalion, 47th Infantry, moved forward cautiously during the morning, covering about 1,500 meters and receiving light sniper fire. At approximately 1250 both Companies A and B, 3d Battalion, 47th Infantry, encountered the enemy. Company A came under heavy automatic weapons fire immediately after emerging from a wood line; it deployed in an attempt to move against the enemy position, but was hampered by heavy undergrowth that made it difficult to see the enemy firing positions. The company sought to improve its position, and called in fire support, including artillery fire, gunships, and eventually three air strikes on the enemy position.

About 1300, Company B, 3d Battalion, 60th Infantry, was placed under operational control of the commander of 3d Battalion, 47th Infantry, and directed to establish a blocking position north of the enemy location. At the same time Company A, 3d Battalion, 60th Infantry, and Company C, 5th Battalion, 60th Infantry, were ordered to close enemy escape routes on the west. Companies B and C, 3d Battalion, 47th Infantry, were ordered to block northeast of the position of Company A, 3d Battalion, 47th Infantry.

Company C, 5th Battalion, 60th Infantry, a mechanized company, using full-tracked armored personnel carriers, moved through inundated areas which had been thought impassable to occupy a position west of the enemy. Company C, 5th Battalion, 60th Infantry, and Company A, 3d Battalion, 60th Infantry, then made the final assault from the west into the enemy position. Company C, 5th Battalion, 60th Infantry, greatly enhanced the firepower of the assault by employing the .50-caliber fire of its full-tracked armored carriers in the assault line. The organic infantry attacked on foot alongside the carriers. The enemy resisted with heavy rifle and automatic weapons fire. Company A, 3d Battalion, 60th Infantry, on the right flank of the assault, charged into the southern line of bunkers, and finally overran it. Seeing that their line was broken, many Viet Cong tried to escape to the east but were killed or wounded as both attacking companies made their final assault into the bunker line. By 1820 enemy resistance was overcome.

Although not a riverine operation, the action at Ap Bac contributed to the brigade tactical experience which was later carried into riverine operations. In developing operational plans, the brigade staff recognized that tactical control measures have to provide for maximum flexibility in controlling the maneuver of units. If the original plan cannot be executed, there must be sufficient latitude to redirect the effort of the participating units according to the control measures previously issued. Check points, a series of intermediate objectives, and an area grid system provide flexibility for redirection of units and shifting of boundaries and fire co-ordination lines.

The Ap Bac operation included in the words of an infantryman "finding, fixing, fighting, and finishing" the enemy. Through the use of simple control measures, units of the two battalions were moved into blocking positions to cut off enemy routes of withdrawal, and other units were maneuvered into assault positions. When this maneuver was combined with use of both air and artillery supporting force, the enemy had to remain in his position or expose himself in an attempt to withdraw.

The operation made it clear that units must be prepared to bring in artillery and air support as close as possible to the front lines. Each battalion commander used an observation helicopter to co-ordinate fire in close support of his unit. The infantry units, once having found the enemy, had to be prepared through fire and maneuver to conduct a co-ordinated assault against the enemy positions. In this engagement, by the use of close supporting artillery fire, the infantry units were able to launch a co-ordinated attack which overcame the enemy.

Mechanized infantry was used most successfully at Ap Bac. The unit commander had to search for routes through very swampy and marshy areas. Once his armored personnel carriers (APC's) were deployed, he dismounted his infantry and moved APC's and infantry in a forward rapid assault on the enemy. The volume of fire delivered by the APC's into the bunker line, along with high explosive and white phosphorous rounds of artillery, enabled the infantry to overcome the enemy in bunkers and foxholes. Once

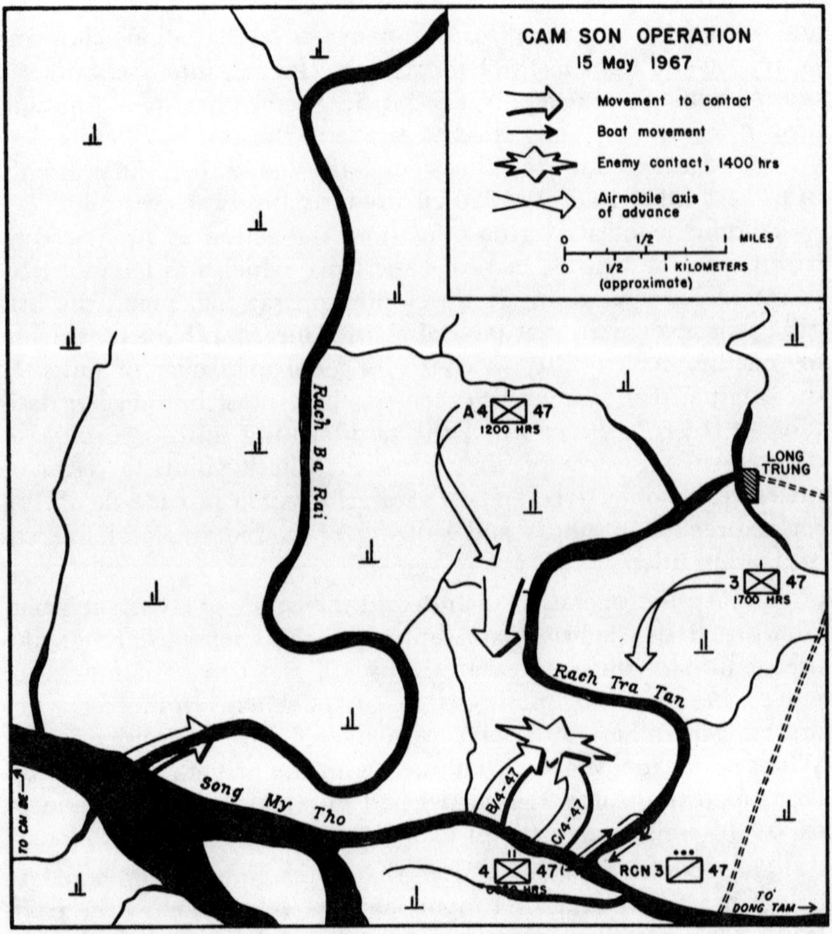

MAP 5

fire superiority had been established, the assault was executed with few American casualties.

General Thanh, commanding the 7th Vietnam Army Division, monitored the course of the 2 May battle with interest. By midnight the intelligence staffs of the brigade and 7th Vietnam Division had estimated that the enemy consisted of the 514th Local Force Battalion with two companies and its heavy weapons. An enemy attack launched at dusk of 2 May on the command post of the 3d Battalion, 60th Infantry, just south of Highway 4, appeared to be the rest of the 514th Local Force Battalion trying to relieve pressure on its units north of Highway 4. On the strength of this estimate, General Thanh sent a Ranger battalion on 3 May into the area which he

considered the most probable location to which the enemy would flee. His Rangers encountered and attacked an estimated company of the 514th Local Force Battalion during the afternoon. The casualties inflicted upon the 514th by the U.S. 2d Brigade and the 7th Vietnam Army Division severely reduced its combat effectiveness. Reports received later suggested that the 263d Main Force Battalion was forced to undertake training of new recruits and operational tasks of the 514th Battalion because of the losses in men and weapons.

On 13 May the 4th Battalion, 47th Infantry, completed operations in the Rung Sat Special Zone and joined the brigade at Dong Tam. Colonel Tutwiler's battalion participated in its first major riverine operation in the Dong Tam area on 15 May as the 2d Brigade conducted the first of several operations in the Cam Son Secret Zone. (*Map 5*) The Cam Son area was considered one of four major Viet Cong bases in Dinh Tuong Province by the intelligence staffs of both the province and 7th Vietnam Army Division. The operation of 15 May relied entirely on intelligence provided by these Vietnamese organizations.

The brigade plan was to search the southern area of Cam Son along the Rach Ba Rai and Rach Tra Tan streams and to capture or destroy the Viet Cong, their supplies, and their equipment. A forward brigade command post was established approximately two kilometers north of Cai Be, and a barge-mounted artillery base was established on the southern bank of the My Tho River, five kilometers southeast of the mouth of the Rach Ba Rai. The two infantry battalions were supported by 22 ATC's, 2 monitors, and 2 CCB's of River Assault Flotilla One. Commander Charles H. Black, the operations officer of River Assault Flotilla One, joined the brigade command group and co-ordinated the support of the Navy assault craft.

The operation began at 0815 when the 3d Battalion, 47th Infantry, landed from assault craft at the mouth of the Rach Ba Rai and began to search northeast along the stream. At 0830 the 4th Battalion, 47th Infantry, landed two companies from assault craft on the north bank of the My Tho River approximately halfway between the mouths of the Rach Ba Rai and the Rach Tra Tan. At 1200 Company A, 4th Battalion, 47th Infantry, was airlifted from Dong Tam, where it had been in readiness as a reserve, and was landed three kilometers north of the river on the west side of the Rach Tra Tan to act as a blocking force against any enemy encountered. After landing the Army troops, the boats of the Navy task force proceeded to blocking stations along the waterways.

At 1400 Companies B and C of the 4th Battalion, 47th Infantry, met a Viet Cong force equipped with small arms, light machine guns, and rocket launchers. Company A maneuvered south and met the enemy within two kilometers of the My Tho river. Although Companies B and C made little progress in moving against the enemy fire, artillery and close air support maintained pressure on the Viet Cong.

In an effort to move more troops to the northeast and rear of the Viet Cong force, the Reconnaissance Platoon, 3d Battalion, 47th Infantry, was moved by ATC into the Rach Tra Tan. When the low tide and enemy antitank rockets prevented the assault craft from penetrating upriver beyond enemy positions on the banks, the platoon was withdrawn.

By 1630 it became apparent that some enemy forces were escaping by moving to the northeast, away from both Companies B and C, which were moving from the south, and from Company A, which was moving from the northwest. At this point Colonel Fulton directed Colonel Bolduc to move one of his companies by helicopter to establish a blocking position northeast of the battle. This was accomplished by 1700, but the company failed to find the enemy, and by 2000 all contact with the Viet Cong was lost.

This fight called attention to the limitations imposed upon maneuver or assault craft during low tide and the importance of artillery and close air support against an enemy in well-prepared bunkers and firing positions. Although most American casualties did not require evacuation because their wounds were superficial, both Army and Navy were concerned by the vulnerability of men aboard the assault craft to rocket fragments. The Mobile Riverine Force was to find vulnerability of troops aboard assault craft one of its continuing problems.

On 18 and 19 May the 2d Brigade moved a forward command post by motor convoy north of Cai Be in western Dinh Tuong Province to control the operations of 3d Battalion, 47th Infantry, and 3d Battalion, 60th Infantry. To reduce the distance the supporting helicopters would have to fly, River Assault Flotilla One assault craft moved both battalions by water thirty-six kilometers west of Dong Tam to landing sites on the north bank of the My Tho River. With the infantry battalions positioned within seven kilometers of the center of the target area, one airmobile company was able to insert each battalion rapidly into the area. In the event of substantial fighting the helicopters could turn around quickly in building up forces.

During this operation the battalions of the 2d Brigade met few of the Viet Cong, but the brigade command post was attacked by mortar, recoilless rifle, and machine gun fire during the early hours of 19 May. A ground attack was thwarted when the Reconnaissance Platoon, 3d Battalion, 47th Infantry, led by Second Lieutenant Howard C. Kirk III intercepted enemy movement toward the western perimeter of the position; assisted by artillery, gunships, and an armed illumination aircraft, the reconnaissance platoon broke up the attack.

Throughout the month of May, a maximum effort was made to establish procedures for close co-operation between Army and Navy elements. Colonel Fulton and Commander Black agreed that the helicopter was invaluable for command and control of riverine operations. Finding important terrain features is a very difficult task for the commander on the surface, but a simpler task for the airborne commander. Foot troop and assault craft maneuver were facilitated by information furnished by the airborne command group. During darkness and in marginal flying weather, the command and communications boats were valuable to brigade and battalion commanders in their forward positions. The combined use of command helicopters and command boats by brigade and battalion commanders permitted close supervision and control of the Mobile Riverine Force in combat.

The operations of the 2d Brigade in Dinh Tuong Province from March through May had already provided invaluable operational experience. All of the brigade's units had met and withstood the enemy; thus a feeling of confidence had been engendered in commanders and men. Of even greater importance, however, was the displacement of Viet Cong units from the Dong Tam area to the western portion of Dinh Tuong Province, from which the enemy could not readily launch a large ground attack on the base. The 2d Brigade had become operational at Dong Tam on 10 March, only seventy-two hours after an engagement involving a platoon of the 3d Brigade and a larger Viet Cong unit less than eight kilometers from the base, and forty-eight hours after the enemy launched an attack on Dong Tam with recoilless rifles and mortars.

In the next ninety days the enemy made one successful sapper attack that damaged a construction vehicle outside the camp and an American patrol ambushed an enemy force of platoon size three kilometers west of the base. To prevent enemy fire and ground attack on the base, a patrolling system was executed by the base defense battalion, using division artillery radar. Patrols were made on foot, by tracked and wheeled vehicles, by boat, and by helicopter, and were sent out by day and by night.

Offensive operations came to be guided by knowledge of the habits of the Viet Cong, who made use of certain areas and routes for bases and for communication, liaison, and supply. Although information provided by the Vietnam Army division and province intelligence agencies seldom arrived in time to serve as the basis for an attack, it was useful in tracking the enemy's routes, bases, and length of stay in bases. It permitted a rough guess as to when a Viet Cong battalion would be in any one of the four major Dinh Tuong base areas at a given time. Operations could be conducted against one or more bases on a priority basis. By co-operation with the Vietnam Army and using economy of force, the brigade could enter the first priority base area with most of two battalions, the Vietnamese forces could enter the second priority area, and the brigade would use a small force to reconnoiter a third base area. Helicopter transport was essential and air cavalry support highly desirable. It was not, however, until May that a portion of Troop

D, 3d Squadron, 5th Cavalry, was used by the 2d Brigade.

By the end of May, the brigade had found the enemy in three of the four Dinh Tuong base areas on many occasions and had contributed to a period of relative security for the men attempting to complete construction of the Dong Tam Base as well as for the province itself.

Mobile Riverine Force Campaign Plan

During early April it had become apparent that the Navy's concept of the employment of the Mobile Riverine Force differed slightly from the original Mobile Afloat Force concept. Captain Wells contended that the force should act as a separate force, divorced from 9th U.S. Division operations and control, with deployments deep into the delta. A period of intensive discussions between the component commanders ensued. Differences were not resolved until the preparation of a wet and dry season campaign plan for the Mobile River Force as well as a draft letter of instruction from the 9th U.S. Division commander to the brigade commander. This letter was prepared by the brigade staff and carried to the commander of the 9th Infantry Division, General Eckhardt, with the recommendation that it be issued by Headquarters, 9th U.S. Division, to the Mobile Riverine Force Army component commander.

General Eckhardt accepted the draft letter and draft campaign plan and personally took them to Captain Wells, who, as the commander of River Assault Flotilla One and Task Force 117, the operational designation of the Navy component of the riverine force, accepted both. These two documents adhered to the original Mobile Afloat Force plan for operation of the river force in conjunction with the other 9th U.S. Division elements in the southern III Corps Tactical Zone and in the northern portion of the IV Corps Tactical Zone north of the Mekong River.

The opinion of the Navy component commander that operations should be conducted exclusively in IV Corps was not supported by Headquarters, MACV, Planning Directive Number 12-66, dated 10 December 1966, entitled Command Relations for Riverine Operations in South Vietnam. Essentially, this document placed Army forces conducting riverine operations in III and IV Corps Tactical Zones under the operational control of the Commanding General, II Field Force, with a stipulation that he might exercise operational control through designated subordinate U.S. Army headquarters. The commander of U.S. Army, Vietnam, would exercise command, less operational control, of all U.S. Army units engaged in riverine operations. Similarly, Navy riverine forces were placed under the operational control of the commander of Naval Forces, Vietnam, and under the command, less operational control, of Commander in Chief, Pacific Fleet.

The planning directive recognized the unique command arrangements peculiar to the Mobile Afloat Force concept. This was not to be a joint task force and the specific command relationships had not been planned under the original concept. The planning directive took note of the fact that "the conduct of riverine operations by Army and Navy forces is a new concept which will require the utmost coordination and cooperation by all concerned. As operations are conducted and lessons learned, command relations will be revised as necessary to insure effective and workable arrangements." There was to be no single commander of the Mobile Riverine Force.

The MACV document stipulated that the base commander for all bases, whether ashore or afloat, would be the senior Army commander assigned. It further stipulated that the relation between the Army and Navy units stationed on both Army and Navy bases would be one of co-ordination and mutual support, with the Navy providing its appropriate share of forces for local base defense, including naval gunfire support and protection against waterborne threats. Operational control of Navy units in these circumstances was to be exercised by the base commander through the Navy chain of command.

Command relationships for riverine operations were further defined as commencing when troops began embarking on assault craft to leave the base and ending when troops had debarked from the boats upon return to the base. During riverine operations, the Army commander would control all participating Army forces and the Navy commander would control all participating Navy forces. The Navy would provide close support to the Army during these operations according to the definition by the Joint Chiefs of Staff:

> When, either by direction of higher authority or by agreement between the commanders concerned, a force is assigned the primary mission of close support of a designated force, the commander of the supported force will exercise general direction of the supporting effort within the limits permitted by accepted tactical practices of the service of the supporting force. Such direction includes designation of targets or objectives, timing, duration of the supporting action, and other instructions necessary for coordination and for efficiency.

Command relationships between the Army and Navy elements

or components during the operational planning phase would be one of co-ordination. This particular aspect of the planning directive posed a basic dilemma in that co-ordination meant agreement at the lowest possible level as to where the force would deploy and how it would fight. If the agreement could not be obtained during the planning phase, the planning directive made provision for the following:

> It is the responsibility of commanders at all levels through liaison, cooperation, coordination, and good judgement to make every effort possible to solve all command relationship problems in the most expeditious and workable manner consistent with the problem. Problems which cannot be solved satisfactorily will not be forwarded to the next higher headquarters until the commanders concerned have made every effort to reach agreement.

In the event that agreement could not be reached, the division of component authority meant that each of the component commanders would proceed up his respective chain of operational control to obtain a solution. A solution would require co-ordination between the headquarters of the parallel Army and Navy echelons. For example, in the event that there was a disagreement between the Navy component commander and the Army component commander of the Mobile Riverine Force, the Army commander would have to pass the problem to the commander of the 9th U.S. Division. It is notable that there was no Navy echelon equivalent to the 9th Infantry Division under the Navy chain of operational control. The commander of the 9th Infantry Division would then have to pass the matter to the commander of II Field Force, who, in turn, would co-ordinate with the parallel Navy commander. (*Chart 2*)

The command relationships had complicated planning of the location of initial operations, and prompted Captain Wells to challenge the role of the 2d Brigade as an integral part of the 9th U.S. Division's over-all operations. This initial disagreement was resolved by Captain Wells' acceptance of the 9th Division letter of instruction. Determination of the mission and area of operation of the Mobile River Force in relation to the 9th Infantry Division, however, was a continuous source of friction between the brigade and flotilla commanders. Generally the commander of River Assault Flotilla One agreed to the Joint Chiefs of Staff provision that the supported force would direct operations: "Such direction includes designation of targets or objectives, timing, duration of the supporting action, and other instructions necessary for the co-ordination and for efficiency."

CHART 2—MOBILE RIVERINE FORCE COMMAND STRUCTURE

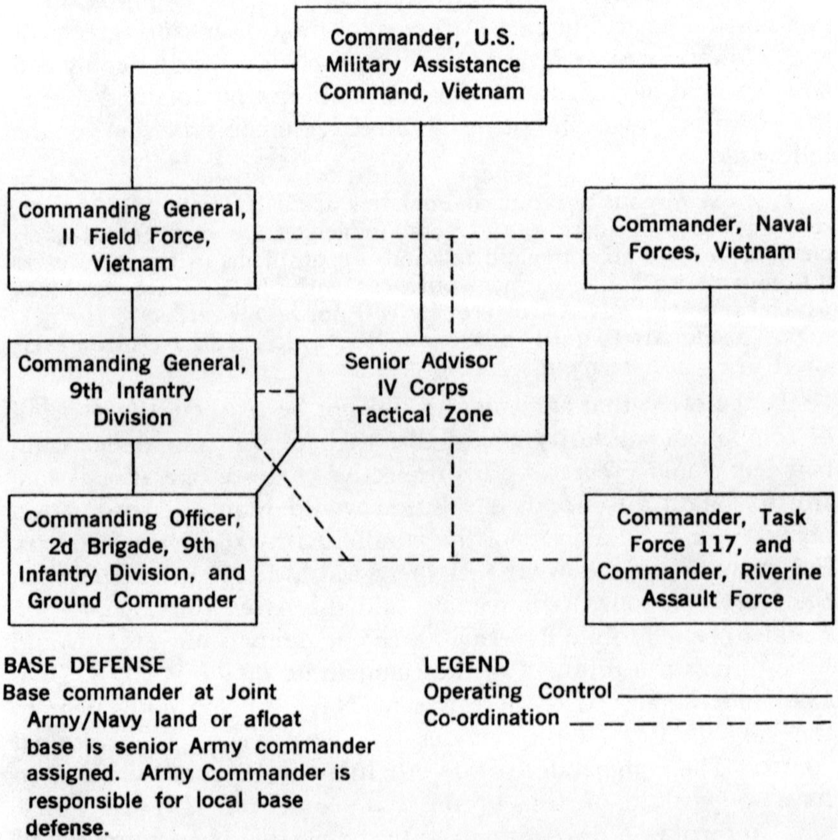

Brigadier General George G. O'Connor, Assistant Commander, 9th U.S. Infantry Division, was responsible to the division commander for the division operations in IV Corps. He provided broad guidance and considerable latitude to the brigade commander in dealing with the command relationships and operational procedures of the Mobile Riverine Force. Without this degree of flexibility, it is unlikely that the brigade and flotilla commanders could have resolved as they did many fundamental issues without recourse to their respective superiors.

Based on the fundamental issues agreed upon and the campaign plan outline of where and how the river force was going to fight, planning continued as the 2d Brigade and its subordinate units began to board the Navy ships of the Mobile Riverine Force at Dong Tam on 31 May.

CHAPTER V

Plans and Operational Procedures for the Mobile Riverine Force

While the Army elements were being moved aboard the ships of River Assault Flotilla One, the staffs of the flotilla and brigade completed the planning for initial tactical operations. Lacking the unity of organization for planning that is present in a joint staff, the brigade and flotilla commanders informally agreed upon the planning roles of each staff.

Intelligence

Colonel Fulton and Captain Wells decided that Mobile Riverine Force operations would be planned and conducted on the basis of intelligence collected from areas in which major enemy forces were most likely to be met and in which the abilities of a river force could be best used. Once an enemy force and area had been agreed upon as a target by the two component commanders, the brigade S-2 and flotilla N-2, working together closely, would collect intelligence to support further planning. The N-2 would concentrate on the navigability of waterways and threats to the Navy ships and assault craft. The S-2 would gather intelligence information necessary to conduct land operations. Both the S-2 and the N-2 would be highly dependent upon the intelligence disseminated by other U.S. and Vietnamese headquarters because the Mobile Riverine Force had a large area of interest and would need to move considerable distances from one location to another.

Since the S-2 and N-2 could not supply all the information needed by the riverine force, intelligence was obtained from several agencies. A seven-man Mobile Intelligence Civil Affairs Team was formed by the brigade to co-ordinate with these agencies. This team was formed from the brigade S-2 and S-5 sections, the prisoner of war interrogation team, the psychological operations team, and military police platoons. It moved into the operational areas of the force to collect intelligence from Vietnamese political officials and from intelligence officers of military units. Working close to the intelligence centers of Vietnamese organizations, the team aided in the exchange of tactical intelligence as well as in the co-ordination of a limited number of civil affairs activities. The Mobile Intelligence Civil Affairs Team was not usually moved into an area during the planning phase of an operation for fear of detection by enemy counterintelligence, but was moved in at the beginning of an operation.

Another means of intelligence collection for the riverine force was the riverine survey team. Controlled by Task Force 117, the team accompanied the task force on missions and recorded depth soundings and clearance measurements, thus providing reliable navigation data for subsequent operations. Under the direction of the 9th Infantry Division engineer, Vietnamese Regional and Popular Forces also collected information on bridges so that the riverine force could be sure of vertical and horizontal bridge clearance on a waterway.

While they were collecting information, the S-2 and N-2 briefed the brigade and flotilla commanders and the planners on the area of the impending operation, and this intelligence along with other information was incorporated in planning guidance provided by the commanders. It was at the point of the formulation of planning guidance that the command relationships of the Mobile Riverine Force received one of its greatest tests. By close co-operation, Colonel Fulton and Captain Wells decided upon the guidance to be issued to their staffs for each operation, and these agreements in time came to be accepted as an informal set of standing operating procedures. They were, however, subject to change at any time by either commander and were not reduced to a written, formally approved document. Task Force 117 published a standing order that contained the results of considerable Army and Navy planning but was not jointly approved.

Planning

The brigade commander or a higher echelon Army commander usually selected the enemy target and area of operations. The two commanders then agreed upon the general task organization, the tentative duration and timing of the operation, and the location of the mobile riverine base to support the operation. The planning often included great detail in order to insure that major issues were resolved early, permitting the two staffs to plan efficiently.

From the outset, Colonel Fulton and Captain Wells recognized the need to plan for future efforts while operations were in progress. Colonel Turner, who had been designated riverine adviser, acted as the planning co-ordinator, with the assistant N-3 (plans), the assistant S-3 (plans), the N-2, and the S-2 forming the planning staff. The planning for operations to take place ten days hence, the planning for the next operation, three to five days hence, and the execution of the current operation were accomplished at the same time, with the S-3 and N-3 dealing with the current operation.

The planning staff, using the commanders' guidance, began by outlining the scheme of maneuver in the objective area. From there the planners worked backwards, covering in turn the landing or assault, water movement, and loading phases. In preparing operations orders they took into consideration factors peculiar to riverine operations such as tides, water depth, water obstructions, bridge clearance, distance of the mobile riverine base from beaches, availability of waterway routes into the area of operations, suitability of river banks for landing sites, and mooring for barge-mounted artillery. Operation orders followed the format of the standard, five-paragraph field order, and were authenticated by the S-3 and the N-3. The bulk of the information peculiar to riverine operations was in the annexes, which included intelligence, operations overlay, fire support plan, naval support plan, signal arrangements, logistics, civil affairs, and psychological operations information. The intelligence annex supplied information on terrain, weather, and the enemy situation. Waterway intelligence was usually provided in an appendix that covered hydrography and the enemy threat to assault craft. A map of the waterways to be used was furnished, showing tides, widths and depths of streams, obstacles of various types, bridges, shoals, mud banks, and other navigation data. The enemy threat to assault craft was covered in descriptions of recent enemy action along the waterways, location of enemy bunkers, kinds of enemy weapons likely to be used in harassing action and ambushes, and water mine and swimmer danger to the small boats. The operations overlay annex showed schematically the area of operations, plan of maneuver, and control measures such as checkpoints. The naval support plan annex contained the naval task organization and referred to the operations order for information concerning the situation, mission, and concept of operations. It assigned specific support tasks to subordinate naval elements together with the necessary co-ordinating instructions. An appendix to the naval support plan provided waterway data.

Battalion orders for operations in a riverine area followed the format used in the brigade orders and were authenticated by the battalion S-3. The supporting river assault squadron water movement plan was prepared by the river assault squadron operations officer in co-ordination with the battalion S-3. It was, in effect, the river assault squadron operations order. This plan did not become a formal part of the battalion operations order but was attached to it. The water movement plan contained the task organization, mission, schedule of events, boat utilization plan, command and communications instruction, and co-ordinating instructions. The schedule of events paragraph listed events critical to the operation and the time they were to take place, for example, where and when each unit was to load, and its scheduled time of arrival at critical water checkpoints. The boat utilization paragraph included numerical designations of boats and the companies to embark on these boats. The co-ordinating instructions paragraph included information on submission of reports, radio silence, recognition lights, reconnaissance by fire, and the use of protective masks.

Once approved, both the brigade and battalion operations orders became the authority for fulfilling the intent of the scheme of maneuver and for providing combat and combat service support. Prior to each operation, a briefing was conducted on the flagship of the Mobile Riverine Force; it included presentation of the plan of each battalion and squadron, as well as the latest S-2 and N-2 intelligence. Briefings seldom required decisions by the flotilla or brigade commander because problems had been resolved between the Army and Navy elements at each subordinate echelon and between echelons during planning. Beginning in June of 1967, plans and orders were in far greater detail than the Army brigade and battalion commanders believed was needed or even optimum for routine land warfare. The detailed nature of the plan, however, included agreements at the Mobile Riverine Force command level; the Navy commander desired to define clearly the tasks to be performed by each service. For the Navy commanders and staffs, the detailed plan was less objectionable, being similar to the planning associated with amphibious, ship-to-shore operations. After June of 1967 as time passed both Army and Navy commanders realized that matters such as the loading of a battalion from a barracks ship onto the assault craft of a river assault squadron and the configuration of a battalion river assault squadron convoy were standing operating procedure. The Mobile Riverine Force was nevertheless to rely heavily on detailed operations orders

Mobile Riverine Force Briefing Aboard USS Benewah

rather than a formal, written standing operating procedure for many months of its operations.

Operational Concept and Procedures

The initial operations of the Mobile Riverine Force during the period 1 June to 26 July 1967 were designated Operation Coronado I. From 3 June through 10 June operations were conducted in the vicinity of Dong Tam, and were designed to make the land base more secure and to test the operational procedures of the force. A tactical operations center manned jointly by the Army and Navy provided a focal point for communications and for monitoring operations and could fulfill the needs of the riverine brigade and flotilla commanders separately.

At the levels of maneuver battalion and river assault squadron, the staffs operated independently but maintained close, harmonious relationships. The maneuver battalion staff outranked and outnumbered the river assault squadron staff. Because of a limited staff, the naval river assault squadron was unable to perform staff functions which corresponded to those of the infantry battalion it supported. This limitation contributed to the centralization of planning at the flotilla level. The two boat divisions organic to the river assault squadrons also were limited in their planning. The rifle company commanders transacted their business with naval enlisted men, who did not have the authority to make decisions. Time could be lost at the company and boat division level in situations requiring quick decision.

Operations consisted of co-ordinated airmobile, ground, and waterborne attacks, supported by air and naval forces. The ground and naval combat elements traveled to the area of operations by river assault squadron craft, helicopter, or a combination of these means. While the boats would serve as a block and could transport troops in the early stages of an operation, once the troops had engaged the enemy more speed was necessary and air transportation of forces was generally more satisfactory.

The basic offensive maneuvers used by the Mobile Riverine Force were to drive the enemy against a blocking force, with the open flanks covered by Army helicopter gunships, or to encircle him. These maneuvers were based on the estimate that the enemy would choose to fight only when he thought he could inflict heavy casualties or when he was surprised and forced to fight. If he chose not to fight, he might attempt to take advantage of the concealment afforded by the numerous tree-lined waterways by dispersing into small groups and leaving the area of operations under the protection of small delaying and harassing fire teams. It was necessary for U.S. forces to establish blocking positions quickly and to be able to deploy troops rapidly. Several maneuver battalions were needed, but the Mobile Riverine Force had usually only two battalions, a situation that provided further incentive for co-ordinating operations with Vietnamese or other U.S. units.

Control of the riverine forces was aided by reliable and versatile parallel Army and Navy communications systems, by operations conducted over flat terrain by units within mutually supporting distances, and by command helicopters used at the brigade and battalion levels. Troop movements were controlled and co-ordinated from the flagship. The focal point for control was the joint tactical operations center, the Army element of which was under the supervision of the brigade executive officer. Staff representation came from the S–3, S–2, N–3, air liaison, Army aviation, and artillery fire support sections, and the center was operational at all times.

During operations the brigade employed a forward command group, usually located at the fire support base, and composed of the

TROOPS PREPARE TO EMBARK FROM AMMI BARGES

brigade commander, the brigade S-3, the brigade assistant fire support co-ordinator, and the air liaison officer. The brigade command group was generally aloft in a command helicopter in daylight hours. The battalion command post was fragmented into a forward and a rear tactical operations center. The forward post was located in a command boat that accompanied the troops during their waterborne movement and normally consisted of the battalion commander, S-3, assistant S-3, artillery liaison officer, an operations sergeant, an intelligence sergeant, and two radio telephone operators. The river assault squadron commander and his operations officer were aboard the same command boat. The rear command post was located aboard ship at the mobile riverine base and usually consisted of the battalion executive officer, S-1, S-2, S-3, S-4, an operations sergeant, and two radio telephone operators. When a command and control helicopter, usually an observation type, was available, the battalion commander and his artillery liaison officer controlled the operation from the air.

After the briefing that took place before each operation, battalion commanders and supporting river assault squadron com-

Monitors and Assault Patrol Boats Head in to Shore

manders issued final instructions to their staffs and subordinate commanders. These confirmed or modified previously issued orders. Each rifle company was allocated three armored troop carriers, and arrangements were made to load bulk cargo and ammunition prior to troop embarkation. At the designated loading time for a particular company, three armored troop carriers were tied alongside the Ammi barges moored to the ship and three platoons of a company embarked simultaneously. In most instances, the loading of a complete company was restricted to twenty minutes. The Navy stationed expert swimmers on the barges prepared to rescue men who might fall overboard. Once a company was loaded, the ATC's proceeded to a rendezvous where they waited for the remainder of the battalion to load. Upon completion of the battalion loading, the ATC's moved at a specified time across a starting point and thence to the area of operation. Army elements observed radio silence; the naval radio was used only for essential traffic control.

The boats moved across the starting point in column formation, the leading assault support boats providing minesweeping and fire support. Each minesweeper was equipped with a drag hook that

ASSAULT CRAFT GOING IN TO LAND TROOPS

was tethered with a steel cable to a high-speed winch. Two of the leading minesweepers preceding on the flanks of the column dragged these hooks along the bottom of the waterway in an effort to cut electrical wires rigged to underwater mines. The river assault squadron commander traveled aboard the leading command and control boat. The battalion commander was either in the control boat or in a helicopter aloft. Each supporting river division was divided into three sections, each section consisting of a monitor and three ATC's supporting the one rifle company. These sections were in such order in the column as to maintain infantry company integrity and to place units on the beach in the order specified by the battalion commander. While underway, the river assault squadron commander exercised command and control of the boats. The rifle company commanders monitored the Navy command and control and the battalion command net in order to stay abreast of developing situations. Radar was the principal navigational aid during the hours of darkness.

Water checkpoints were designated along the routes as a means of control, and as march units passed these a report was made to the joint tactical operations center. Whether on large rivers or small streams, river assault units were faced with the threat of hostile attack. However, when the boats left the large rivers for the smaller waterways the danger from recoilless rifles, rocket fire, and mines increased. The waterways negotiated by the boats varied from a width of 100 meters where the smaller waterways joined the river to widths of 15 to 25 meters. The formation that the boats assumed was similar to that used on the main river except that the leading minesweepers moved to positions nearer the column. While the column proceeded along the small waterways, suspected areas of ambush (if in an area cleared by the Vietnamese government) were often reconnoitered by fire from the small boats and by artillery.

When the lead boats of the formation were approximately 500 meters from the beach landing sites, artillery beach preparations were lifted or shifted. The leading minesweepers and monitors then moved into position to fire on the beaches on both sides of the waterway. This fire continued until masked by the beaching ATC. If no preparatory fire was employed, the boats landed at assigned beaches in sections of three, thus maintaining rifle company integrity. Boats within a section were about 5 to 10 meters apart, and a distance of 150 to 300 meters (depending on the beach landing sites selected for each company) separated each boat section or assault rifle company. After the units had disembarked, the boats remained at the beaching site until released by the battalion commander. Upon release, the river assault squadron craft either moved to provide fire support to the infantry platoons or moved to interdiction stations and rendezvous points. Subsequent missions for the boats included independent interdiction, resupply, and extraction of troops.

TROOPS GO ASHORE FROM ARMORED TROOP CARRIER

After landing the troops secured initial platoon and company objectives and moved forward in whatever formation the terrain and mission required. (*Diagram 6*) When contact with the enemy was made, commanders immediately acted to cut off possible enemy escape routes. The most frequently used tactic was to move units to blocking positions to the flanks and rear of the enemy and direct extensive artillery fire, helicopter gunship fire, and air strikes into the enemy positions. After this softening up process, troops swept the area.

The Mobile Riverine Force had little trouble finding suitable helicopter landing and pickup zones. Pickup zones used to mount airmobile operations were normally located in the vicinity of the fire support base or on terrain adjacent to the waterways. When there were not enough aircraft to move an entire company at one time, platoons were shuttled into the area of operations. The brigade standing operating procedure called for helicopter gunships to escort each serial, and for an airborne forward air controller to operate along the route of aerial movement.

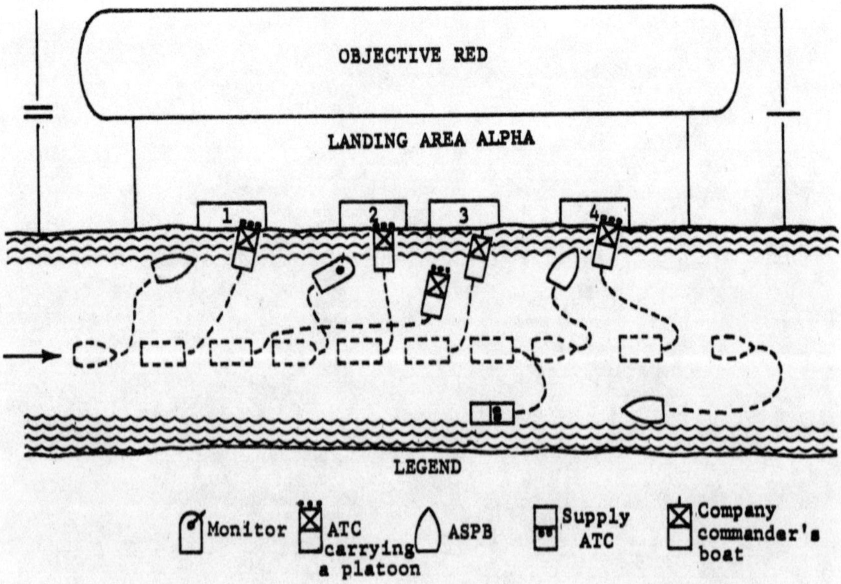

Diagram 6. Typical company landing formation.

During each day plans were made to arrive at a night defensive position before dark unless troops were engaged with or pursuing the enemy. After resupply, the night defensive position was organized against possible enemy attack.

The fourth rifle company of each battalion was usually employed at the fire support base under operational control of the base commander; for mobile riverine base security it was under direct control of the Mobile Riverine Base commander.

When the river-assault craft remained overnight on the small waterways in the operational area, the brigade and battalion commanders planned for security of the boats, which were usually kept near infantry elements ashore. The boat fire was integrated with the fire of other units.

Withdrawal of riverine forces from the area of operations was accomplished chiefly by boat. When units operated far inland from navigable waterways, however, they were extracted by helicopter and taken to a landing zone near a navigable waterway. They were then transported by boat to the Mobile Riverine Base or to another area of operations. Sites designated for picking up troops were often on streams lined with dense banana groves, coconut groves, or nipa palm that made it difficult for both the ground unit commander and the river assault squadron commander to spot. Ground and water movement to the site was therefore controlled and co-ordinated from the battalion commander's helicopter. The commander marked specific beach and unit locations with colored smoke and directed the Army and Navy elements to them by radio.

The same boat that was used to put an Army element ashore was also used to bring it out. Each boat carried an identifying number and flew a distinctive colored pennant from the mast that could be recognized by troops who were behind dikes and vegetation. Each boat also carried three running lights tiered near the top of the mast. Through the use of varying color combinations in the top, center, and bottom running lights, the boat designated for each boarding element could be readily identified.

Tides, draft, and maneuver room were primary considerations when boats were scheduled to rendezvous with Army forces for pickup because tides not only affected the water depth in canals, but caused significant changes in current velocity and direction. Traveling a distance of thirty kilometers upstream could take up to six hours against an ebbing tide, whereas the same route might be covered in four and a half hours on an incoming tide.

The threat of ambush during troop removal was considered as great as during movement to landings. When possible, an alternate to the route used for entering an area was selected for picking up troops. Beaching of the boats was usually accomplished with little difficulty because the infantrymen on shore had reconnoitered the banks for obstacles. Army security elements were placed 100 to 150 meters inland from the extraction site. After the troops were aboard, the boats resumed tactical formation and moved along the canal or stream and into the major waterway where the Mobile Riverine Base was anchored.

During offensive operations, the commander of the Army element of the Mobile Riverine Force in his position as base commander for all joint Army and Navy bases was also responsible for the defense of the Mobile Riverine Base. The Navy provided its appropriate share of forces, which included those for gunfire support and protection against waterborne threats. Defense of the base also involved arrangements for curfew and other restrictions for water craft with appropriate Vietnamese civilian and military officials in the immediate vicinity.

River assault divisions were assigned the responsibility for waterborne defense on a rotating basis. They conducted patrols to control river traffic, enforce curfews, and deter attack by water;

swept the vicinity of the Mobile Riverine Base for water mines; sent demolition teams to inspect underwater anchor chains, hulls of ships, and pontons for limpet mines; and dropped random explosive charges in the anchorage area to deter enemy swimmers.

One rifle company under the base commander was responsible for shore defense of the Mobile Riverine Base. Normally the company employed one platoon on each bank of the river and held the remainder of the company in reserve. Since anchorage space was 2,000 to 2,500 meters in length, it was impossible to conduct a closely knit defense with the relatively small number of troops committed. Platoon ambush sites were established on the banks opposite the flotilla flagship and during daylight hours security patrols were dispatched to provide early warning of enemy attack. The security troops were reinforced as needed by elements of the company defending the fire support base. Artillery and 4.2-inch and 81-mm. mortar fire as well as fire from the boats was planned in support of the defense of the base. The flat trajectory of naval weapons fire required careful planning for both shore and waterborne defense.

The planning and operational procedures initially used by the Mobile Riverine Force were refined as the staff and the force gained experience. The first significant test of these procedures came during operations in Long An Province in the III Corps Tactical Zone.

CHAPTER VI

III Corps Operations and the Threat to Dong Tam

On 11 and 12 June 1967 the fully constituted Mobile Riverine Force made its first major move. Leaving Dong Tam, it sailed down the Mekong River and across a stretch of the South China Sea to a temporary anchorage at Vung Tau, and thence to an anchorage southeast of Saigon at Nha Be—a total distance of sixty miles. At Vung Tau it received additional Navy assault craft that had arrived from the United States. Since the assault support patrol boats that had been scheduled to join the force at this time were delayed, armored troop carriers continued to perform minesweeping and security operations until arrival of the assault support patrol boats in September and October. Upon reaching the Nha Be anchorage, the force returned to the Vietnamese Navy the borrowed craft it had used since February. With the new assault craft, the flotilla had 52 armored troop carriers, 10 monitors, 4 command boats, and 2 refuelers.

From the Nha Be anchorage operations were conducted from 13 through 17 June in the Rung Sat Special Zone as part of the U.S. 9th Division operation, GREAT BEND, which brought greater security to the Long Tau shipping channel. Although the force found a base camp believed to have been the recent site of the headquarters controlling Viet Cong actions in the Rung Sat Special Zone, no contact was established with the enemy.

On 18 June the Mobile Riverine Force moved eight miles to a mobile riverine base anchorage at the junction of the Soi Rap and Vam Co Rivers in preparation for operations in the Can Giuoc District of eastern Long An Province. One battery of supporting 155-mm. self-propelled artillery was moved by LCU to the west bank of the Soi Rap River adjacent to the mobile riverine base at the confluence of the Soi Rap and Vam Co Rivers. Ammunition supply for the battery was transported from Vung Tau by Army LCM-8's while the barge-mounted artillery continued to receive ammunition support from the LST supply ship in the base.

Before entering Long An Province, the brigade commander briefed the battalion and company commanders on their new area of operations. The battalions of the 2d Brigade had fought in Dinh Tuong and northern Kien Hoa Provinces where trees lined the banks of most streams and major canals. Although the soldiers were familiar with moving in the rice paddies near Dong Tam, they had seldom encountered such wide expanses of open paddy as existed in eastern Long An Province. These open areas provided observation and fields of fire that dictated greater dispersion of men and greater reliance on the "scouts out" technique. A long proven infantry tactic in open terrain, scouts out provided for point and flank security men to move out on foot as much as 500 meters from the remainder of their squad to provide early warning.

In further preparation for entering eastern Long An Province the brigade commander, S-2, and S-3 visited the 3d Brigade, 9th Infantry Division, and the 2d Battalion, 3d Infantry, 199th Infantry Brigade (Separate). Both of these units had operated in Long An and furnished helpful information. The group also visited the headquarters of the 46th Regiment, 25th Division, Army of Vietnam, and the Can Giuoc District headquarters. Although such visits risked exposing planned operations to compromise, the risk was accepted in order to exploit local intelligence and take advantage of operating in conjunction with other U.S. and Vietnamese units. For the Can Giuoc activities, the Mobile Intelligence Civil Affairs Team set up operations with the 2d Battalion, 46th Regiment, Army of Vietnam, and Can Giuoc District headquarters on 19 June, the first day of Mobile Riverine Force operations in Long An.

Can Giuoc Operation

Can Giuoc District contained a good network of navigable waterways, permitting the assault craft to enter an area that intelligence reports indicated was used extensively by Viet Cong regional forces for rest and training. Civilian travel in the locality was chiefly by water, since most bridges and the one ferry were no longer serviceable. Previous military actions here had depended for movement on boats and aircraft. The U.S. 9th Infantry Division's 3d Brigade was disposed in Long An Province west of Can Giuoc District to lend security by its operations to Highway 4; however, Can Giuoc District was outside the brigade's routine area of operations.

The fact that the Mobile Riverine Force could move its afloat base permitted the establishment of a brigade base within three

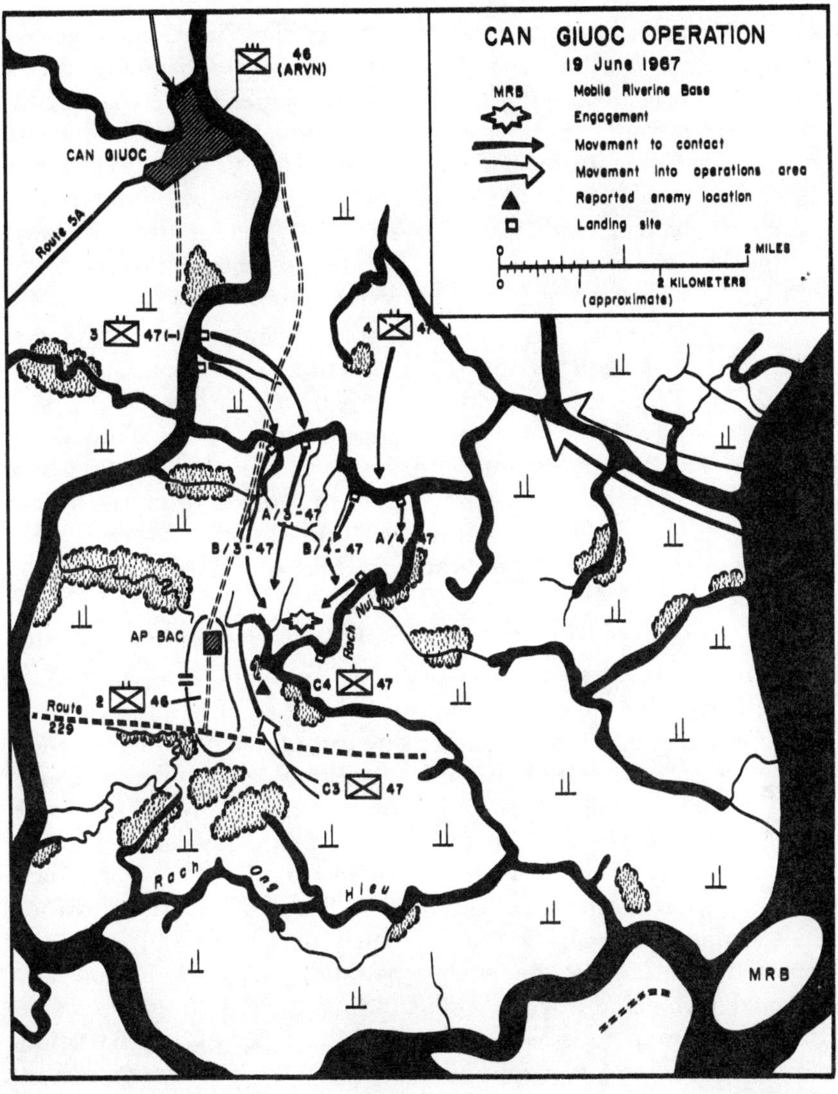

MAP 6

kilometers of a location that had been a remote Viet Cong base area enjoying considerable security. To attack this area, Colonel Fulton and Captain Wells had agreed to anchor the riverine ships as close as practicable to the area of operations. The time needed by assault craft to enter the area and the turnaround time of both helicopters and water craft conducting resupply and medical evacuation would thus be reduced. The base was moved into its anchorage on the evening before operations. The risk of disclosing the intended area of operations by this move was accepted because the force had not been in the area before and the Viet Cong were not thought to be familiar with the capabilities of the ships and assault craft. The brigade and flotilla commanders agreed that assault craft would go up only those streams wide enough to permit them to make 180-degree turns. Colonel Fulton and Captain Wells also agreed to use a portion of the assault craft as a blocking force once Army troops had landed. The boats were to enter the waterways as the tide was rising, permitting greater speed and a long period of high tide level immediately following entry.

The Mobile Riverine Force sent five companies of the two U.S. infantry battalions into the operations area by assault craft. (*Map 6*) The sixth company, Company C, 3d Battalion, 47th Infantry, moved by water to an air pickup zone to stand by as reserve. The troops entered the area and searched south, using assault craft to cross water barriers and to provide communications and fire support. The 2d Battalion, 46th Infantry, Army of Vietnam, moved during darkness and established a blocking position near the town of Ap Bac, oriented to the east.

At approximately 1000 Colonel Fulton was notified through the Mobile Intelligence Civil Affairs Team, located near Can Giuoc District headquarters, that the district chief had information of a Viet Cong battalion-size force due east of the blocking position of the 2d Battalion, 46th Infantry. The brigade commander issued a fragmentary order at 1010 informing the commanders of the 3d and 4th Battalions, 47th Infantry, and the U.S. adviser to the Vietnam Army battalion of the reported enemy strength and location. The order directed the two U.S. battalions to continue their maneuver south toward the newly designated objective—the reported location of the enemy battalion. Colonel Fulton also directed Colonel Tutwiler, commanding the 4th Battalion, 47th Infantry, to prepare to assume control of Company C, 3d Battalion, 47th Infantry, and to deploy the company by helicopter south of the reported enemy location.

Colonel Tutwiler moved Company C at 1105 by air south of the reported enemy location with the mission of moving northeast to reconnoiter the enemy position. He sent Company C of his battalion by assault craft south on the stream and landed the company at 1135 northeast of the reported enemy position.

By 1150 Company C of the 3d Battalion had swept the reported enemy location without finding the Viet Cong. Company C of the 4th Battalion was moving west from its landing area when it was fired upon from the north. At the same time Company A of the 4th

Battalion, moving south but at a distance of some 800 meters north of Company C, 4th Battalion, encountered heavy automatic weapons and small arms fire from its front and right flank. The enemy position had turned out to be north of the reported location. Company A, lacking cover, suffered heavy casualties. The Viet Cong had occupied well-fortified firing positions in an L-shape along the north bank of the stream that separated Company A from both Company C of the 3d Battalion and Company C of the 4th Battalion, 47th Infantry.

Colonel Tutwiler shifted Company B of his battalion, which had been moving on the battalion right flank, into the area behind Company A to assist by fire and with medical evacuation. He held his Company C on the south side of the stream to maintain contact and maneuvered Company C, 3d Battalion, north across the stream. Once on the north bank, Company C, 3d Battalion, fought slowly to the east, with its right flank on the stream. Major H. Glenn Penny, executive officer and acting commander of the 3d Battalion, 47th Infantry, meanwhile moved his Companies A and B southeast to link up with Company C of the 3d Battalion on that company's north flank. At 1545 Major Penny resumed operational control of his Company C. Company B attacked east on line with Company C while Company A moved into a blocking position 600 meters north of the left flank of Company B. By 2000 darkness and enemy fire prompted a halt to maneuvers and placed Companies B and C, 3d Battalion, some 600 meters west of Company C of the 4th Battalion where the units remained throughout the night of 19–20 June.

In the movement of the two U.S. battalions toward the first reported enemy location, the naval assault craft were limited to movement on the stream paralleling the 4th Battalion's left flank. When Company C of the 4th Battalion was fired upon at 1150, the naval assault craft that had brought in the company provided fire support for it and, later, for Company C of the 3d Battalion as it crossed the stream west of the actual enemy positions.

Although the rifle companies and the naval assault craft quickly returned the enemy fire, artillery and helicopter gunship fire could not be immediately brought to bear because the heavy casualties initially suffered by Company A of the 4th Battalion prevented the company commander from determining the dispositions of his platoons. Artillery fire began at approximately 1200; it was delivered at the request of the forward observers and co-ordinated by both ground and airborne artillery observers. Support was provided during the daylight hours and well into the night by helicopter gunships, medical evacuation helicopters, and assault craft.

The movement of Companies A, B, and C, 3d Battalion, 47th Infantry, required the entire afternoon, but not all companies were able to link up before dark. The 2d Battalion, 46th Vietnam Army Infantry, remained in its original position during the engagement because Colonel Fulton decided that maneuver of the battalion to the east would be complicated by the presence of U.S. companies between the Vietnam battalion and the enemy.

Viet Cong and U.S. troops exchanged fire throughout the daylight hours and into the night. U.S. troops found that the enemy's reinforced bunkers could be destroyed only by 90-mm. recoilless rifle fire and helicopter rockets and bombs; the 20-mm. and 80-mm. rounds fired by the assault craft penetrated a bunker only after multiple hits.

Casualties of Company C of the 3d Battalion were evacuated during the afternoon and evening of the battle by plastic assault boat and helicopter. Company C of the 4th Battalion was unable to use the assault craft for medical evacuation and relied on helicopters. Whether casualties were taken directly by helicopter from a ground pickup zone or from an armored troop carrier aid station after treatment, they were sent either to the barracks ship USS *Colleton* or to a field hospital.

During the afternoon and evening of 19 June most of the enemy losses came from U.S. supporting fire concentrated on a small area. A portion of the enemy battalion eluded the U.S. blocking positions during the night, probably by crossing the stream to the west of Company C, 4th Battalion, 47th Infantry, and then moving south. On 20 June the 4th Battalion, 47th Infantry, searched south to regain contact with the enemy. Moving by helicopter and on foot the battalion found the enemy north of the Rach Gion Ong stream at Ap Nam and, aided by a company of the 2d Battalion, 60th Infantry, encircled and eliminated an enemy platoon. The company from the 2d Battalion, 60th Infantry, was provided from the 3d Brigade by the Commanding General, 9th Infantry Division.

Following the battles of 19–20 June, the Mobile Riverine Force remained in the Can Giuoc area, capitalizing on the knowledge obtained of the area and attacking small elements of the Viet Cong 5th Nha Be Battalion and local guerrillas with whom battle had been joined on 19 June. On 23 June Company A, 4th Battalion, 47th Infantry, which had taken heavy losses, was moved by air to Dong Tam to begin a two-week period of refitting and retraining. Operations were conducted in the Rung Sat Special Zone, the Can

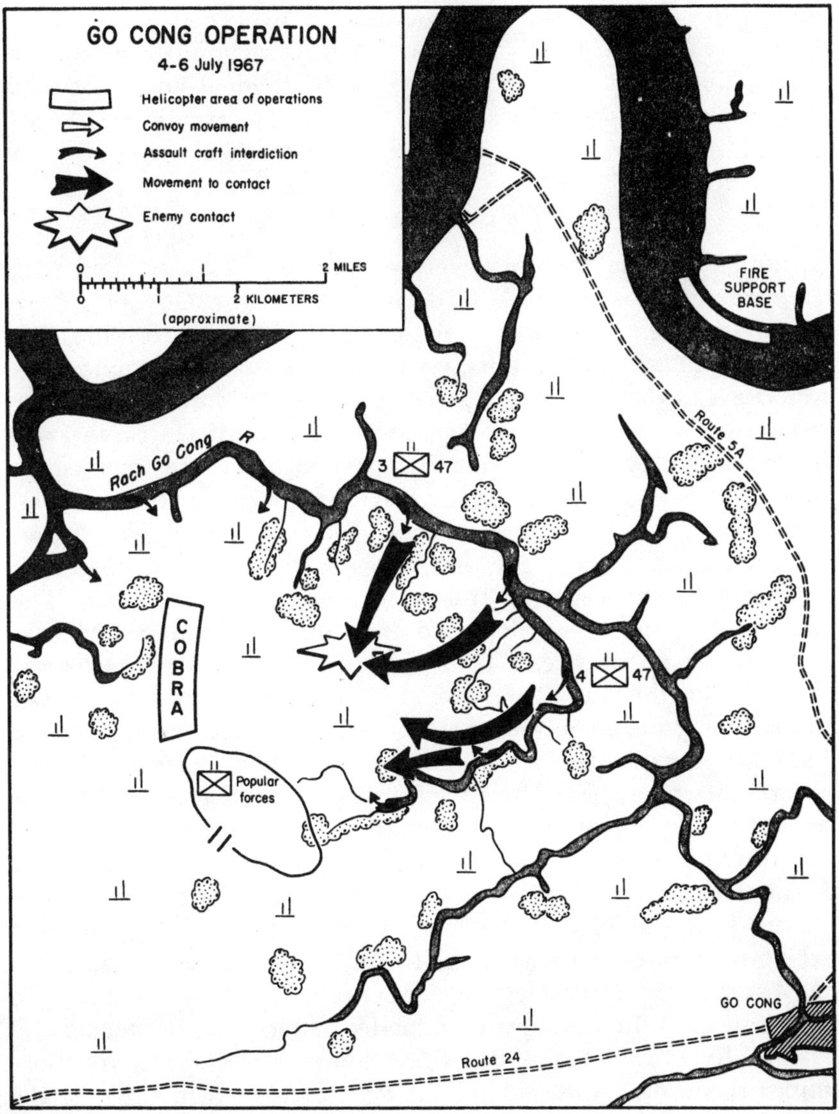

MAP 7

Duoc District of Long An Province, and Go Cong Province of IV Corps. Companies on independent missions entered the smaller waterways by ATC at night to establish widely dispersed ambushes. Infantry platoons set up ambushes ashore in co-ordination with ATC's and monitors to interdict land and water routes. Co-operating with the 199th Infantry Brigade (Separate) and the 2d and 3d Battalions of the 46th Vietnam Army Infantry Regiment, the force ranged in widely dispersed formations to find the enemy. An assault helicopter company provided by II Field Force was used extensively to move troops when the riverine assault craft were limited by the lack of navigable streams or by their relatively slow movement.

Go Cong Operation

On 4 July the Mobile Riverine Force again co-operated with Vietnamese forces to attack an enemy base area in Go Cong Province. The base, reportedly used for training recruits for the Viet Cong My Tho Province units, lay in an area nearly surrounded by waterways. (*Map 7*) The scheme of maneuver for the operation required a Popular Forces provisional battalion of Go Cong Province to move overland during darkness to block the land escape route that the Viet Cong might use—if attacked—on the southwest boundary of the reported base area. To assist the Popular Forces battalion in blocking on the west, helicopter gunships watched over an area into which ground troops were not allowed to move. The Mobile Riverine Force deployed into the area and moved into positions along the stream nearly encircling the enemy base area.

Entering the Vam Co River before daylight, five companies under the command of two battalion headquarters moved off the Vam Co and into the streams that formed a three-quarter circle around the enemy base. Once the companies had landed, the ATC's, augmented by all other assault craft available, moved to stations to prevent enemy movement across the small streams. An assault helicopter company stood ready at first light to move one infantry company as a reserve under brigade control. This company was set down before daylight by ATC's at a pickup zone adjacent to the barge-mounted artillery fire support base.

Early on 4 July troops were landed without encountering the enemy. By 1800 the sweeping operation had produced only three minor skirmishes; three of the enemy were killed, ninety-one detained, and two weapons were captured. There had been no U.S. or Popular Forces casualties. The U.S. battalions established dispersed ambush sites and shortly after dark began to encounter small groups of Viet Cong in a number of places. These encounters continued sporadically throughout the early evening; several of the enemy were killed and more were detained.

On 5 July, discovering cleverly disguised bunkers and so-called spider holes in which the enemy had escaped detection the previous day, U.S. troops made a more methodical search of the area.

On the same day the Viet Cong who had been detained were sent to a combined interrogation center established by the Mobile Intelligence Civil Affairs Team and Vietnamese provincial officials at the province capital. Later, the interrogation reports provided information that the enemy elements encountered had been a platoon-size cadre and a newly recruited Viet Cong company. The cadre was reportedly equipped only with small arms, and the company had few weapons. The search for the Viet Cong continued through 5 July and ambushes were again established during the night.

The Go Cong operation ended on 6 July without casualties to U.S. or Popular Forces troops. Throughout the operation, the assault craft guarded the waterways, stopping over seven hundred native watercraft and screening the people, some of whom were held for further interrogation. On 4 July the reserve company had been inserted by the assault helicopter company into the area near the COBRA zone. This company, operating under control of its parent battalion, had subsequently searched and maintained patrols and ambushes in the area. The impact of the operation on the enemy was not fully known until several days later when the interrogation center had completed its work and a Popular Forces company had re-entered the area to check information provided by the prisoners. Enemy losses included sixty-six killed, sixty-two prisoners of war, and five weapons. Under the Vietnamese government program of granting amnesty to Viet Cong who returned to the government, seven returnees, or Hoi Chanhs, were received.

The operation emphasized the importance of using a combination of land, air, and water transportation to take advantage of terrain, and the necessity for close co-operation with South Vietnamese officials and intelligence units. The combined transportation means enabled the Mobile Riverine Force to gain control over an area quickly. By seizing sampans along the waterways the Mobile Riverine Force prevented the enemy from using them to escape.

During this operation the Army initiated air resupply directly from the support LST. Previously supplies were moved from the LST by boat to a landing zone ashore, whence they were carried by helicopter to the field, an operation that required four separate transfers and considerable time. With the new method, loads were broken to unit size on the LST, each helicopter was loaded directly from the LST deck, and the material was delivered to the troop landing zone. To resupply two battalions using 10 UH–ID's (one assault helicopter company) required one hour and ten minutes.

This time was bettered as the crew teamwork and the landing cycle on the LST's were smoothed out.

During the period of the Go Cong operation, another innovation was fielded by the Mobile Riverine Force that significantly increased flexibility. The first of several armored troop carriers was modified by adding a helicopter landing pad sixteen feet square over the troop compartment. An H-23 successfully operated from the new pad on 4 July and a UH-ID on 5 July.

On 15 July Captain Wells requested that the Commander, Naval Forces, Vietnam, obtain twelve Vietnamese national policemen of the river police branch for assignment to Task Force 117. The experience of searching over seven hundred native boats during the Go Cong operation highlighted the need for more men to screen waterway traffic. Although no Vietnamese river policemen were subsequently assigned, the force had the co-operation of the river police on most operations.

Further Can Giuoc Operations

On 21 July 1967 the Mobile Riverine Force concluded a two-day operation employing two U.S. infantry battalions in the southern part of Can Giuoc District. During the preceding thirty days, the force had conducted three operations in Can Giuoc District, killing 316 Viet Cong, taking 15 prisoners, capturing 68 weapons, and detaining 337 people. This fourth operation was part of a program to strike at different sections of Can Giuoc until the whole district had been fully covered. Reports that company-size groups of Viet Cong were in the area had been received by the combined intelligence center, the 46th Vietnam Army Regiment, and Can Giuoc District headquarters at Can Giuoc.

At 0545 on 20 July the 3d Battalion, 47th Infantry, and the 4th Battalion, 47th Infantry, boarded ATC's that joined in column with the heavy-gunned monitors and steamed west from the Mobile Riverine Base along the Vam Co River. From the fire support patrol base adjacent to the mobile riverine base the artillery supported the operation with two barge-mounted batteries of 105-mm. howitzers and one land-based battery of 155-mm. self-propelled howitzers from the 2d Battalion, 35th Artillery. At dawn Company C of the 4th Battalion, 47th Infantry, landed at the fire base as an airmobile or waterborne reserve force. Three ATC's stood by as water transport until a company of UH-ID helicopters arrived to support the operation and to provide transportation of the reserves to any part of the battle area. When the convoy left the base

ARMORED TROOP CARRIER WITH HELIPAD

it had a unique combat element. Both reconnaissance platoons of the two battalions had been designated Team Recon and were under the control of the 4th Battalion.

At 0700 the ATC's landed along a four-kilometer stretch of the east bank of the Song Rach Cat River, and 800 troops moved ashore under the watchful support of the monitors. The 3d Battallion, 47th Infantry, landed on the north beaches, the 4th Battalion on the south beaches, with Team Recon going in on the right flank. The landing was unopposed and all units quickly secured initial objectives beyond the beach, moving steadily to the east.

The operational area was bounded by the Song Rach Cat on the south and west and by the Song Nha Be on the east. On the north, a company of the 3d Battalion guided its left flank along Highway 229 running generally west to east. From the Song Rach Cat units moved slowly across the rice paddies, picking up all male Vietnamese, who were then evacuated and checked for identification at the combined intelligence center at Can Giuoc.

Overhead the brigade and battalion commanders directed movement from helicopters. Artillery observers and Air Force forward air controllers surveyed the battlefield, waiting to bring in supporting fire. By 1000 the companies had moved east approximately 2,000 meters without meeting the enemy while the Navy support craft moved up close behind them on the narrow streams with guns ready. At 1030, Company A in the center of the 3d Battalion formation reported fire from well-fortified bunkers. It was reported that 10 to 15 Viet Cong were sighted, but later a prisoner gave the number as 50 to 60. A point scout from Company A, operating well forward, was the only friendly combatant killed by enemy fire in the operation. As troops maneuvered to bring small arms fire upon the enemy, close supporting fire by 105-mm. and 155-mm. artillery was adjusted forward of the advance. Shortly after 1100 the first air strike began to lay 750 pound bombs and napalm on the Viet Cong bunkers. Of the five strikes called in on the target, three were directed while the artillery continued to attack.

Units began moving rapidly to block enemy escape routes. Companies B and C of the 3d Battalion to the north and south of the enemy deployed on a line facing the enemy. Company B, 4th Battalion, 47th Infantry, maneuvered northeast across the rice paddy to block to the east. Company A of the 4th Battalion moved to join the block of the 3d Battalion's Company C on the south.

During the whole maneuver, the Navy ATC's and monitors were used to help find the enemy. Moving forward, the assault craft took up positions alongside the ground troops to add their fires to the battle and assist the infantry to cross the Rach Ong Hieu, a small stream. When Company A, 4th Battalion, 47th Infantry, arrived from the south at the Rach Ong Hieu the Navy ATC's provided lift across the stream, accomplishing in minutes what might have taken hours, and furnishing fire support as needed. By 1300 all blocks were in position with the exception of Company C of the 4th Battalion. At 1415 this unit was lifted by helicopters from the artillery fire support patrol base near the Mobile Riverine Base and landed to complete the block on the east next to Company B of the 4th Battalion. The encirclement of the Viet Cong was complete by 1515.

This encirclement was accomplished with a smoothly operating team of infantry, artillery, Navy and Air Force components. The tricky tides were known, and the boat commanders knew when and how far up a stream they could go to provide support. The infantry commanders maneuvered their troops across the rice paddies carefully, alert for booby traps and ambushes. Just in advance of lead elements, artillery delivered white phosphorus rounds which exploded 200 feet above the ground. Constantly re-adjusted, this marking fire insured that rapid and accurate artillery fire could be placed on the ground in front of the U.S. troops when they were engaged with the enemy. The Navy moved up close to the infantry positions to add the fire of the monitor's 40-mm. guns and 81-mm. mortars to reduce Viet Cong bunkers and machine gun emplacements. The Air Force and the artillery worked in close co-ordination, simultaneously laying on air strikes and artillery fire, while the Navy monitors maintained direct fire. When the helicopter company arrived in the battle area with Company C, 4th Battalion, 47th Infantry, it was able to land in a zone already secured by a U.S. ground unit, thus speeding the encirclement.

Action continued during the afternoon of 20 July, with units tightening their ring on the enemy as helicopters shuttled back and forth bringing a resupply of munitions and food. Seventeen Viet Cong dead had been accounted for by nightfall of the 20th. The pressure of artillery and small arms fire was maintained. The infantry positioned 90-mm. recoilless rifles and began to punch holes in the enemy bunkers. With darkness the Viet Cong fire became sporadic. U.S. troops maintained vigilance over the area during the night, using artillery illumination and allowing the Viet Cong no rest.

On 21 July a methodical sweep of the battle area revealed fifteen enemy bodies, one pistol, and seven rifles. More than eighteen bunkers had been reduced to rubble. Ten prisoners of war were taken, one of whom stated that on meeting U.S. troops the Viet Cong company had split into small groups and attempted to get out.

On 22 July the first helicopter barge was delivered to the Mobile Riverine Base. It was prepared for movement with the 3d Battalion, 34th Artillery, to the brigade forward command post at the barge-mounted artillery fire support base on 24 July.

On 24 July, in co-operation with the 3d Battalion, Vietnam Marine Corps, the 3d Battalion, 46th Vietnam Infantry Regiment, and GAME WARDEN patrol boats, the Mobile Riverine Force began operating in the northern part of Can Giuoc District in an effort to reduce the enemy threat to the district capital. (*Map 8*) At 0320 elements of the 3d Battalion, 34th Artillery, left the Mobile Riverine Base and went into position to support the operation at Fire Support Base TANGO. Elements of the 3d Battalion, 46th Vietnam

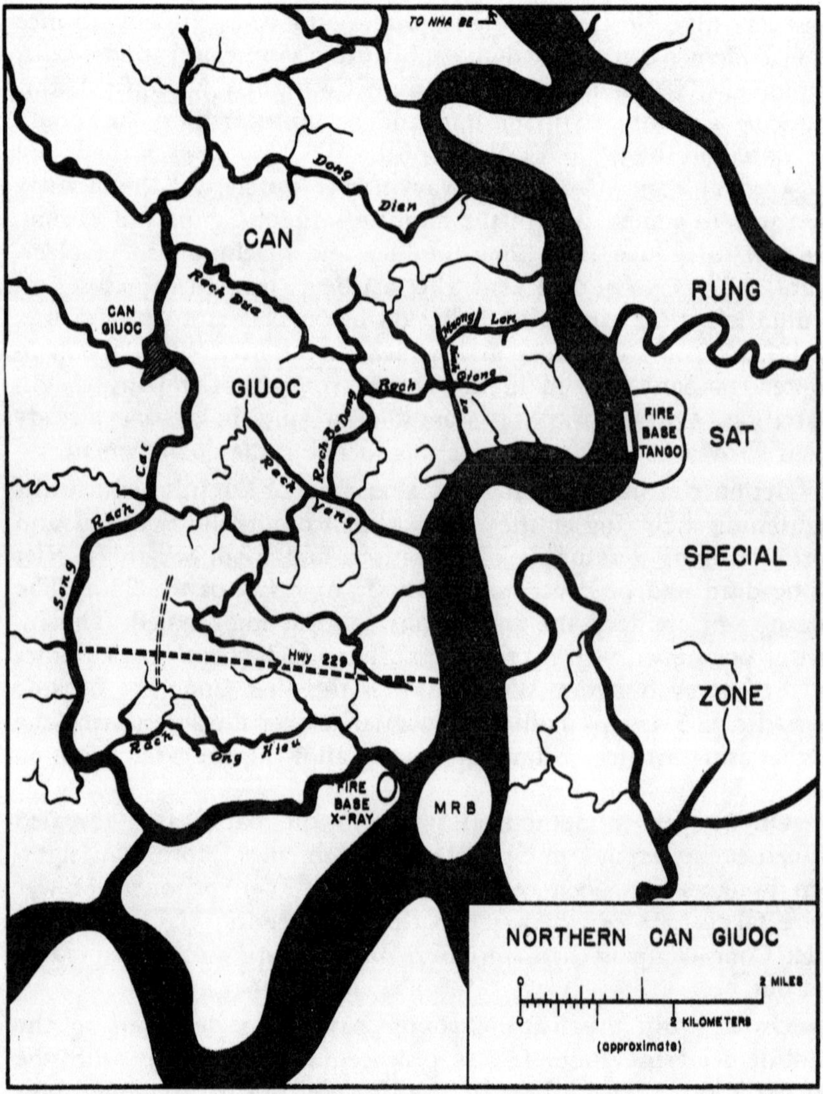

MAP 8

Infantry, moved from their cantonment area at Can Giuoc directly east across the Song Rach Cat to land unopposed. They moved northeast through selected control points to the Rach Dua River without meeting the enemy.

The 2d Brigade troops approached the area from the south, moving up the waterways in ATC's protected by monitors. The 3d Battalion, 47th Infantry, reinforced by the reconnaissance platoon of the 4th Battalion, 47th Infantry, went ashore on the north bank of the Rach Vang River, moved north, and secured its first objectives without opposition. The 4th Battalion remained afloat near the mouth of the Rach Vang as the brigade reserve. Company C of the 4th Battalion was landed at Fire Support Base X-RAY, from which it would later be deployed as needed by helicopter. The waterborne units of the 3d Battalion patrolled the waters of the Kinh Lo, Rach Giong, Rach Ba Dang, and Rach Vang to detect the enemy. The 2d Battalion, 3d Infantry, 199th Infantry Brigade, also participated in the operation, landing two companies by air south of the Dong Dien stream. The Vietnamese Marine battalion was next to enter the operation, having been lifted by ATC's from loading points at Nha Be to beaches along the north bank of a stream called Muong Lon. The landings were unopposed, and all units quickly secured their initial objectives.

At 0915 one company of the 4th Battalion, 47th Infantry, was inserted by ATC's at a beach on the east bank of the Rach Ba Dang and at 1110, the battalion's remaining two companies were brought into the operation, one landing by helicopter and the other by assault craft west of the Rach Ba Dang. A few bunkers and booby traps were found and destroyed. Team Recon discovered freshly broken ground guarded by booby traps; further search disclosed an arms cache containing two 57-mm. recoilless rifles, one 75-mm. recoilless rifle, and one 81-mm. mortar with bipod. Other elements of the 3d Battalion, 47th Infantry, also discovered arms. The caches contained a total of sixteen individual and four crew-served weapons.

Throughout the day of 24 July no enemy was sighted. On the morning of 25 July the Vietnam Marine Corps battalion and the 3d Battalion, 47th Infantry, cleared the remainder of the assigned areas of operation. The marines consolidated in place along the banks of Muong Lon facing north, while the 4th Battalion, 47th Infantry, was taken aboard ATC's from beaches on the south bank of the Rach Dua and Rach Giong Rivers to begin movement south. In the northern operational area the 2d Battalion, 3d Infantry, had moved to the east, while the Vietnam marines held their position. The 3d Battalion, 46th Vietnam Infantry, had swung about to search again to the southwest, arriving at the original beaches about 1540. By 1715 all units were on their way to their home stations by water or air.

A Hoi Chanh who had rallied to the republic during the operation said that his unit had been directed to hide its weapons and equipment, break up into small groups, and temporarily cease operations in the Can Giuoc area. He said that his unit had oper-

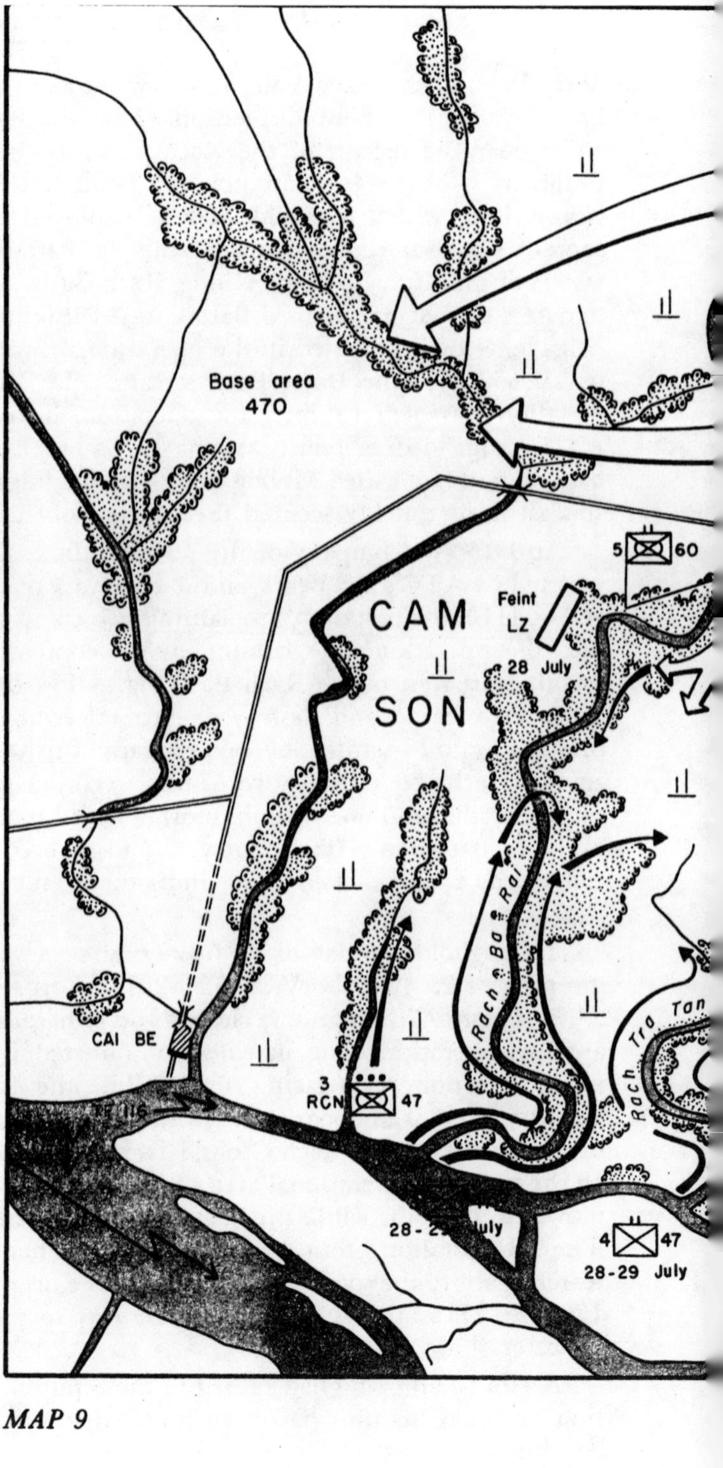

Base area
470
CAM
SON
Feint
LZ
28 July
5
60
CAI BE
TF 116
3
RCN
47
Rach Ba Rai
Rach Tra Tan
28-29 July
4
47
28-29 July

MAP 9

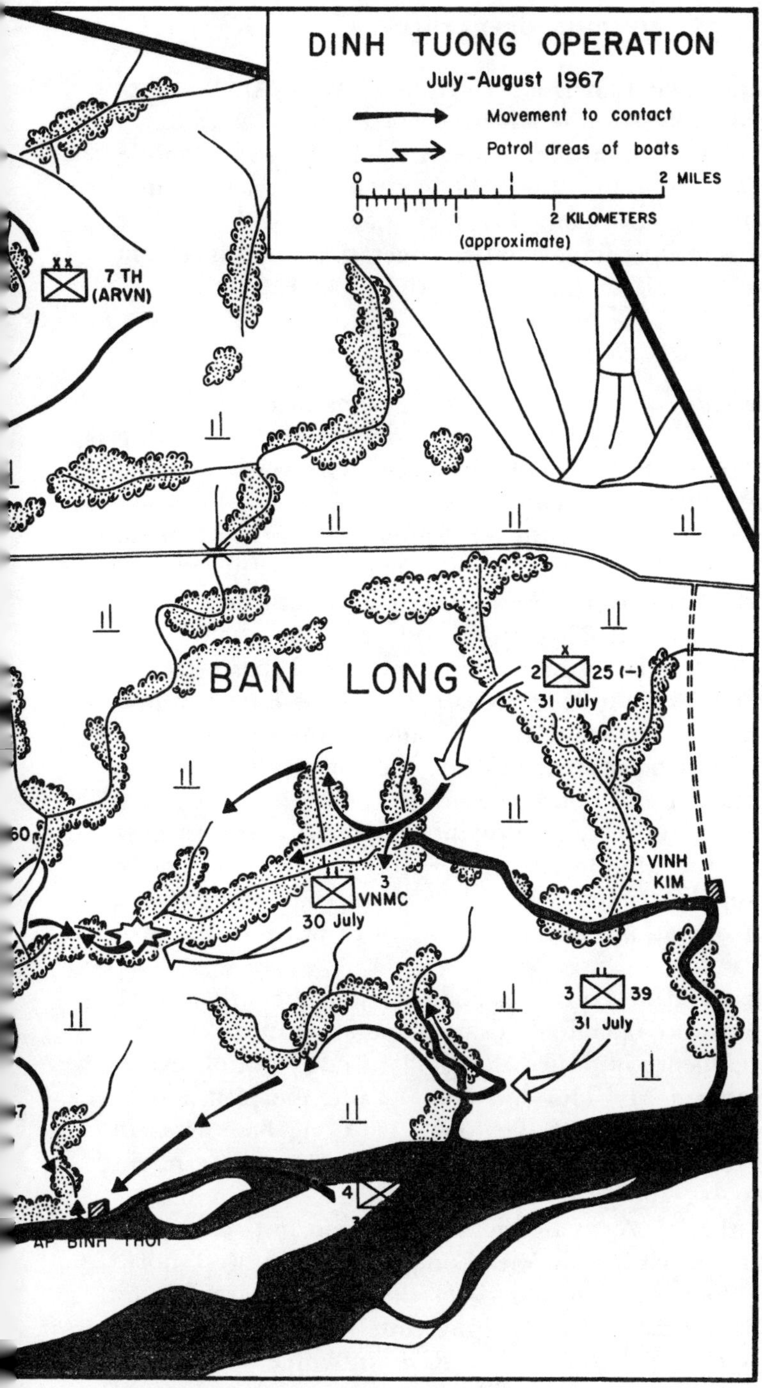

DINH TUONG OPERATION
July-August 1967
Movement to contact
Patrol areas of boats
0
1
2 MILES
0
1
2 KILOMETERS
(approximate)
7 TH
(ARVN)
BAN LONG
2
25 (-)
31 July
3
VNMC
30 July
VINH
KIM
3
39
31 July
4
AP BINH THOI

ated in Can Giuoc and Can Duoc Districts of Long An Province prior to battles with the Mobile Riverine Force.

At the end of Operation CORONADO I on 25 July the Mobile Riverine Force, operating in eastern Long An Province, the Rung Sat Special Zone, and Go Cong Province, had killed 478 of the enemy since 17 June. The force had been operating in areas seldom frequented by the South Vietnam Army and other U.S. units.

Dinh Tuong Operation

The Mobile Riverine Force ended operations in the Long An area because of reliable intelligence indicating an enemy buildup west of My Tho in Dinh Tuong Province. The force received word on 25 July that the Mobile Riverine Base would move on 27 July from the confluence of the Soi Rap and Vam Co Rivers to the vicinity of Dong Tam. During the afternoon of 25 July ground forces were picked up by the assault craft and returned to the Mobile Riverine Base. At 0200 on 27 July riverine assault craft began leaving the base for minesweeping and patrol stations along the route to Dong Tam. At 0550 the last ship of the force was proceeding south on the Soi Rap River. Because of the slow speed of the towed APL moving against the tide the journey took eleven and a half hours. This did not, however, delay the commencement of the operation in Dinh Tuong Province on 28 July. In just over forty-eight hours the Mobile Riverine Force was able to relocate a base supporting 3,900 men over a distance of sixty miles and to shift its area of operations a total of eighty-five miles to the area west of Dong Tam.

The Mobile Riverine Force was about to join the largest force with which it would co-operate in a single operation in its Vietnam experience. Intelligence indicated that a Viet Cong force of several battalions threatened My Tho and Dong Tam; the plan was to attack simultaneously three of the four Viet Cong base areas in Dinh Tuong Province from which an attack by the enemy might be staged. (*Map 9*)

On 27 July the 7th Army of Vietnam Division initiated operations designed to search for the Viet Cong from east to west, north of Highway 4. The search would cover the territory around the Ap Bac Viet Cong base and end in the eastern portion of enemy base area 470. On 28 July the Mobile Riverine Force would move into the Cam Son base area; on 29 July one or more battalions of the Vietnam Marine Corps would move into the Ban Long base area. The U.S. 9th Division was to place the 5th Battalion, 60th

Infantry (Mechanized), under the operational control of the 2d Brigade for the Cam Son operation, and was to hold the 3d Battalion, 39th Infantry, on call at that battalion's Long An base camp. The 1st Brigade, U.S. 25th Division, was to arrive at Dong Tam on 28 July for commitment under the operational control of the 9th U.S. Division. The 7th Army of Vietnam Division was given the 44th Ranger Battalion by the commander of IV Corps for insertion by helicopter into the northwestern portion of Cam Son on 28 July. The U.S. Navy Task Force 116 (GAME WARDEN) was to patrol the My Tho River from My Tho to Sa Dec with thirty river patrol boats. To facilitate command and control, the U.S. 9th Division moved a forward command post to Dong Tam for the operation.

The Mobile Riverine Force operation in Cam Son began during the night of 28 July with the movement of the 5th Battalion, 60th Infantry (Mechanized), from its Long An base camp along Highway 4 to the town of Cai Lay. A battalion command post was established there as the maneuver companies continued south into the Cam Son area. As the mechanized battalion moved into the area of operations from the northeast, the 3d and 4th Battalions of the 47th Infantry moved by assault craft into the waterways in the southern portion of Cam Son.

Troop D, 3d Squadron, 5th Cavalry, minus the aerial rifle platoon, was operating with the Mobile Riverine Force for the first time. The troop had a reconnaissance mission covering the eastern Cam Son and western Ban Long areas on the brigade's flank. One rifle company of the 3d Battalion, 60th Infantry, was on call to the 2d Brigade for airmobile employment from Dong Tam.

Two assault helicopter companies were available to the 2d Brigade from II Field Force. At 0800 on 28 July they conducted feint landings at two landing zones just north of known enemy fortifications in northern Cam Son for the purpose of delaying enemy movement north until both the 5th Battalion, 60th Infantry, and the 44th Ranger Battalion could move into blocking positions near the feint landing zones.

On 28 July troops of the 7th Army of Vietnam Division north of Highway 4 received a little enemy fire and the Mobile Riverine Force encountered a few snipers in Cam Son. Troop D detected a squad of the enemy in the Ban Long area and killed five men with gunship fire.

Throughout the late morning on 29 July both the 3d and 4th Battalions, 47th Infantry, discovered widely dispersed small enemy groups. From their movements it was deduced that these groups were trying to fall back to the north into a fortified area. As the 3d Battalion moved companies into this area from the north and south on the east bank of the Rach Ba Rai, the enemy resisted. Between the hours of 1700 and 1900, Company C of the 3d Battalion pressed north; small enemy groups moving northeast delayed the company's advance. Sometime during these two hours an ATC was hit by B-40 rockets and 57-mm. recoilless rifle fire; twenty-five men—Army and Navy—were wounded by fragments. The 5th Battalion, 60th Infantry, fired upon individuals and small groups of the enemy during the late afternoon and evening. None of the Mobile Riverine Force units were able to fix the enemy position and by 1930 contact with the enemy was lost. Most of the Viet Cong dead were found when the infantry moved into areas which had been attacked by artillery and helicopter gunships.

By the night of 29 July, the fact that the 7th Vietnam Army Division north of Highway 4 had found few Viet Cong and that the Viet Cong in central Cam Son had evaded major battle prompted General O'Connor, 9th Division, and Colonel Lan, commanding the Vietnam marines, to consider the probability that the enemy was in the Ban Long area. Although what the Mobile Riverine Force had learned about the enemy in central Cam Son was far from conclusive, the highly evasive tactics of the enemy encountered by the force was considered an indication that the Viet Cong units that the force had met might be protecting the movement of larger units into the Ban Long area. This was in keeping with the pattern of movement in southern Dinh Tuong Province, and while no enemy was detected in Ban Long by D Troop on 29 July, an enemy squad had been attacked there by gunships on 28 July.

At approximately 2000 on 29 July Colonel Lan selected a landing zone for his 3d Battalion of Vietnam marines to begin landing by helicopter in Ban Long on 30 July. The area selected by Colonel Lan as a likely enemy position was near the place where D Troop had discovered the enemy on 28 July.

When it landed on 30 July the 3d Vietnam Marine Corps Battalion met heavy resistance. The troops immediately attacked the enemy, who were in a wooded area north of the landing zone. More marines were airlifted into the landing zone, still under enemy fire. For five hours the marines attacked prepared Viet Cong defensive positions. The enemy armament consisted of light and heavy machine guns and mortars. The marines relied on helicopter gunships and artillery. The 3d Marine Battalion fought the enemy throughout the afternoon, taking a few casualties and reporting more and more of the enemy killed and more equipment captured.

General O'Connor, noting the long east-west belt of trees that could provide concealment for the enemy, employed the 1st Brigade, 25th U.S. Division, east of the marines' location to block movement of the enemy to the east. In midafternoon General O'Connor directed Colonel Fulton, commanding officer of the 2d Brigade, to assist the 3d Marine Battalion in evacuating casualties and in preparing for an attack against the Viet Cong. Colonel Fulton directed Lieutenant Colonel Bruce E. Wallace, commander of the 3d Battalion, 47th Infantry, to establish a blocking position west of the battle area, facing east, a maneuver accomplished by 2000. The 4th Battalion, 47th Infantry, in the field for three days, was returned to the Mobile Riverine Base with instructions to be prepared to deploy early on 31 July. The 5th Battalion, 60th Infantry, was detached to 9th Division at 1230.

During the action on 29 July several assault boats were hit with small arms, rocket, and recoilless rifle fire. The monitor most seriously hit suffered no major structural damage. Hits and minor damage were received by five other craft, but the boats were able to absorb punishment and remain in operation.

At approximately 2030 on 30 July, Colonel Lan requested illumination for a night attack against the enemy positions. The subsequent attack by the 3d Vietnam Marine Corps Battalion silenced several 12.7-mm. machine guns and inflicted losses on the enemy. The attack was stopped by the 3d Marine Battalion commander because his own losses were heavy. Illumination was maintained during the night; at approximately 0430, 31 July, the enemy counterattacked to the east, with heavy losses to both sides.

Later in the morning of 31 July, the 5th Battalion, 60th Infantry, was again placed under the operational control of Colonel Fulton. At 0835, the battalion went to the assistance of the 1st Squadron, 6th Vietnamese Army Cavalry, and the 44th Ranger Battalion, which had met the enemy while moving to assist the 3d Marine Battalion. By 0825 the 5th Battalion, 60th Infantry, occupied a blocking position northeast of the 3d Battalion, 47th Infantry, where it remained during the day. During the morning of 31 July, the 3d Battalion, 39th Infantry, also was placed under the operational control of Colonel Fulton, bringing the Mobile Riverine Force to four battalions and Troop D, 3d Squadron, 5th Cavalry. The 3d Battalion, 39th Infantry, landed south of Vinh Kim and searched west.

Reports from the 44th Ranger Battalion and 3d Marine Battalion indicated that the Viet Cong, tentatively identified as the 263d Main Force Battalion, had dispersed during the predawn counterattack and were making their way south. Airborne reconnaissance by the 3d Battalion, 39th Infantry, revealed movement south in the direction of the village of Ap Binh Thoi.

Colonel Fulton directed the 3d Battalion, 39th Infantry, to conduct reconnaissance using helicopters southeast of the battle area and working west to Ap Binh Thoi. He directed Colonel Wallace to move his battalion southeast and to search the area as he closed on Ap Binh Thoi. This movement was initiated in midmorning and by 1700 both battalions were on the outskirts of Ap Binh Thoi. During that time Viet Cong were observed moving into Ap Binh Thoi in groups of twenty-five to thirty.

The 4th Battalion, 47th Infantry, augmented by elements of a Vietnamese field police force company, landed by ATC and entered Ap Binh Thoi. One company moved out to search northwest of the town while the rest of the battalion assisted the Vietnamese police in rounding up and interrogating people suspected of being Viet Cong. Several of the prisoners reported that the Viet Cong units encountered by the Vietnamese marines were the 263d Main Force Battalion and elements of the 514th Local Force Battalion. The prisoners were classified as Viet Cong when they confessed to having hidden their arms as they left the battle area during the early morning darkness. Company C, 4th Battalion, 47th Infantry, captured four men northwest of Ap Binh Thoi, all of them members of the 263d Main Force Battalion and one of them the battalion deputy commander. Of the more than 400 suspects detained by the National Police, 83 were from the 263d Main Force Battalion. The cordon around Ap Binh Thoi was completed by dark on 31 July, and no more of the Viet Cong were sighted.

The four-day operation, primarily because of the outstanding performance of the 3d Vietnam Marine Battalion, caused severe losses to the Viet Cong 263d Main Force Battalion, destroyed major fortifications in the Cam Son base area, probably thwarted planned enemy operations against Dong Tam, and eased the pressure on Highway 4. It also demonstrated the ability of U.S. and Vietnamese forces to work together. After the operation intelligence sources reported that the enemy had attempted to organize boats for a crossing of the My Tho River into Kien Hoa Province but were stopped by the cordon at Ap Binh Thoi and the river patrols. During the five-day operation on the My Tho River more than fifty patrol craft were employed; 283 Vietnamese watercraft were stopped and searched by naval craft from GAME WARDEN and the Mobile Riverine Force in the most ambitious attempt to control river traffic during the force's operations in 1967.

During operations from 28 July to 1 August, a large number of soldiers in the 3d Battalion, 47th Infantry, developed foot trouble as a result of spending five successive days on flooded land. The 4th Battalion, which had had one night of rest aboard ships of the Mobile Riverine Base, experienced a similar but lower rate of fungus infection and immersion foot.

The Mobile Riverine Force Returns to III Corps

CORONADO III was conducted in the Rung Sat Special Zone from 5 through 17 August after the Mobile Riverine Base had moved from Dong Tam to an anchorage at the junction of the Soi Rap and Vam Co Rivers. The purpose of the operation was to disrupt possible Viet Cong attacks on shipping in the Long Tau channel. Although no attacks were made on shipping during the operation, the Mobile Riverine Force fought sporadically with the Viet Cong and captured some munitions.

The Commander of Naval Forces, Vietnam, provided the following evaluation of the Mobile Riverine Force through CORONADO III:

> Perhaps the best evaluation of MRF achievements can be attained by examining the results of frequent riverine operations in Can Giouc District of eastern Long An Province. In its first operation in this area on 19 and 20 June, the MRF became engaged in the toughest fight it has experienced to date. Over 250 of the enemy were killed at a cost of 46 US KIA and 140 wounded. As the MRF returned to Can Giouc for further operations in late June, during July and again in late August, it never failed to make contact with the enemy. The size of the enemy units encountered has grown smaller and the percentage of prisoners taken versus enemy killed has risen steadily. Increasingly large caches of weapons have been uncovered. River Assault craft now move freely through areas where two months ago ambush with RPG–2's or recoilless rifles could be anticipated at any moment. In summary, it appears that a VC haven and stronghold, rarely ventured into by ARVN or FWMAF in the past, has been reduced to an area containing only scattered and poorly organized VC Guerillas.

Ben Luc Operation

CORONADO IV was conducted from 19 August through 9 September, with operations in Long An, Co Cong, and Kien Hoa

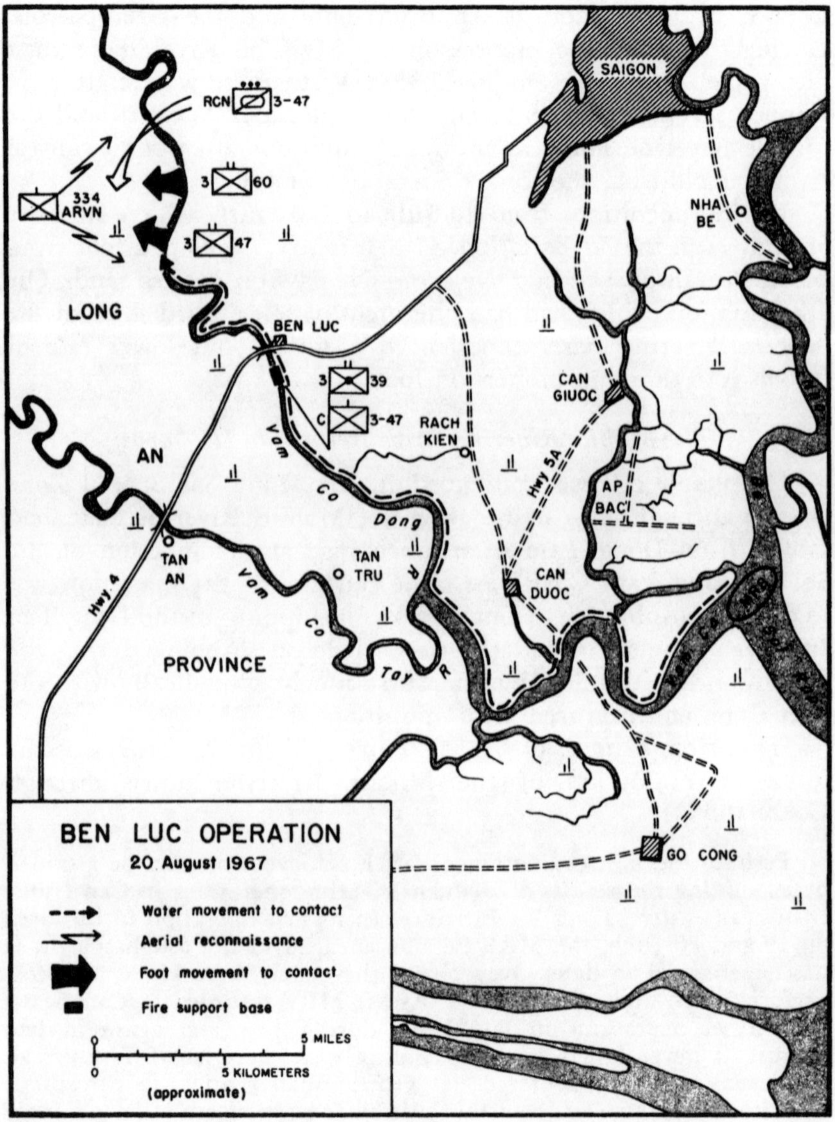

MAP 10

Provinces. On 20 August the assault craft left the Soi Rap and Vam Co River anchorage of the Mobile Riverine Base just after midnight and landed troops at 0904 in the target area north of Ben Luc on the Vam Co Dong River, a distance of over fifty kilometers. (*Map 10*) Because waterways off the Vam Co Dong in the target area were not navigable, the two infantry battalions were landed to move west and search the area on foot. Company C of the 3d Battalion, 47th Infantry, remained at a pickup zone near the fire support base at Ben Luc as an airmobile reserve. To intercept enemy forces, the 334th Aviation Company's supporting gunships maintained surveillance of the areas forward of the infantry battalions.

At 1400 the movement of the 3d Battalion, 47th Infantry, forced an enemy platoon from a lightly fortified area. The gunships were placed under control of the battalion commander, and were directed against the enemy, who was attempting to evade contact with the ground troops. The gunships sighted the enemy troops and took them under fire, after which the reconnaissance platoon of the 3d Battalion, 47th Infantry, was brought in by helicopter to mop up. The platoon encountered some fire from snipers and co-ordinated fire of the supporting gunships on the enemy. A search of the area revealed that thirty-four of the enemy had been killed. From documents found in the area the enemy was identified as an element of the 506th Local Force Battalion.

The success of this operation was attributed to the surprise achieved by the ground troops landing from the river; the Viet Cong were forced into the open where gunships could take them under fire. During the operation, which ended on 22 August, the Mobile Riverine Force suffered six wounded and the enemy lost fifty-nine killed.

For the remainder of August and the first week of September, the Mobile Riverine Force operated in Can Giuoc District, encountering minor enemy resistance. On 7 and 8 September the force operated in conjunction with the 1st Brigade, 9th Division, in the southeastern part of Nhon Trach District of Bien Hoa Province and the northeastern part of the Rung Sat Special Zone. Few Viet Cong were encountered but a cache containing medical supplies, eight crew-served weapons, and ninety-seven small arms was discovered. This operation was one of the first in which Colonel Bert A. David commanded the 2d Brigade. Colonel David assumed command as Colonel Fulton, promoted to brigadier general, became assistant division commander of the 9th Infantry Division. General Fulton was responsible to General O'Connor, now commander of the 9th Division, for operations in the Mekong Delta. At this point in early September the Mobile Riverine Force had operated extensively in the III Corps provinces north of the Mekong River. As the second week of September began, the force prepared to return to Dinh Tuong, an area of great interest to the senior adviser of the IV Corps Tactical Zone.

CHAPTER VII

Cam Son to the Rach Ruong Canal

On 11 September 1967 the Mobile Riverine Force returned to Dong Tam to prepare for an operation that would start in the Ban Long area on 12 September, the first operation of CORONADO V. Brigadier General Nguyen Manh Thanh, commander of the Army of Vietnam 7th Division, furnished information that the Viet Cong 263d Main Force Battalion had been in the Cam Son and Ban Long area during the preceding ten to fourteen days. Although the 7th Division intelligence was known to depend largely on reports of agents and informers, the Mobile Riverine Force had found it highly reliable in identifying enemy base areas. In Dinh Tuong Province particularly the force repeatedly had found the Viet Cong in regions reported to be base areas.

Dinh Tuong Province and Coronado V

On 12 September the Mobile Riverine Force entered the Ban Long area with three battalions. The 3d and 5th Battalions of the 60th Infantry—the 5th again released from operational control of the 3d Brigade to operate under the 2d Brigade—relied on helicopter and overland movement to get into the major east-west forested portion of the Ban Long area. The assault craft of the force were unable to navigate the waterways of the area.

As the 3d Battalion, 60th Infantry, moved into the forest it found an enemy force in well-prepared positions. Assisted by artillery and close air support, the battalion advanced to the east. The Viet Cong, under the pressure of the infantry advance and supporting fire, attempted to evade to the north and northwest, exposing themselves along thinly vegetated rice paddy dikes. The 5th Battalion, 60th Infantry, northwest of the 3d Battalion, engaged a platoon of the enemy; fire from M113 armored personnel carriers and the battalion's mortar platoon killed or dispersed the enemy.

At approximately 1430 a provisional battalion of Dinh Tuong Province Regional Forces was sent in by helicopter northeast of the 3d Battalion, 60th Infantry. The provisional battalion engaged widely dispersed enemy elements that had been forced from hiding by the 3d and 5th Battalions, 60th Infantry, attacks. Mobile Riverine Forces losses were nine soldiers killed and twenty-three wounded —all from the 3d Battalion, 60th Infantry. The three battalions accounted for 134 Viet Cong killed and 39 captured. Although the main forces of the enemy had escaped on 12 September, the Mobile Riverine Force continued to search the Ban Long area until it returned to the Mobile Riverine Base on 14 September. *(Map 11)*

Colonel David, after consulting with General Fulton, concluded that if an operation was launched in the Cam Son area on 15 September the enemy force, tentatively identified as the 514th Local Force Battalion, might be found. The plan was to strike the area in central Cam Son where the enemy's heaviest fortifications had been identified on previous operations. To reach this area before the major enemy force could escape, Colonel David decided to withhold preparatory and reconnaissance fire until the assault craft of the Mobile Riverine Force passed a wide curve in the Rach Ba Rai referred to as "Snoopy's Nose." Helicopter flights over the area were to be limited until the assault craft cleared Snoopy's Nose. The movement of the 5th Battalion, 60th Infantry, by ground vehicles into the area from Cai Lay was to be delayed until the 3d Battalion, 60th Infantry, and 3d Battalion, 47th Infantry, entered the Rach Ba Rai aboard ATC's. Finally, to provide a higher degree of flexibility if the enemy was found, the 2d Battalion, 60th Infantry, 3d Brigade, was designated a reserve force by the 9th Division. If required, the battalion would be employed by helicopter, staging from Dong Tam after movement from the battalion's Long An Province base.

Key elements of the maneuver were the landing of the 3d Battalion, 60th Infantry, north of an eastward bend in the Rach Ba Rai and the movement of the 5th Battalion, 60th Infantry, from the northeast. Both battalions would attack into a series of tree lines which the brigade planners believed had been used by enemy troops in the past to escape fighting.

As the 3d Battalion, 60th Infantry, moved up the Rach Ba Rai at approximately 0715 on 15 September, fire was withheld, and the assault craft moved steadily around Snoopy's Nose. By 0730 lead boats were nearing Beach White Two where a company of Lieutenant Colonel Mercer M. Doty's 3d Battalion, 60th Infantry, was to land when the boat formation came under heavy rocket, automatic, and small arms fire from both sides of the stream.

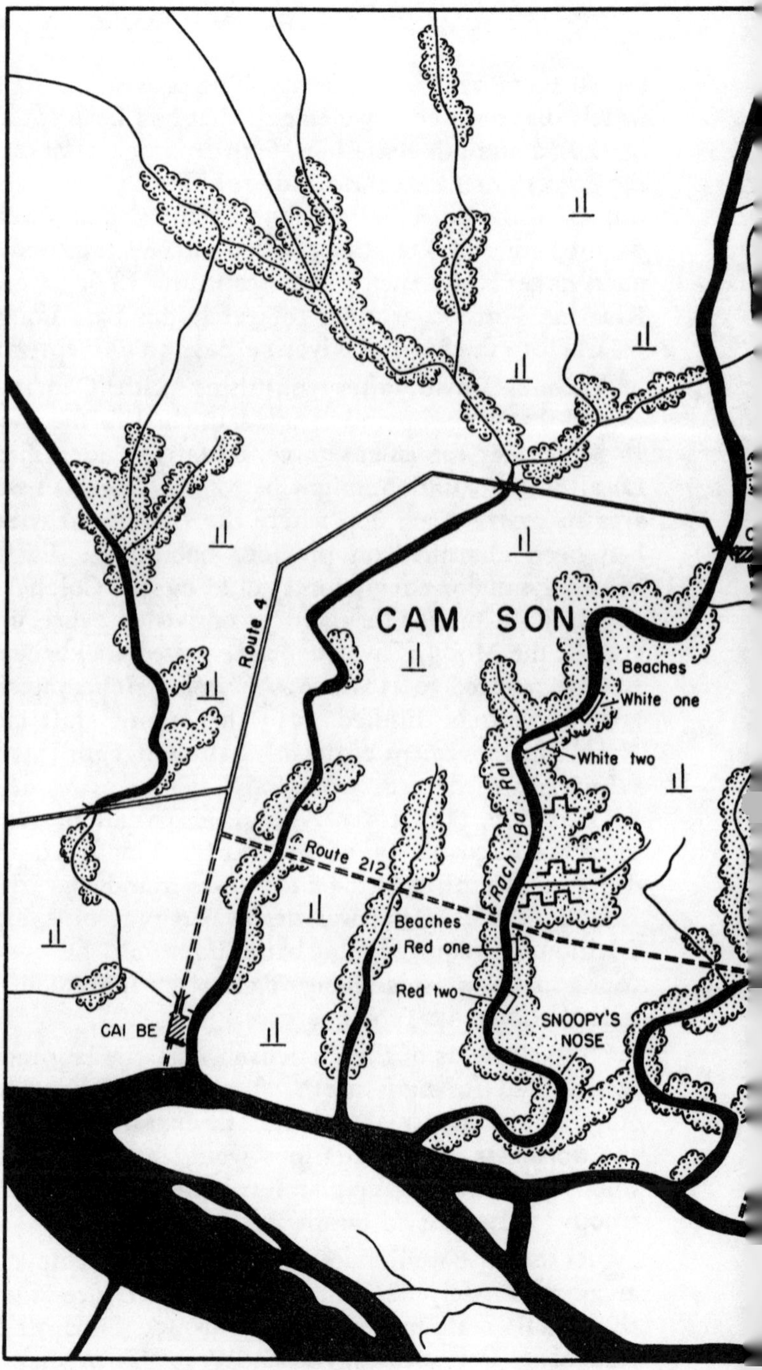
CAM SON
Route 4
Route 212
Beaches
White one
White two
Rach Ba Rai
Beaches
Red one
Red two
SNOOPY'S NOSE
CAI BE

MAP 11

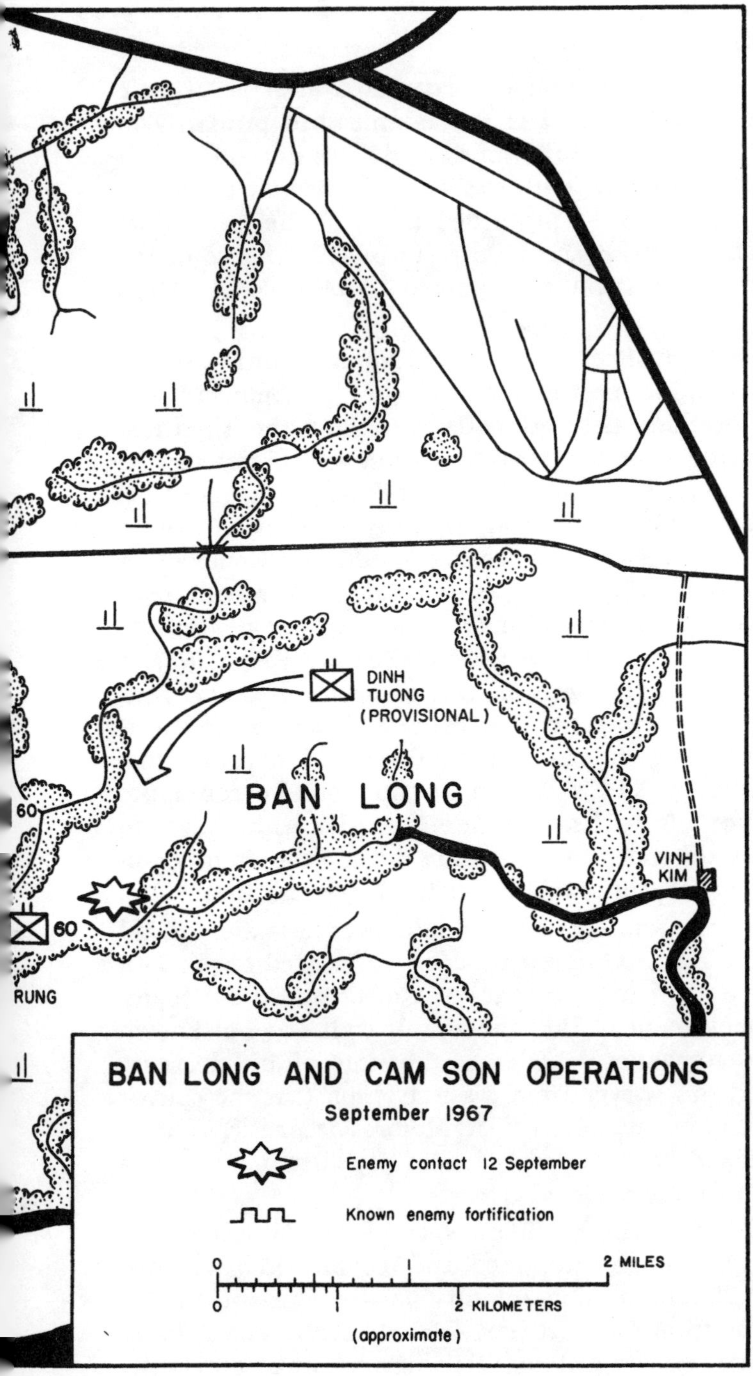

60
DINH
TUONG
(PROVISIONAL)
BAN LONG
60
VINH
KIM
RUNG
BAN LONG AND CAM SON OPERATIONS
September 1967
Enemy contact 12 September
Known enemy fortification
0
1
2 MILES
0
1
2 KILOMETERS
(approximate)

Enemy fire was heavier from the east bank, and the organic firepower of the riverine assault craft was unleashed primarily to the right flank of the force. In the smoke and confusion the assault craft maneuvered to fire weapons or to avoid other craft temporarily out of control. One ATC proceeded north of the lead minesweepers and landed on Beach White Two with the company commander and one platoon of Company B of Colonel Doty's battalion.

During the critical fifteen to twenty minutes following initial enemy fire, the flow of information through the command and control communications net did little to reflect the situation. Colonel Doty, flying over the boat formation and observing the apparent mobility of all assault craft and the success of one ATC in arriving at Beach White Two, was convinced that his unit could continue and land at the assigned beaches. Lieutenant Commander Francis E. ("Dusty") Rhodes, Jr., commanding the assault craft supporting Colonel Doty, issued an order at 0758 for all boats to turn back and assemble in the vicinity of Beaches Red One and Two. Commander Rhodes' decision that the convoy should turn back was based on casualties to boat crews and damage to minesweepers. The standing orders of Task Force 117 required that minesweepers precede ATC's carrying troops, but he could not continue minesweeping to Beach White One. To act contrary to this procedure would constitute an action outside the "limits permitted by accepted tactical practices" of the Navy task force.

The boat captain who passed the minesweepers and landed his ATC at White Beach One was probably influenced to press on by the fact that the infantry company commander was on board. The successful movement of this one assault craft was not known to Lieutenant Commander Rhodes at the time of his decision. Colonel Doty did not waiver from his conviction that the convoy could and should continue. His S-3, Major Richard H. Sharp, aboard the command boat relayed Colonel Doty's decision to "send in the troops" to Commander Rhodes.

While the 3d Battalion, 60th Infantry, and River Assault Squadron 11 evacuated casualties, resupplied, and reorganized at the Red Beaches, the 5th Battalion, 60th Infantry, moved overland toward Beach White One from the northeast. The 3d Battalion, 47th Infantry, was commanded by Colonel Tutwiler, who had previously commanded the 4th Battalion, 47th Infantry. He held his battalion south of the congested area of Beach Red, prepared to resume movement on order.

At approximately 1000 Colonel Doty's battalion began to move upstream, supported by artillery gunships and helicopters. The volume of fire was as great as before but the convoy landed at Beaches White One and Two. Companies B and C had few men wounded in this second run, while Company A had eighteen men wounded in one platoon. Both the assault craft and the infantry, who had joined freely in returning the enemy fire, required resupply of ammunition. Once ashore, the 3d Battalion, 60th Infantry, attacked south against stubborn enemy resistance. The 3d Battalion, 47th Infantry, landed at Beaches Red One and Two and pushed north. The 5th Battalion, 60th Infantry, moved close enough to see the 3d Battalion, 60th Infantry, by early afternoon.

To encircle the enemy south of Colonel Doty's battalion, the 2d Battalion, 60th Infantry, was placed under the operational control of the 2d Brigade and landed by helicopter south of the 5th Battalion, 60th Infantry. By dark the 3d Battalion, 60th Infantry, unable to overcome the enemy resistance, was ordered back to improve its defensive position. One Vietnam Army battalion was landed by helicopter at approximately 1600, northwest of the 3d Battalion, 60th Infantry, and moved to set up a position along the west bank of the Rach Ba Rai. The four U.S. battalions were in an irregular arc on the east side of the Rach Ba Rai. The stream was a possible enemy escape route west, although the 3d Battalion, 47th Infantry, had seized a number of sampans just north of route 212 during the late afternoon. Assault craft supporting the 3d Battalion, 47th Infantry, and 3d Battalion, 60th Infantry, were positioned to observe and place fire along the stream; however, no U.S. boats were deployed into the stream unless there were American or Vietnamese troops ashore.

During darkness air and artillery illumination was maintained over the area and artillery fire was placed within the partially encircled area on likely enemy locations. Between 0200 and 0430, small groups of enemy soldiers were observed and fired upon forward of the 2d Battalion, 60th Infantry, and later the 3d Battalion, 47th Infantry. After 0430 on 16 September no Viet Cong were sighted. On 16 September the 5th Battalion, 60th Infantry, led the sweep into the area, followed by sweeps by the two southern battalions forward of their positions. Resistance was light; most of the enemy force encountered on 15 September had been killed or had slipped away during the night.

The Navy assault craft expended, during the period 0730–1600 on 15 September, 10,273 rounds of 40-mm. ammunition, sixteen

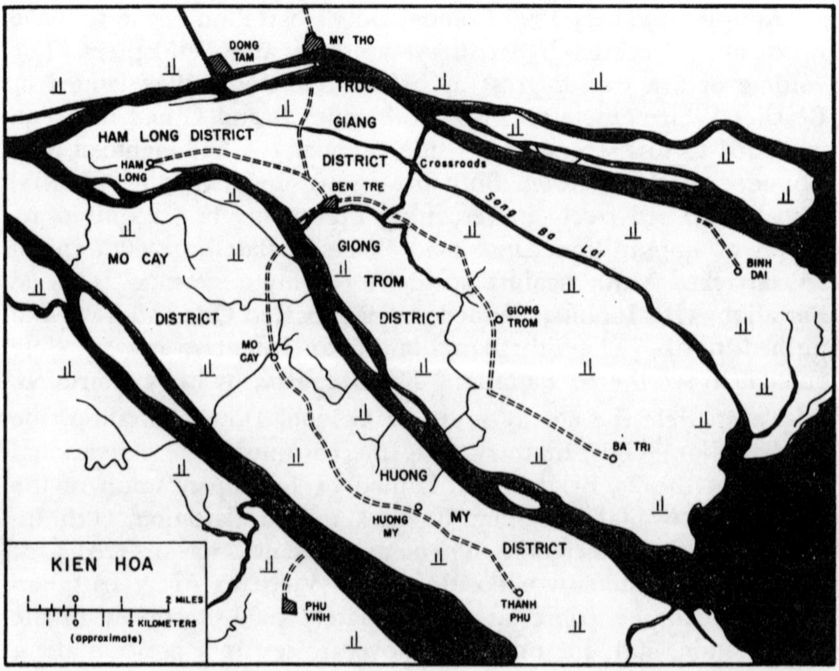

MAP 12

rounds of 81-mm., 7,445 rounds of 20-mm., 20,934 rounds of .50-caliber, and 40,216 rounds of .30-caliber. The operation ended on 16 September, after four days of heavy fighting in which the Americans and Vietnamese lost 16 killed and 146 wounded and the Viet Cong lost 213.

Following the Cam Son operation, the Mobile Riverine Force moved into Kien Hoa Province. (*Map 12*) Although operations during the remainder of September were widely separated in Ham Long, Giong Trom, and Huong My Districts, interrogation of local civilians revealed that they had prior knowledge of the operations. In Giong Trom District local inhabitants said that a Viet Cong unit, believed to be part of the 516th Local Force Battalion, had been in the area, but had left the night before the Riverine Force arrived. This experience became characteristic of Mobile Riverine Force operations conducted in Kien Hoa Province in late 1967. Operations usually involved brushes with enemy rocket launcher and recoilless rifle teams which delayed operations but inflicted few losses. Helicopters became invaluable during movement to detect and engage small enemy teams armed with antitank weapons. These operations in Kien Hoa Province saw the first use of the long-awaited assault support patrol boats.

During the period 5-7 October, the Mobile Riverine Force terminated major operations of CORONADO V with an operation in the Ban Long area. It was conducted in close co-operation with the 7th Army of Vietnam Division and resulted in a battle with the Viet Cong 263d Main Force Battalion. The Mobile Riverine Force had 1 killed and 26 wounded, while the Vietnam Army 7th Division suffered 6 killed and 36 wounded. The Viet Cong losses totaled 163 killed.

The Mobile Riverine Force moved to Vung Tau on 10 October and CORONADO VI commenced on 11 October in the Rung Sat Special Zone. Minor engagements took place and small lots of weapons and supplies were discovered. On the night of 16 October the Mobile Riverine Force sent out forty-eight ambush patrols and twenty-two boat patrols in order to insure the security of the Long Tau shipping channel. No ships were attacked during the Mobile Riverine Force operations.

On 20 October the Mobile Riverine Force moved to the juncture of the Soi Rap and Vam Co Rivers. From this base CORONADO VII was initiated, with operations in the northern part of Can Giuoc District to secure the waterways while elections were being held in the Republic of Vietnam. Both infantry and assault craft were widely dispersed to get as many American soldiers into the area as possible. The usual search of water craft was discontinued. After the elections the commander of the 46th Vietnam Army Regiment told Colonel David that the turnout for the election had been 83 percent of the registered voters.

CORONADO VIII was conducted in co-ordination with the Royal Thai Regiment and elements of the 3d Battalion, 5th Cavalry, on 27, 28, and 29 October in the southern Nhon Trach and the northern Rung Sat Special Zone. There were few encounters with the enemy.

Coronado IX

CORONADO IX began with the movement of the Mobile Riverine Base from its late October anchorage off Vung Tau to an anchorage in the My Tho River near Dong Tam. The series of operations that constituted CORONADO IX was conducted primarily north of the My Tho River and directed against the enemy bases of Dinh Tuong Province.

The Mobile Riverine Force arrived off Dong Tam 1 November 1967 and during the first days of the month concentrated on equipment maintenance and preparations for coming operations. The 3d Battalion, 60th Infantry, debarked and assumed the defense mission for Dong Tam Base. The battalion's waterborne replacement was the 3d Battalion, 47th Infantry, which began tactical operations in the southeastern part of the Giao Duc District in western Dinh Tuong Province at 1500 on 2 November. During the nine-hour operation, the battalion destroyed 141 enemy bunkers and evacuated 1,100 pounds of rice and an assortment of enemy engineering and medical materials from a cache. The evacuated materials were delivered to the Dinh Tuong Province Headquarters for distribution within government programs.

On 5 and 6 November, a two-battalion operation was conducted in the Cam Son Secret Zone. Barge-mounted artillery gave support from a position on the north shore of the My Tho River. In this operation the Mobile Riverine Force destroyed 34 bunkers, captured 800 pounds of rice and 125 pounds of salt, and killed five of the enemy.

With the arrival of the 5th Battalion of the Vietnamese Marine Corps at a shore camp near My Tho on 6 November, the Mobile Riverine Force had a new and valuable asset. The 5th became the third maneuver battalion. Possessing four rifle companies and a heavy weapons company, it had a strength equal to that of the two embarked Army battalions. The Vietnamese marines brought a special esprit to the Mobile Riverine Force and fought extremely well throughout the CORONADO IX operation.

The battalion commander, Major Nam, participated fully with the advisers in the planning of Mobile Riverine Force operations. Major Nam, Colonel David, Captain Wells, and Captain Salzer, who succeeded Captain Wells on 2 December, agreed on plans and each commander approved and signed the original operation order prior to each operation. The Navy assault craft, Army artillery, and Air Force aircraft supported the Marine battalion as they did the Army battalions.

After a short time spent on training and maintenance, the Mobile Riverine Force resumed CORONADO IX on 9 November. Again the targets were the 263d and 514th Viet Cong Battalions in the Cam Son Base area. While the 3d Battalion, 47th Infantry, and the 5th Marine Battalion made beach assaults early on 9 November, the 4th Battalion, 47th Infantry, moved by ATC to the Dong Tam airstrip, and then in a series of helicopter lifts entered the area of operations. All landings were unopposed and few of the enemy were sighted.

On the second day the search for the enemy shifted to the east; troops were moved by boat and by helicopter into the Ban Long

PORTABLE FIRING PLATFORM WITH 105-MM. HOWITZER

and the Ap Bac base areas. Only the Marine battalion, which remained in its original area of operation, saw action, killing seven of the Viet Cong.

On 14 November, to increase security for Highway 4 and the Dong Tam Base area, a new operation began, with support from the artillery at Dong Tam. While the 3d Battalion, 47th Infantry, remained at the Mobile Riverine Base for maintenance, the other battalions were transported by boat and helicopter to the north along the Kinh Xang Canal and east of Dong Tam Base. The 5th Marine Battalion and the 4th Battalion, 47th Infantry, destroyed 63 bunkers and seized 2,000 pounds of rice and 200 pounds of salt. This operation continued through the night. Ambush patrols of platoon size were sent out along Highway 4 north of Dong Tam but saw few of the enemy.

On 16 November the Mobile Riverine Force began an operation with the 3d Brigade, 9th U.S. Division, and with elements of both the 7th and 9th Army of Vietnam Divisions along the border of Kien Phong and Dinh Tuong Provinces. The target was the

502d Local Force Battalion and 267th Main Force Battalion, which IV Corps and II Field Force intelligence estimated were in Base Area 470. Troops of the 3d Brigade were landed by helicopter in the northern part of the area along with the 3d Battalion, 47th Infantry, which was initially under the operational control of 3d Brigade. Since Base Area 470 lacked firm ground for artillery fire support bases, and artillery positioned along Highway 4 could not cover the area, experimental artillery firing platforms were used.

One platform accommodated an M102, 105-mm. artillery piece, ammunition, and enough space for the crews to operate. The legs of the platform were adjustable to various heights and a large metal "foot," mounted on the bottom of each leg, provided support in the mud of rice paddies. A CH-47 helicopter carried the platform, artillery piece, ammunition, and crew in four lifts. One battery of 105-mm. artillery was used throughout the operation. The second night of the 3d Brigade's operations, on 17 November, the Viet Cong attacked one of the brigade's fire support bases. The attack was repulsed several hours before the Mobile Riverine Force entered the operational area off the My Tho River on the Rach Ruong Canal. In order for the Riverine Force to enter the operational area, IV Corps Vietnamese engineers, who were accompanying the assault forces early on the morning of 18 November, had to remove the center span of the bridge on the Rach Ruong Canal.

Before the bridge span was removed, a barge-mounted artillery fire support base was set up so that the artillery could fire on any enemy troops encountered by the engineers. A 155-mm. fire support base was also established on Highway 4, six kilometers east of the bridge. For better control, the Mobile Riverine Base was moved upriver from Dong Tam to an anchorage near Sa Dec. While the 5th Marine Battalion conducted riverine assaults in the southern portions of the target area, the 4th Battalion, 47th Infantry, landed troops by helicopter in the north.

Early on 18 November both battalions discovered the enemy. In the Mobile Riverine Force fighting alone, forty-five of the enemy were killed, nearly half of them by helicopter gunships, and a large medical cache was uncovered. The Mobile Riverine Force had four wounded. Total losses for all American and Vietnamese units were 26 killed and 155 wounded, while the Viet Cong suffered 178 killed and 33 taken prisoner.

Following a period at the Dong Tam anchorage for rest and maintenance, the force returned to the Cam Son Base area on 23 November. After the first air attack—a B-52 strike in the heavily populated Dinh Tuong Province—three battalions entered the area by riverine assault craft. Only a few of the enemy were found and eight of these were killed. Several caches were discovered.

From 27 to 30 November operations were conducted to clear the Kinh Xang Canal, which runs northwest by Dong Tam. Company D, 15th Engineer Battalion, removed all water blocks along the canal while the maneuver battalions searched the Ap Bac Base area. Five of the enemy were killed and two taken prisoner. Four major blocks were removed from the Kinh Xang Canal and sixty-two bunkers were destroyed. The opening of the upper reaches of this canal permitted the Mobile Riverine Force to use the assault craft of the Navy to attack the enemy's Ap Bac Base.

On 4 December the Mobile Riverine Base moved to Sa Dec and the 3d and 4th Battalions, 47th Infantry, with the 5th Marine Battalion, began operations to find and destroy elements of the 267th Main Force and 502d Local Force Battalions in western Dinh Tuong and eastern Kien Phong Provinces. The battle that ensued on 4–5 December proved to be one of the most severe the Mobile Riverine Force had yet experienced.

Early on 4 December the force encountered major elements of the 502d Local Force Battalion in a fortified base on the west bank of the Rach Ruong Canal. (*Map 13*) The enemy attacked the boats with rockets and automatic weapons and a decision was made to land the Marine battalion to the north of the enemy position. Shortly afterward the 3d Battalion, 47th Infantry, was landed south of the enemy position. Fighting was intense and Colonel David directed the 4th Battalion, 47th Infantry, which was standing by at a pickup zone, to land west of the enemy location. In midafternoon of 4 December, the Vietnamese Marine Battalion made a frontal assault that overran the enemy's major bunker complex. Supporting fire from armed helicopters and assault craft contributed largely to the success of the assault. To the south the 3d Battalion, 47th Infantry, encountered stubborn resistance from scattered enemy bunkers that prevented it from linking with the Vietnamese marines.

This action demonstrated the importance of a quick decision by a waterborne force commander when the force was under fire. Major Nam decided to land immediately on what he judged to be the enemy flank. The commander of the supporting river division immediately gave the order to his boat captains, and the landings were made. Total enemy casualties for 4 and 5 December were 266 Viet Cong killed, with the Vietnamese marines accounting for the

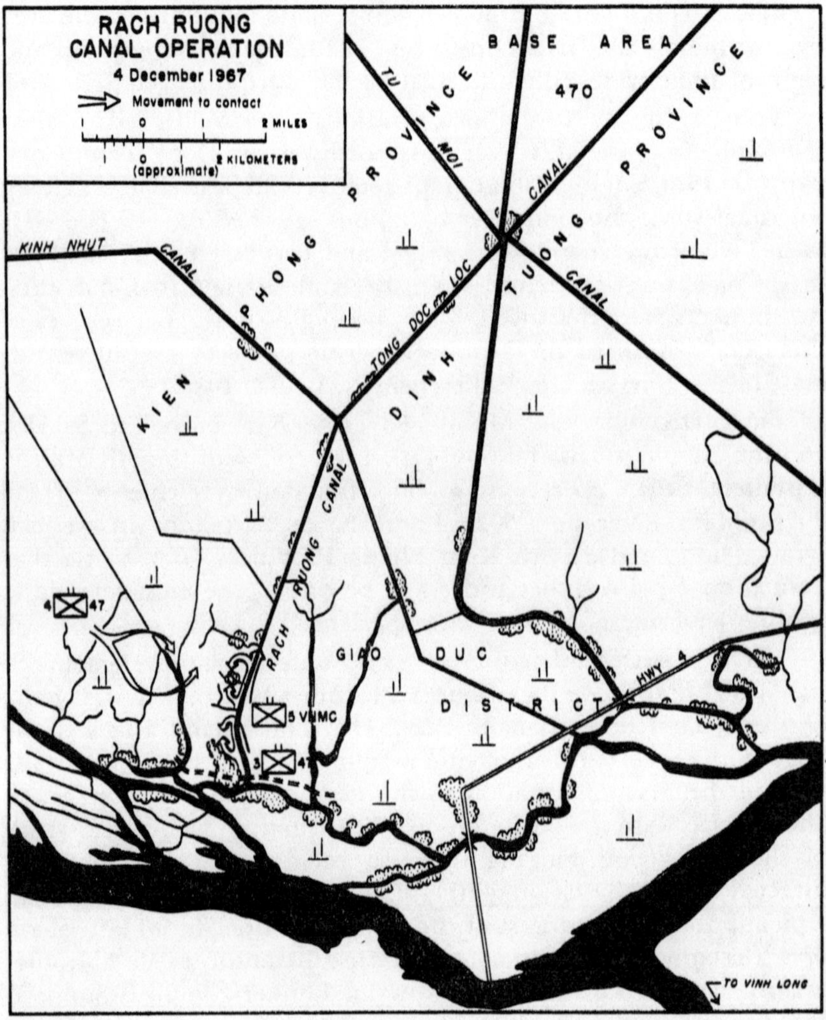

MAP 13

heaviest enemy losses. The Vietnamese marines had 40 killed and 107 wounded. Nine American soldiers were killed and 89 wounded.

The assault craft were able to land the marines with light casualties on 4 October chiefly because of a flame thrower aboard one of the armored troop carriers. A vehicle with a flame thrower had been driven aboard, and the ATC placed in the convoy to fire on targets as required. The flame thrower had not only a physical but also a psychological effect on the enemy manning bunkers south of the Marine landing site. The first successful test of a flame thrower aboard an ATC had been made on 4 October 1967.

On 6 December the Mobile Riverine Base moved to an anchorage on the Mekong River north of Vinh Long. After three days of local operations and maintenance work during which new fire support bases were established in support of forthcoming operations, the Mobile Riverine Force undertook operations in the southern part of Cai Be District and in the western part of Dinh Tuong Province against local guerrillas and their installations. Initial landings were made from ATC's but later in the first day of operations troops were landed by helicopter. Very few of the enemy were found.

On 14 December the Mobile Riverine Force again searched for the Viet Cong in Cam Son. The force made assaults by boat in the southern portion of the base, followed by helicopter landings by the 3d Battalion, 47th Infantry. It was not until the last day of the operation that the enemy was discovered and in a firefight nine of the Viet Cong were killed.

On 17 December the Mobile Riverine Base moved to Dong Tam to permit the Mobile Riverine Force to land troops from the two barracks ships. By the afternoon of 18 December the brigade and one battalion had moved ashore to Dong Tam. The USS *Colleton* left the area of operations to refit at Subic Bay in the Philippine Islands and the USS *Benewah* moved to Vung Tau in Vietnam to refit. At this time, the 3d Battalion, 60th Infantry, replaced the 4th Battalion, 47th Infantry, as part of the Mobile Riverine Force, and the 4th Battalion assumed the Dong Tam defense mission.

On 19 December a two-battalion operation was initiated in northern Cai Lay District while a third battalion operated near Dong Tam. On the night of 19 December, two companies of the 3d Battalion, 47th Infantry, were landed along the Kinh Xang Canal to set up ambushes. The other two battalions of the Mobile Riverine Force were landed by assault craft in the northern Ap Bac area. Effective artillery coverage was provided by the barge-mounted artillery and by Battery C, 2d Battalion, 35th Artillery (155-mm. self-propelled) . This operation covered most of the north central part of Dinh Tuong Province and used both helicopters and boats to land troops. Although few of the enemy were found, the maneuver battalions killed eleven Viet Cong. Navigability of the Kinh Xang Canal was extended when engineers removed a major canal obstruction. The operation was concluded late on 22 December and the Mobile Riverine Force returned to the afloat base to conduct maintenance and prepare for Christmas truce operations.

The Mobile Riverine Force was instructed that operations should be defensive during the truce period; troops could fire on groups of enemy soldiers who "seemed to be trying to breed contact," or who were more than "platoonsize" in number. The truce ran from 1800 on 24 December through 1800 on 25 December. Prior to 1800 on the 24th, one Mobile Riverine Force battalion moved to each of the two areas in which saturation patrols were to be conducted. The 3d Battalion, 47th Infantry, moved to Long Dinh District, while to the southeast the 3d Battalion, 60th Infantry, moved into northern Kien Hoa Province. During the truce there was occasional enemy sniper and harassing fire.

The force's next operation was in Cai Lay District of Dinh Tuong Province. On 28 December the 3d Battalion, 60th Infantry, was landed by aircraft and waterborne craft in an area approximately eleven kilometers west of Dong Tam. It conducted operations directed westward toward Cai Be, with supporting fire from barge artillery batteries located to its south along the north shore of the My Tho River. Few of the enemy were seen during the operation; monitors and assault support patrol boats provided surveillance of inland waterways. On 29 December the 3d Battalion, 60th Infantry, continued operations to the west toward Cai Be, while the 4th Battalion, 47th Infantry, remained in the same area and destroyed eighty-five bunkers and captured two prisoners. During the day the 3d Battalion, 60th Infantry, found only a few of the enemy and concluded its operations in Cai Lay District.

On 30 December the 4th Battalion, 47th Infantry, was moved from Kien Hoa north and across the My Tho River to assist the 3d Battalion, 60th Infantry, in continuing operations in Cai Be and Cai Lay Districts. Although troops were shifted by boat from one place to another, the battalions could find no large groups of Viet Cong. On the following day both battalions went into positions where they stayed until the end of the New Year's truce at 0600 on 1 January 1968. In groups of platoon and company size, the battalions were dispersed to prevent the enemy from using important lines of communication during the truce period. Following the truce period the units arrived in Dong Tam on the afternoon of 2 January.

The next major mission of the Mobile Riverine Force was an operation in the eastern part of Vinh Long Province. On 7 January the battalions were landed by air and water but found no enemy until midafternoon, when a company of the 3d Battalion, 60th Infantry, came under heavy automatic weapons and small arms fire from an estimated two platoons. Artillery fire and air strikes were called in on the enemy, who were firing from well-prepared, concealed positions. By the end of the fight, late on 7 January, two more companies of the 3d Battalion, 60th Infantry, were engaged. Twenty-eight of the enemy were killed and three weapons were captured. The Mobile Riverine Force concluded the operation the following day, killing two more of the enemy, and reached the riverine base late that afternoon.

The next target was the 261st Main Force Battalion in the Cai Be District, western Dinh Tuong Province. On 10 January assault craft and helicopters landed the 4th Battalion, 47th Infantry, and 3d Battalion, 60th Infantry, and by midafternoon Company A, 3d Battalion, 60th Infantry, was in heavy combat and had sustained moderate casualties. The battalion had been set down on a "hot" landing zone. Company E was flown in to support Company A. For both companies the fighting was heavy until after dark on 10 January. The following day fighting was sporadic. Over the two days, forty-seven of the enemy were killed. American forces suffered eighteen killed and fifty wounded; most of the casualties occurred at the landing zone where the enemy was in well-prepared, excellently camouflaged positions with good fields of fire.

On 12 January an operation was conducted in conjunction with the 3d Brigade in Binh Phouc District of Long An Province. The 3d Battalion, 60th Infantry, and 4th Battalion, 47th Infantry, moved by boat along the Cho Cao Canal to assigned beaches. In landing, troops met heavy enemy rocket and automatic weapons fire but killed seven of the enemy. The rest quickly escaped and there was no further fighting during the two-day operation.

On 14 January the 2d Brigade embarked on the USS *Benewah*, and was followed aboard on 21-22 January by the rest of the Mobile Riverine Force. A cordon was thrown around the village of An Quoi, near Dong Tam, by the 3d Battalion, 47th Infantry, which had the day before relieved the 4th Battalion, 47th Infantry, as a Mobile Riverine Force battalion. The object of the cordon operation was to capture or kill guerrillas, but it was unsuccessful; the operation brought CORONADO IX to a close.

Six Months in Retrospect

As the Mobile Riverine Force prepared for the *Tet* truce, it could look back over six months of unusual experiences. The force had entered the Mekong Delta in June as the first U.S. force free to conduct sustained operations against Viet Cong main force units whose ability was respected. Republic of Vietnam armed forces were widely dispersed, with battalions of infantry and batteries of artillery fragmented to spread a degree of security throughout populated areas along the major land and waterway lines of communication. South Vietnamese offensive operations were limited in number and duration during the hours of darkness by the need to maintain security posts at political, military, and commercial centers and on highway bridges.

The 2d Brigade did not escape the duty of maintaining security at fixed installations; one of its battalions was required at Dong Tam. The Mobile Riverine Force as a whole—a force of nearly 4,000 men—was not tied to a static security mission, but was available for wide-ranging movement.

Whether operating in southern III Corps Tactical Zone or northern IV Corps Tactical Zone, the Mobile Riverine Force added to the capabilities of the corps commanders. It provided more troops with which to expand Vietnam armed forces and Free World Military Assistance Force influence. Also it possessed significant water mobility to complement air and ground movement. The contribution of the Mobile Riverine Force on the waterways is difficult to separate from its contribution as an additional combat force even if it had not relied extensively on water mobility. The Mekong Delta in June 1967 was a place where the operations of an airmobile brigade could also have had significant impact. The Mobile Riverine Force was, however, able to attack areas such as Cam Son, the Rung Sat Special Zone, eastern Long An Province, Go Cong, and western Dinh Tuong Province where the enemy relied heavily on waterways in bases seldom violated by operations of the South Vietnamese armed forces.

These areas were lucrative targets for a force free to operate within them. They were generally remote in terms of being outside the range of established artillery positions, accessible only with great difficulty by tracked vehicles, and requiring substantial use of air or water craft for troop movement. The mobility of the barge-mounted artillery and the Mobile Riverine Base enabled the Mobile Riverine Force to give effective artillery coverage to troops and to bring other substantial combat and combat service support to operations immediately adjacent to the base area. Further, the Navy assault craft, more heavily armed and armored than the craft of the Vietnamese river assault groups and enjoying far more artillery support, were able to enter base areas into which the craft of the river assault group dared not venture. Finally, the

Mobile Riverine Force was an unknown and, therefore, intimidating force to the Viet Cong. Intelligence estimates of June 1967 were that it would take the Viet Cong six months to obtain adequate knowledge of Mobile Riverine Force equipment, tactics, and techniques and to react with a program of mining and recoilless rifle and rocket attacks. Wide-ranging operations across the boundaries of responsibility of the major enemy organizations would gain more time before highly effective countermeasures were fielded by the enemy.

Operations were planned, therefore, so that the Mobile Riverine Force would move freely among the provinces north of the My Tho River; subsequently move south of the My Tho; eventually move into the southern Mekong Delta. In each area the force was to attack enemy main forces and local forces. By inflicting major losses on these units, the Mobile Riverine Force would take away the security provided to local guerrillas and the secret political organization by the presence of the Viet Cong main forces.

It was in the pursuance of this major mission that operations were conducted from June through December 1967. Within the widely separated base areas, the Mobile Riverine Force inflicted losses on the 5th Nha Be Battalion and 506th Local Force Battalion of the Long An and Gia Dinh areas, on the 514th Local Force Battalion, 263d Main Force Battalion, and the Viet Cong district companies of Dinh Tuong Province, on the 502d Local Force Battalion of Kien Phong Province, and on training cadres and companies of Long An and Go Cong Provinces. These units were most frequently met in areas where water mobility permitted U.S. forces to reach fortifications and caches at the heart of the enemy base. Most enemy bunkers were chosen for defense against likely helicopter landings, and covered trails entering the base from the limited land routes; few were designed to cover an approach by water.

The Mobile Riverine Force routinely requested and planned for the use of aircraft in the conduct of operations during the last half of 1967. Often an assault helicopter company was shared during the day with the 3d Brigade, 9th Infantry Division. This arrangement, while not ideal, provided aircraft which the commanders considered an inherent part of riverine operations.

During the six-month period, Mobile Riverine Force operations departed from the original planning in respect to duration of operations and the authority for and frequency of major relocations of the Mobile Riverine Base. Plans had called for a four- to five-day operation, to be followed by a two- or three-day period for rest, skin care, and equipment maintenance. Beginning with Operation RIVER RAIDER 1 in the Rung Sat Special Zone, however, it was learned that foot problems caused by wetness and fungi increased rapidly after a few hours of exposure, and operations generally were limited to forty-eight hours, with a rest period of twenty-four to thirty-six hours. When it was necessary to keep troops on land for longer periods, a high percentage of foot problems occurred and rest periods of three to four days were required. Since the operations were shorter, eight instead of four operations took place each month.

A June 1967 planning directive of the Military Assistance Command, Vietnam, stated that the Mobile Riverine Base could be relocated within the assigned tactical area of responsibility by the base commander in co-ordination with the senior Navy commander embarked. For relocation to a new area of responsibility, the commanding general of II Field Force would co-ordinate the move with the commander of Naval Forces, Vietnam, and the senior adviser of IV Corps, as appropriate, keeping Headquarters, Military Assistance Command, Vietnam, informed. This procedure was followed; however, the base commander was able to initiate co-ordination for a move to a new area of operations and inform the commanding general of II Field Force, through the Commanding General, 9th Infantry Division. This practice was often followed; but the requirements of the planning directive issued by Headquarters, Military Assistance Command, Vietnam, were met on movements across the boundary between III and IV Corps.

The original plan to keep the Mobile Riverine Base in the same anchorage for four to six weeks was not adhered to; more than twenty major relocations of the anchorage were made during the six months of operations—an average time at one anchorage of less than two weeks.

During the months of October and November, the Mobile Riverine Force operations in Dinh Tuong and Long An Province, where substantial numbers of the enemy had been found during previous months, met with limited success. The Viet Cong had become familiar with riverine equipment and tactics and was using small teams armed with rockets and recoilless rifles. Stationed along the waterways entering enemy base areas, the teams harassed the Mobile Riverine Force, delaying operations and inflicting casualties.

It was clear that if the Mobile Riverine Force could find the large enemy units it could destroy them. In the 4–5 December engagement, the 502d Local Force Battalion had suffered heavy losses either because the Americans achieved surprise or because the enemy, aware of a pending attack, had decided to stand and fight. Despite this successful experience, both Colonel David and Captain Salzer noted that the enemy was becoming more difficult to find. On the eve of the *Tet* truce period, the Mobile Riverine Force published an order that would return the force to the scene of its last battle—western Dinh Tuong Province. The Viet Cong *Tet* offensive was to find the Mobile Riverine Force widely dispersed in that area and well removed from the scene of the major battles that erupted throughout the Mekong Delta on 30 January 1968. The Mobile Riverine Force would have to move quickly to the scene of the major actions during *Tet*.

CHAPTER VIII

Tet Offensive of 1968 and U.S. Reaction

Shortly before the beginning of the three-day cease-fire declared by the government of South Vietnam to celebrate *Tet,* the lunar new year, the Mobile Riverine Force was ordered to the western portion of Dinh Tuong Province and the eastern part of Kien Phong Province to prevent the enemy from using communication routes running east and southeast through the area. There had been continuous and credible intelligence reports of enemy activity within the area, which was readily accessible to assault craft. The Mobile Riverine Force planned to establish bases along the waterways to provide fire support, as it had done during operations in the preceding November and December.

The operation began with the movement north by stages of supporting artillery batteries; as each battery moved, an infantry unit was sent ahead to secure the next fire support base. Four bases were established, three of them north along the Rach Ruong Canal from the Song My Tho to an agroville, one of the many agricultural resettlement areas established by President Diem. Three CH-47 helicopters were used to set down the artillery on the agroville site and the battery was laid and ready to fire by 1800 on 29 January 1968, the beginning of the *Tet* truce. The fourth base was on Highway 4, about two kilometers north from the river. The Mobile Riverine Force elements met only sporadic sniper fire on the 29th although the CH-47's were fired upon with .50-caliber machine guns.

The brigade's two battalions, in addition to defending the fire support bases, actively patrolled in the area of operations. Surveillance was aided by the radars mounted on the assault support patrol boats. At 2100 on 29 January, fifteen rounds of 82-mm. mortar fire were received at one fire support base without causing casualties or damage. No further enemy activity occurred during the remainder of the evening of 29 January and the Mobile Riverine Force dispersed to ambush positions to prevent major enemy movement.

On 25 January 1968, the senior adviser of IV Corps Tactical Zone had warned all subordinate elements in the IV Corps that

during the impending *Tet* holiday cease-fire period the Viet Cong were expected to resupply and move into position for a post-*Tet* offensive. The warning was based on past experience and recent intelligence reports. On 29 January the senior adviser dispatched the following message:

> Desire immediate dissemination of following information to all provinces without delay. There are a number of positive intelligence indicators that the enemy will deliberately violate the truce by approaching friendly installations during night of 29 January or early morning of 30 January. All provincial senior advisors will take action to insure maximum alert posture through the *Tet* period. Be particularly alert for enemy deception involving use of friendly vehicles and uniforms.

About 1000 on 30 January, the Mobile Riverine Force was informed that the Military Assistance Command, Vietnam, had canceled the *Tet* truce because of Viet Cong attacks on cities in the three corps to the north. The force was directed to resume offensive operations "with particular attention to the defense of the Headquarters complexes, logistical installations, airfields, population centers and billets." The Mobile Riverine Force ordered increased and aggressive reconnaissance in force within the original area of operations, but the infantry was directed to operate close to the major waterways to make feasible a rapid move by water craft toward the population centers. While two companies of the 3d Battalion, 47th Infantry, remained to provide security for the fire support base, the rest of the 3d Battalion and the 3d Battalion, 60th Infantry, on 30 January conducted saturation patrolling to the east toward Cai Be. At the end of the day, forty suspects had been detained, forty bunkers destroyed, and several small caches found.

On 31 January My Tho, Ben Tre, Cai Lay, Cai Be, and Vinh Long were attacked by the Viet Cong. The Viet Cong units involved included at My Tho, the 261st, 263d, and 514th Battalions; at Vinh Long, the 308th, 306th, 857th Battalions and local forces; at Cai Be and Cai Lay, the 261st Main Force Battalion, supported by the 540th and 530th District Companies and local forces. The Mobile Riverine Force however had not found any Viet Cong in the populated area along the Rach Ruong. When the force moved from this area local guerrillas made an effort to delay its return movement to the My Tho River. Although planning and coordination were evident in the enemy attempt to prevent movement of the Mobile Riverine Force to the scene of the major battles, the boats and their embarked battalions were able to reach the

Mobile Riverine Base by 0220 on 1 February. After less than four hours rest, the Army and Navy elements were ordered to conduct operations in the vicinity of Cai Be. Before the landing could be executed, however, orders were changed by the senior adviser of IV Corps Tactical Zone and the river assault divisions were diverted to My Tho where allied forces were still heavily engaged. Elements of the two battalions were landed by water craft in My Tho at 1520, 1 February. The five major ships of the Mobile Riverine Base moved from Vinh Long to Dong Tam in order to be in a better position to support operations.

After landing unopposed in My Tho, Company B, 3d Battalion, 47th Infantry, secured landing sites on the southwestern edge of the city for its parent battalion and was joined by Companies A and C. As the troops began to move north into the city, they met heavy fire. With the 3d Battalion, 60th Infantry, moving on the west, both battalions advanced north through the western portion of the city, receiving small arms, automatic rifle, and rocket fire. Fighting was intense and continuous and of a kind new to the riverine battalions. The city had to be cleared slowly and systematically; pockets of enemy resistance had to be wiped out to prevent the Viet Cong from closing in behind allied troops.

While advancing through the city, Company A, 3d Battalion, 47th Infantry, met heavy fire at 1615 and Company E was ordered to reinforce. On the way, the lead elements of Company E also met intense fire and were eventually pinned down at the western edge of My Tho. At this time both maneuver battalions were involved in pitched battles and were taking casualties. The 3d Battalion, 60th Infantry, continued its movement north, advancing under heavy enemy fire, and air strikes were requested at 1740 to assist the battalion's forward elements. Troops moved in and out of doorways, from house to house, and from street to street. Artillery was employed against enemy troops who were fleeing the city. At 1955 a group of Viet Cong who had been in a previous engagement with troops of the Vietnam Army 7th Division attempted to enter the streets where Company B, 3d Battalion, was fighting, but by 2100 Company B had eliminated them.

Company A, 3d Battalion, 47th Infantry, requested a light fire team to support its point element, which had met intense resistance from small arms and rocket fire and had suffered several casualties. At 1825 the light fire team arrived and was used to relieve the pressure on Companies A and E by firing on Viet Cong positions. The team made runs directly over Company A and placed fire within twenty-five meters of the company's lead elements. To evacuate the wounded, a platoon leader sprinted through enemy fire, jumped into a Vietnam Army jeep parked in the street, and drove to the wounded. Ignoring the fire directed against him, he helped the wounded men aboard the jeep and drove back to his company lines. By 2100 most of the firing had ceased and the enemy began to withdraw under cover of darkness. Throughout the night sporadic sniper fire and occasional grenade attacks were directed against the Americans and Vietnamese but no major engagements developed.

On 2 February the 2d Brigade continued to attack strongholds within the city, which was encircled by U.S. and Vietnamese units. At 0630 both U.S. battalions continued a sweep to the north in the western portion of the city, encountering only light resistance. At 0915 a Viet Cong force was engaged on the northern edge of the city. Tactical air strikes with napalm were called in and dislodged Viet Cong troops holding a guard tower near a highway bridge. The resulting damage to the bridge was repaired under fire by the Mobile Riverine Force's supporting engineer platoon. Upon completion of the sweep, the city was cleared of enemy units and the Mobile Riverine Force battalions loaded onto armored troop carriers at 1201 for redeployment to Cai Lay District in Dinh Tuong Province.

By this time, the Viet Cong offensive had lost much of its original intensity in Dinh Tuong Province and the enemy appeared to be withdrawing to the north and west. Base Area 470, where the Mobile Riverine Force had taken up positions before *Tet,* was thought to be a likely location for the Viet Cong to regroup. The Mobile Riverine Force therefore moved the twenty-five kilometers from My Tho to the Cai Lay area to cut off enemy escape routes from eastern Dinh Tuong Province. There were no significant engagements during the following two days as the Viet Cong apparently remained close to My Tho and did not immediately withdraw to their normal base areas.

On 4 February at the direction of the senior adviser of IV Corps Tactical Zone, the 3d Battalion, 60th Infantry, and 3d Battalion, 47th Infantry, moved to Vinh Long to relieve continued Viet Cong pressure on Vietnamese units. The two battalions were transported by helicopter and boat to positions south of Vinh Long, and together with allied elements they established a cordon around the city. The Mobile Riverine Base relocated during the day to an anchorage on the Mekong River north of Vinh Long. The 3d Bat-

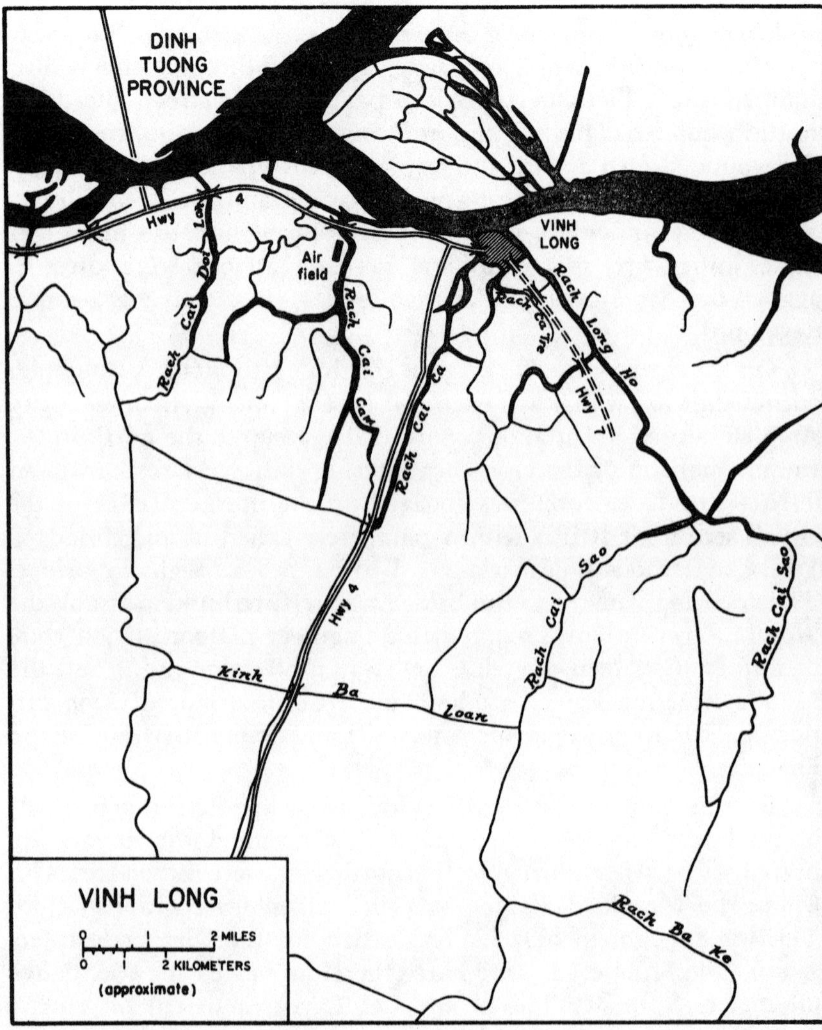

MAP 14

talion, 60th Infantry, completed the first airlift at 1655 with no opposition, but at 1733, on the east bank of the Rach Ca Tre Company A began to receive sniper fire. At the same time Company E was attacked with small arms and automatic weapons fire. The company returned fire and commenced movement against the Viet Cong, while artillery was used against the enemy's position. Company A meanwhile came under intense fire as it moved to its assigned sector. At 2030 Company E met a heavily armed Viet Cong company, and the fight was still in progress at 2145. As a result of this engagement, the 3d Battalion, 47th Infantry, sent

Company C to reinforce the 3d Battalion, 60th Infantry. (*Map 14*)

Thus far the battalions were successfully blocking enemy movement from Vinh Long at several points. Boats of the river assault divisions conducted patrols on the Rach Long Ho and Song Co Chiem throughout the night, reporting only a few incidents. Division boats received small arms and automatic weapons fire from the west and east banks of the Rach Long Ho which was suppressed with no casualties. During the remaining hours of darkness on 4 February the 3d Battalion, 60th Infantry, continued to engage the enemy in a fight that subsided gradually. Companies A and C were low on ammunition and required resupply. At 0200 a resupply helicopter was taken under fire and downed while attempting to land, but an infantry force rescued the craft and its crew. Throughout the night the enemy probed both battalion positions, but suffered a considerable number of casualties. At dawn both battalions conducted search operations within their immediate areas and confirmed Viet Cong losses.

Operations south of Vinh Long continued on 5 February with American and Vietnamese forces attempting to clear the area by pushing south against blocks of infantrymen inserted by helicopter. Intelligence indicated there was a Viet Cong battalion in the area. Company E, 3d Battalion, 60th Infantry, conducted airmobile search operations and Company A cleared the area near the Vinh Long airfield. The 3d Battalion, 47th Infantry, operated east of the Rach Cai Cam River, encountering several small enemy forces during the afternoon. Upon completion of the sweep, the infantry was loaded aboard ATC's and by 1725 had returned to the Mobile Riverine Base, after eight days and nights of continuous movement and combat. Company A, 3d Battalion, provided security for Vinh Long airfield and Company C, 3d Battalion, 60th Infantry, provided security for the Mobile Riverine Base and for the 3d Battalion, 34th Artillery.

On 6 February, in response to intelligence reports that the Viet Cong had succeeded in moving large forces southwest through the cordon around Vinh Long, Company B, 3d Battalion, 60th Infantry, departed the Mobile Riverine Base by boat in the early morning in an attempt to overtake the Viet Cong. The area to be searched was west of the Vinh Long airfield and south of National Highway 4. Company B made its first landing just south of the Highway 4 bridge over the Rach Cai Cam at 0810. Conversation with Popular Forces troops at a nearby outpost revealed that a large Viet Cong unit was in the woods and along the stream approximately 500 meters south of the bridge. Re-embarking, Company B commenced reconnaissance along the banks of the Rach Cai Cam to the south of the bridge. At 1100 the lead element of monitors and assault support patrol boats received fire from automatic weapons, recoilless rifles, and RPG's (Russian-built antitank rockets) on both banks of the river. Company B, supported by artillery, gunships, and fire from the river craft, assaulted the west bank of the Rach Cai Cam just north of the area of the ambush and swept south. No Viet Cong were found and the company re-embarked on the ATC's and continued along the stream, landing patrols at irregular intervals.

When the Viet Cong opened fire at 1100, Company E, 3d Battalion, 60th Infantry, was dispatched by boat from the Mobile Riverine Base and arrived in the area at 1430. Company B was again landed on the west bank of the Rach Cai Cam near the 1100 firefight area, and Company E was beached at that time just opposite Company B on the east bank of the Rach Cai Cam. Almost immediately both companies came under heavy RPG, grenade, and 60-mm. mortar fire. Company B charged the Viet Cong positions in its zone, killed the enemy troops, and took four weapons, suffering two soldiers wounded. Company E had twelve wounded in the first clash and was held up while the wounded were evacuated. By 1510 the enemy had withdrawn to the southwest.

Company A, 3d Battalion, 60th Infantry, beached just south of the Regional Forces and was able to move rapidly south through the rice paddies and act as a blocking force to the west of Company B. Men of Company A observed twenty Viet Cong in the river to their west, apparently trying to escape, and called in artillery fire that caused several secondary explosions. Shortly thereafter, at 1700, all three companies received heavy automatic weapons and RPG fire from the wooded stream line in front of them and became heavily engaged.

The battalion commander, having committed all of his available infantry, requested that the brigade reserve force be committed in an attempt to encircle the Viet Cong positions. By nightfall, however, enemy forces had broken contact and the 3d Battalion, 60th Infantry, returned to the Mobile Riverine Base early on 7 February.

During the fighting from 30 January to 6 February the Mobile Riverine Force made several rapid moves over a wide area. The Mobile Riverine Force moved from the Rach Ruong Canal area of western Dinh Tuong Province to My Tho; then to Cai Lay; and, finally, to Vinh Long. The effectiveness of the Mobile Riverine Force at each city resulted in a reduction of the Viet Cong attacks to harrassing actions and elimination of the threat to the city. By using in combination the Mobile Riverine Base, which moved large numbers of troops and support elements between the areas, assault water craft, and supporting helicopters the Mobile Riverine Force not only moved quickly to each new area, but also arrived in strength and was able to sustain operations as needed.

From 8 through 12 February the Mobile Riverine Force deployed to the northwest of My Tho and to Gia Dinh Province near Saigon. The entire CORONADO X operation, which ended on 12 February, proved the ability of the Mobile Riverine Force to move rapidly over a large geographic area. The counteroffensive to relieve My Tho and Vinh Long highlighted the importance of having adequate air resources to use in conjunction with the ships and small assault craft of the Navy Task Force 117.

The back of the Viet Cong *Tet* offensive had been broken in the My Tho and Vinh Long area by the middle of February through the combined efforts of the Mobile Riverine Force and South Vietnamese armed forces. However, Viet Cong units continued to maintain pressure on Can Tho, the capital of Phong Dinh Province. The Senior Advisor, IV Corps Tactical Zone, having current operational control of the Mobile Riverine Force, decided to employ it to relieve this pressure on Can Tho. Thus CORONADO XI, the last of the CORONADO series of Mobile Riverine Force operations, was initiated. The use of the Mobile Riverine Force in the central delta was made possible by the movement of the 1st Brigade, 9th U.S. Infantry Division, from the III Corps Tactical Zone to Dinh Tuong Province. All three brigades of the 9th Division were thus placed in the delta for the first time, signaling the opportunity for the Mobile Riverine Force to move south into the Bassac River area to carry out further the original Mobile Afloat Force concept.

Before CORONADO XI, intelligence indicated that the Viet Cong, instead of withdrawing to base areas after being routed from the cities, had remained near the heavily populated areas. Later it was apparent that the enemy had left only enough men to maintain pressure on the cities so that American and Vietnamese forces would also remain nearby. Numerous intelligence reports indicated that the enemy had improved his strength throughout Phong Dinh Province, in some cases by assigning young recruits to units and sending them to battle with minimum training. This enabled the Viet Cong to display considerable force on the battlefield. The Tay Do Battalion was believed to have recruited substantial numbers on the strength of its good reputation as a fighting unit. Enemy forces within Phong Dinh Province were identified as the 306th Main Force Battalion, 303d Main Force Battalion, Tay Do I and II Battalions, U Minh 10th Battalion, and Military Region III headquarters, accompanied by a security element of 200 men. The over-all mission for CORONADO XI was based on the suspected location of Viet Cong units and the Military Region III headquarters.

The mission of the Mobile Riverine Force in CORONADO XI, as developed in co-ordination with the Senior Adviser, IV Corps Tactical Zone, was to conduct riverine, air, and ground search operations in Cai Rang and Phung Hiep Districts of Phong Dinh Province, to locate and destroy Military Region III headquarters, and to conduct waterborne cordon and infantry search operations on the island of Cu Lao May in the Bassac River.

Operation CORONADO XI commenced on 12 February 1968, with the movement of the Mobile Riverine Force from Dong Tam to an anchorage in the vicinity of Can Tho. The force proceeded up the Mekong River through the waterway which connects the My Tho and Bassac Rivers, and down the Bassac to Can Tho. The force arrived shortly after 1300 on 13 February, having completed a journey of 109 miles from Dong Tam. (*Map 15*)

On 14 February the two infantry battalions landed from boats and conducted sweeps north along the canals immediately south of Can Tho. Army of Vietnam troops of the 9th and 21st Divisions conducted operations north of the city, sweeping to the southwest. Company A, 3d Battalion, 47th Infantry, found a cache which contained 460 B–40 rounds, 200 pounds of explosives, 89 120-mm. mortar rounds, and 500 pounds of medical supplies.

During the period 15–19 February, the Mobile Riverine Force conducted river and air operations west of Can Tho without encountering significant enemy forces. When the Can Tho airfield suffered a heavy rocket and mortar attack on 16 February, the main task of the Mobile Riverine Force was to sweep the area in the vicinity of the airfield.

On 19 February, at the request of the senior adviser of the IV Corps Tactical Zone, General Eckhardt, Task Force 117 units initiated joint waterborne patrols with units of the Vietnam Navy River Assault Group along a 13-mile stretch of the Song Can Tho to halt all sampan traffic. At 2217 a monitor was struck by B–40 rocket rounds that penetrated the 40-mm. turret. Although seven people, including a Vietnam Navy interpreter on board, were wounded, the monitor was able to suppress the enemy automatic

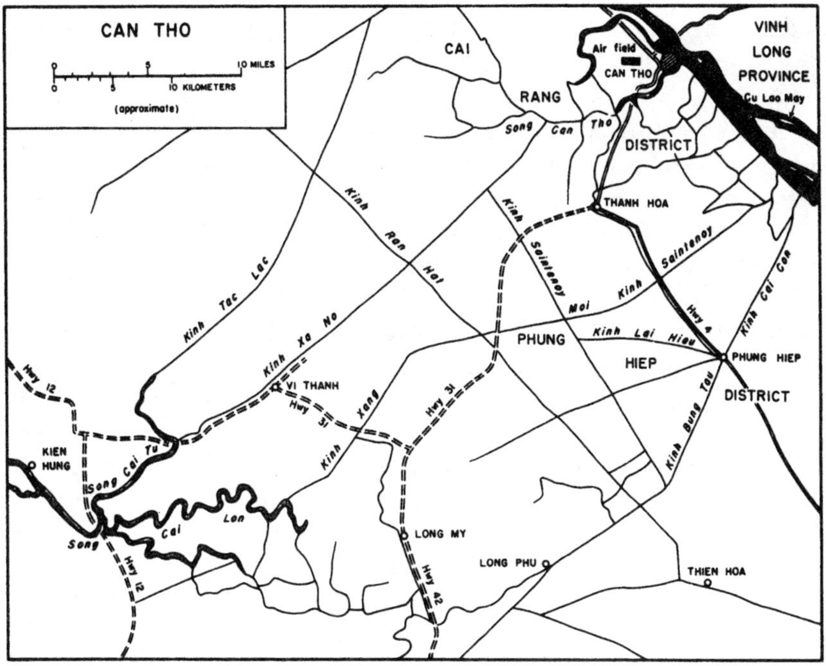

MAP 15

weapons and small arms fire. Four of the wounded were evacuated after a rendezvous with a medical aid boat. The patrols continued throughout the night in an effort to prevent escape of Viet Cong units from the area.

On 22 February the Mobile Riverine Force and government of Vietnam forces initiated a riverine and air operation in Phung Hiep District to locate the Military Region III headquarters. The 3d Battalion, 60th Infantry, and the 3d Battalion, 47th Infantry, moved to the area of operations by means of the Kinh Saintenoy Canal. Fire support was provided by Battery C, 2d Battalion, 35th Artillery, and 3d Battalion, 34th Artillery.

To obtain the overhead clearance that the boats needed to proceed beyond the Phung Hiep Bridge, the Vietnam Army engineers raised the center span of the bridge with jacks. As the assault boats proceeded west from Phung Hiep, sporadic sniper fire from the north bank of the canal wounded four U.S. Navy men. The riverine movement beyond the bridge apparently caught the Viet Cong by surprise. When Companies B and C, 3d Battalion, 47th Infantry, beached along the Kinh Lai Hieu Canal, just northeast of Hiep Hung, the enemy was in bunkers whose fighting ports faced the rice paddies in anticipation of airmobile attacks. The

Viet Cong ran into the open fields away from the canal where they were taken under fire by artillery and gunships and suffered heavy casualties. No additional U.S. casualties occurred.

On 23 February, the Mobile Riverine Force concluded the unsuccessful attempt to locate Military Region III headquarters and was withdrawn from the area of operations. Throughout the day there was no sight of the enemy or significant finding. The operation marked the deepest penetration yet of the Mekong Delta by U.S. forces.

On 24 February the Mobile Riverine Force conducted a waterborne cordon and search operation on the island of Cu Lao May during which both infantry battalions conducted medical civil action and dental civil action programs at enclosures where Vietnamese were detained for questioning. There was no contact with the enemy in this one-day operation. Northwest of Can Tho on 26 February, the Mobile Riverine Force met a large Viet Cong force. Company B, 3d Battalion, 60th Infantry, landed under fire that wounded many men and damaged twelve helicopters. Other elements of the Mobile Riverine Force moved to support Company B; Company E was airlifted at 1130 and landed approximately 800 meters east of Company B and Company A followed at 1405. At 1545, more than five hours after the first fire, Companies B and E were still heavily engaged and had not linked up. Linkup was effected at 1705, and because of the number of casualties sustained by Company B the company was placed under operational control of Company E. Companies A, B, and E established a night defensive position and were resupplied by 2200. The 3d Battalion, 47th Infantry, to the northwest encountered little fire throughout the day, although its scheme of maneuver was modified to allow it to provide additional support to the 3d Battalion, 60th Infantry.

Task Force 117 meanwhile had established patrols on the Song Can Tho along the southern boundary of operations to prevent escape of the enemy. About 2030 an armored troop carrier received a hit in the port bow causing an explosion. An assault support patrol boat went to the aid of the ATC and was taken under fire by automatic weapons. The enemy fire was returned and suppressed. Ten minutes later a second ATC was fired upon by a recoilless rifle. The round passed over the ATC, which immediately returned and suppressed the fire. There were no casualties among those on board in either attack. The units continued their patrols without incident until 0215 when a major action occurred as a large force of Viet Cong attempted to escape. An assault support patrol boat came under heavy fire from both banks and sustained several B-40 rocket hits causing major flooding and wounding two crewmen. Other river assault craft moved into the area and suppressed the hostile fire, but one assault support patrol boat sank as it was being towed by a monitor. All crew members were rescued, but the monitor received several hits while moving to assist the disabled assault support patrol boat. During the same period, another assault support patrol boat, operating four kilometers east of the first attack, was hit by heavy rocket and automatic weapons fire. The boat captain and radio men were killed instantly and the three other crewmen were wounded but were able to beach the boat. The enemy attack lasted an hour and a half, with four assault craft involved in the battle. A light helicopter fire team helped to cut down the enemy fire.

The Viet Cong were unable to escape south across the Song Can Tho and continued to suffer casualties as the blockade was maintained successfully throughout the action. U.S. losses were moderate. During the night the Viet Cong continued harassing the Mobile Riverine Force battalions with probing attacks and sniper fire. On 27 February the area was swept again, confirming additional enemy losses and discovering caches, including five crew-served weapons, sixteen small arms, and assorted ammunition.

On 1 March, also, other elements of the Mobile Riverine Force and three Vietnam Army Ranger battalions operated approximately five kilometers southwest of Can Tho. Heavy fighting developed in the afternoon and continued into the night. The enemy slipped away before daylight and only scattered groups were found the next day.

CORONADO XI required some unusual supply operations because of the geographic location, tempo of operations, and change in control headquarters from the 9th Infantry Division to the senior adviser of IV Corps. Operations took the Mobile Riverine Force away from the normal lines of communication thus straining resupply. The severe and continuous fighting caused a heavy expenditure of ammunition and Class I and Class III supplies. The control exercised by IV Corps created a new set of logistics channels to support operations. The potential logistics problems were solved by personal liaison between the Mobile Riverine Force and Army logistics representatives located at Can Tho. Items such as C rations, fuel, and construction materials were provided by 1st Logistics Command. The IV Corps provided for evacuation of dead and wounded and responded to all Army and Navy logistics needs.

Within the Can Tho area, most movements by waterway and canal were accomplished without significant opposition because the enemy had no prepared fighting positions near the canals. The enemy, however, had taken excellent defensive measures against airmobile operations conducted near open rice paddies. Bunkers were well constructed, with good overhead protection against artillery and air strikes, and commanded adequate fields of fire. In one instance the Viet Cong could not engage the Mobile Riverine Force; their bunkers faced away from the waterway. The enemy attempted to escape, making themselves vulnerable to the fire of the advancing U.S. troops and supporting gunships.

The Viet Cong demonstrated their ability to employ automatic weapons fire in all battles. They characteristically used an initial heavy volume of automatic weapons fire, followed by sporadic sniper fire. Sniper fire was directed particularly at unit leaders and radio operators; snipers were well trained and extremely effective in the Can Tho area. The Viet Cong continued to fight until the late hours of the night, 2200 to 2400. They then withdrew but continued to harass U.S. positions with mortar and rocket fire.

All operations conducted in the Can Tho area made maximum use of naval and air assets, and demonstrated that logistic support planning and timely intelligence were essential. The use of airmobility vastly influenced the course of tactical situations, especially when reserves were employed to reinforce a unit under fire or to exploit the enemy situation.

Combat operations in CORONADO XI ended on 3 March when the Mobile Riverine Force left the Can Tho area for Dong Tam. From 4 to 6 March the force assumed the division reserve role while the 3d Battalion, 47th Infantry, was replaced by the 4th Battalion, 47th Infantry, in the rotation of battalions within the brigade.

Operation TROUNG CONG DINH was initiated by the 9th Infantry Division on 7 March 1968. Its purpose was to destroy enemy forces in Dinh Tuong Province and to reduce the threat west of My Tho to Highway 4, which was being constantly menaced by the Viet Cong. The operation involved the 1st and 2d Brigades, 9th U.S. Infantry Division, the 7th Vietnam Army Division, and provincial forces. The commanding general of the 9th U.S. Infantry Division was able to employ the 2d Brigade for the first time in a continuing co-ordinated role with another division brigade. The Mobile Riverine Force conducted a series of combined riverine and airmobile operations, beginning east of My Tho. Operations were supported by the 3d Battalion, 34th Artillery, which established a fire support base on the north bank of the My Tho River, ten miles east of My Tho.

During initial airmobile assaults on 7 March enemy fire was light and no major firefight resulted. During the afternoon, the two battalions shifted their area of operations west-northwest of My Tho in response to intelligence reports. At 1920 the 4th Battalion, 47th Infantry, came under heavy small arms and automatic weapons fire just west of My Tho. Heavy fire continued until 2225. The following day troops met no Viet Cong in the area; at midday in response to intelligence the two battalions moved again into the area of operations of early 7 March. There were several firefights during the rest of the day. The most significant occurred at 1715 when Company B, 4th Battalion, 47th Infantry, made an assault landing by helicopter and was fired upon by a Viet Cong force from well dug-in positions along the southern edge of the landing zone. Five helicopters were downed during the first landing. Throughout the evening and into the night, as other elements of the two battalions maneuvered in support of Company B, there was sporadic but heavy fighting in the area. At 0300 the fire support base was attacked by mortars that sank two artillery barges carrying four 105-mm. howitzers. The infantry continued their sweep of the previous day's battlefield without finding any Viet Cong and returned by ATC to the Mobile Riverine Base in the late afternoon.

On 10 March the Mobile Riverine Force shifted operations near Cai Lay and Long Dinh, towns of Dinh Tuong Province. Troops of the 1st and 2d Brigades, 9th Infantry Division, conducted day and night patrolling and reconnaissance in force against suspected Viet Cong locations along Highway 4 until 16 March. On 16 March the 1st Brigade terminated its participation in the TROUNG CONG DINH operation. On 18 March, boats of River Division 92 received heavy automatic weapons and rocket fire while patrolling west of Dong Tam. The rockets damaged several assault support patrol boats and one monitor. The operation continued without opposition on 19 March, and the infantry battalions returned by ATC to the Mobile Riverine Base in the vicinity of Dong Tam.

On 22 March the Mobile Riverine Base, still located in the My Tho River south of Dong Tam, was attacked at 0320 by enemy using mortars and recoilless rifles. The *Benewah* received two 75-mm. recoilless rifle hits that caused minor damage, and near misses were registered by Viet Cong mortars on an LST, the *Washtenaw County*.

Through the remainder of March the Mobile Riverine Force continued operations in Dinh Tuong Province with occasional light to moderate firefights. On 1 April the 3d Battalion, 60th Infantry, debarked and assumed the Dong Tam security mission and the 3d Battalion, 47th Infantry, joined the Mobile Riverine Force. Operation TROUNG CONG DINH was terminated on 2 April, after a one-battalion airmobile operation in the Ham Long District in Kien Hoa Province, just south of Dong Tam.

During TROUNG CONG DINH the Mobile Riverine Force used extensively a riverine assault reconnaissance element, a small unit first employed in December 1967 that consisted of three or four monitors and several assault support patrol boats. The riverine assault reconnaissance element led ATC convoys and employed reconnaissance by fire against likely Viet Cong ambush positions. The technique reduced casualties because of the firepower and mobility of the craft in the riverine assault reconnaissance element and the placement of ATC's carrying infantry well back in the column. Airmobility was used during TROUNG CONG DINH to increase the flexibility of the Mobile Riverine Force by providing increased intelligence, firepower, and escort coverage for convoys during troop movement.

On 4 April a significant battle was fought near the intersection of the Song Ba Lai and canals, called the Crossroads, in the Truc Giang District of Kien Hoa Province. As the boats of River Division 92 carrying the 2d Battalion, 47th Infantry, entered the Song Ba Lai they were ambushed with rockets, small arms, and automatic weapons. The battalion put into effect its counterambush plan. Company B passed through the ambush and landed unopposed just beyond the Viet Cong positions. Company E was to land just short of the ambush and the two companies were to pinch the Viet Cong between them. Instead, Company E was landed directly into the ambush, suffered heavy casualties, and was forced to withdraw. Heavy fighting with the well-protected Viet Cong continued throughout the day. The 4th Battalion, 47th Infantry, crossed from the north to assist the 3d Battalion on the south bank. Casualties among the infantry were heavy as they encountered an extensive bunker complex containing .50-caliber and other automatic weapons. The action ceased during the evening as the Viet Cong slipped away in the darkness. The two battalions continued to sweep the marshes south of the Song Ba Lai through 7 April.

From 10 through 12 April the Mobile Riverine Force conducted successive operations near the towns of Vinh Kim and Long Dinh, and east of My Tho without major encounters. An operation in the Giong Trom and Ben Tre Districts of Kien Hoa Province on 14–15 April failed to find the enemy. At 1400 on 15 April the Mobile Riverine Base was attacked by 57- and 75-mm. recoilless rifles while at anchor. The USS *Benewah* received three hits; the supply LST received eight hits—all above the water line. One LCM-6 refueler was hit and later burned and sank. There were no casualties and only minor damages to the *Benewah* and the LST.

During the remainder of April, the Mobile Riverine Force conducted four separate operations in the Cai Lay area of Dinh Tuong Province, the western part of Kien Hoa and Dinh Tuong Provinces, and the Cam Son Base area of Dinh Tuong Province. Significant engagements were fought in three of the four operations, with the Mobile Riverine Force inflicting losses on the enemy in each encounter. Two of the operations were conducted in co-ordination with the 2d Vietnamese Marine Corps Battalion.

On 2 and 3 May, the Mobile Riverine Force again returned to Kien Hoa Province in response to enemy attacks on government outposts. On 5 May a survey was made of Regional Forces and Popular Forces outposts in Cai Be District to determine the extent of damage. Operations were directed from 7 through 11 May against Military Region II Viet Cong headquarters in the Giao Duc District of Dinh Tuong Province. The Mobile Riverine Force and the 2d Battalion, Vietnam Marine Corps, conducted a reconnaissance in force but encountered no large groups of enemy troops. From 14 through 16 May the Mobile Riverine Force was employed in the Mo Cay District of Kien Hoa Province and engaged the Viet Cong 516th Battalion in several firefights. The Mobile Riverine Force and elements of the 3d Brigade, 9th Infantry Division, carried out operations from 16 through 18 May, in the Than Duc District of Long An Province in co-operation with III Corps Tactical Zone Vietnam Army forces in order to reduce Viet Cong and North Vietnam Army infiltration of the Saigon area. The brigade continued operations in Long An and Dinh Tuong Province until 26 May. At that time a two-day operation was launched to reconnoiter and exploit the area of a B–52 strike in the Giong Trom District of Kien Hoa Province.

During the month of June the enemy generally avoided contact with the maneuver battalions and intensified his attacks against naval assault support craft of Task Force 117. On 5 and 6 June the Mobile Riverine Force conducted reconnaissance in force in the Sa Dec area. Effective use was made of the E8—a portable expendable launcher that fired riot-control cannisters—and flame-boats. The period 4 through 8 June saw the Mobile Riverine Force conducting operations in the Sa Dec area and eastern Kien Phong Province. Returning to Kien Hoa Province, the force initiated operations on 10 June in the Giong Trom and Truc Giang Districts. On 16 June it moved to Can Tho, and began operations again directed by the senior adviser of IV Corps Tactical Zone to prevent a suspected Viet Cong offensive against the city. A four-day operation commenced on 17 June with a major firefight in which the majority of the enemy's losses resulted from fire support by Company A, 7th Battalion, 1st Air Cavalry, in support of the maneuver battalions. Completing operations in Phong Dinh Province on 19 June, the Mobile Riverine Force moved to Dong Tam. After four days of operations near Dong Tam, it proceeded on 26 June to Long An Province where it was again employed to prevent Viet Cong and North Vietnam Army forces from moving in and out of the vicinity of Saigon. Unlike the brigade's experience in early 1968 operations in Long An Province, the enemy avoided contact with the maneuver battalions throughout the operation.

On 2 July the 2d Brigade was directed to place the 3d Battalion, 60th Infantry, under operational control of the 3d Brigade, 9th Infantry Division, which was in contact with the enemy in Dinh Tuong Province. The battalion remained under operational control of the 3d Brigade through 5 July. During that time the Mobile Riverine Force continued its operations in Long An Province, moving to Dong Tam on 5 July. On 6 July the 3d Battalion, 47th Infantry, relieved the 4th Battalion, 47th Infantry, of its security mission at Dong Tam Base. The 2d Brigade continued combat operations on 7 July in Kien Hoa Province near the canal Cross-roads on the Song Ba Lai, where the 2d Brigade had previously fought one of its heaviest engagements. The 4th Battalion, 47th Infantry, entered its objective area and beached without incident. The 3d Battalion, 60th Infantry, air-landed assault troops at several spots south of the 4th Battalion beach sites. The only incidents of the day occurred when Company E of the 4th Battalion, 47th Infantry, received sporadic small arms fire and D Troop, 3d Battalion, 5th Air Cavalry, was subjected to sporadic automatic weapons fire. The limited enemy activity in the area was unlike prior experience of the Mobile Riverine Force along the Song Ba Lai.

On 10 July the Mobile Riverine Force began operations to

locate and destroy enemy forces and equipment within the Huong My and Mo Cay Districts of Kien Hoa Province. Operations continued, through 13 July, with both battalions using boats and helicopters to search for the enemy. During the period 15 through 17 July the Mobile Riverine Force conducted riverine operations in Vinh Binh Province in co-operation with the 9th Vietnam Army Division. Completing operations in Vinh Binh Province the Mobile Riverine Force moved to Dong Tam Base on 18 July. While anchored off Dong Tam, the 2d Brigade employed the 4th Battalion, 47th Infantry, on 20 July to conduct saturation patrolling and to establish night ambushes on the south bank of the My Tho River in the Truc Giang and Ham Long Districts of Kien Hoa Province. On 21 July the 3d Battalion, 60th Infantry, was employed in a cordon and search operation in co-operation with Regional Forces and Popular Forces elements on Thoi Son Island. Operations continued on 23 July in the Giong Trom and Truc Giang Districts of Kien Hoa Province in co-operation with the Vietnam Army. On 25 July the 2d Brigade terminated its operations in Kien Hoa Province; the next day the Mobile Riverine Force moved to Vinh Long Province.

After completing final plans and preparations for its journey the Mobile Riverine Force left its Vinh Long anchorage on 28 July and arrived in Phong Dinh Province the same day. On 30 July the force began offensive operations in co-ordination with the 5th Battalion, Vietnam Marine Corps, in the Vi Thanh area of Chuong Thien Province. To accomplish its mission, the 2d Brigade debarked from the Mobile Riverine Base and established its headquarters and tactical operations center inland in the vicinity of Vi Thanh. The Mobile Riverine Force moved into the U Minh Forest, forty-eight miles southwest of Can Tho in early August in a co-ordinated combined operation that included U.S. Army, Navy, and Air Force units and Vietnam Marine Corps and Army forces. This was the first major Allied ground operation in that area in more than a decade and another amplification of the original Mobile Riverine Force operational concept that had envisioned operations no more than twenty to thirty miles from the Mobile Riverine Base. The ten-day operation was also significant in that it substantially exceeded in scope the two- to three-day operations of the force contemplated in original plans. The operation was the first penetration by an American ground force into the U Minh Forest region and it was the deepest penetration by the Mobile Riverine Force into the Mekong Delta. The 2d Brigade established a land base and forward logistic support area with lines of communication extending fifty miles to the riverine base anchored near Can Tho. The operation was also destined to be the last major strike operation conducted by the Mobile Riverine Force.

By early August the Mobile Riverine Force had conducted many tactical operations in co-ordination with the other brigades of the 9th U.S. Division and with Vietnamese Army, Marine Corps, and paramilitary units. The tempo of strike operations had been maintained at a high level as the force moved from one province to another, across corps boundaries, and in response to missions originating with the commanding general of the 9th U.S. Infantry Division and with II Field Forces Vietnam through the senior adviser of the IV Corps Tactical Zone. On several occasions operations were carried on to block infiltration routes in order to cut down the threat of enemy forces present in the Capital Military District around Saigon, and near Ben Tre, Sa Dec, and Can Tho. The Mobile Riverine Force had operated in eight provinces of the Mekong Delta since early February 1968. In all operations its efforts were complemented by the co-ordinated operations of other U.S. or Vietnamese units.

CHAPTER IX

Pacification and Kien Hoa Province

The Third Battalion

As the Mobile Riverine Force began its second year of operations in 1968, the 2d Brigade still lacked a third maneuver battalion and full use of the 3d Battalion, 34th Artillery. Successive commanders of the brigade had reiterated the need for a third battalion to increase the flexibility of the force and to enable it to operate with greater independence, but the brigade's overall strength had remained basically unchanged. Two of its three battalions remained afloat with the Mobile Riverine Force, while the third infantry battalion was employed in defense of Dong Tam Base. In the absence of a third maneuver battalion the Mobile Riverine Force operated extensively in conjunction with Vietnam Army units.

During the first half of 1968 the Navy component of the Mobile Riverine Force continued to grow. In June a third river assault squadron was formed and in July the Navy component was reorganized into two groups, Mobile Riverine Group Alpha and Group Bravo. By the fall of 1968, the force was scheduled to reach its full strength of 4 river assault squadrons, 184 river assault craft, 4 barracks ships, 3 repair ships, 2 barracks barges, 2 support ships, 2 resupply ships, and various other support craft.

At a riverine concept briefing on 5 January 1968, General Abrams, deputy commander of the U.S. Military Assistance Command, Vietnam, had directed the U.S. Army, Vietnam, to reexamine the organization for the Army riverine battalions and the composition of the land-based brigade. The 9th Infantry Division, Headquarters, II Field Force, Vietnam, and Headquarters, U.S. Army, Vietnam, concluded that the mission of the Mobile Riverine Force could best be accomplished by a reorganization of the seven infantry battalions of the division, deleting equipment and units not essential in riverine operations. General Westmoreland approved the reorganization on 21 February 1968.

This new organization of the battalions lent itself readily to operations other than riverine, particularly airmobile operations, without the investment in equipment and men required for continuing land-based operations. In firepower the riverine battalion, less four 81-mm. mortars, was equivalent to the standard infantry battalion even without the considerable firepower support of the Navy assault craft. By borrowing equipment, the battalion was capable of sustained operations on dry land at a saving of some 600 spaces which would be required by a standard battalion and its support elements.

The value of and continuing need for one Vietnam Marine Corps battalion to operate with the Mobile Riverine Force was also recognized. The battalion was not, however, permanently assigned to the force because Vietnam Marine Corps units were part of the Army of Vietnam general reserve and therefore subject to recall at any time. Vietnamese marines had been operating with the Mobile Riverine Force on this basis since 15 November 1967 and had contributed to successes of the force against the Viet Cong.

The CORONADO series of operations conducted from June 1967 to July 1968 had demonstrated the effectiveness of the Mobile Riverine Force in the use of waterways to deny the enemy areas where he had previously operated with relative freedom. This success led to an examination of how the riverine effort could be expanded cheaply in order to step up the tempo of operations in the Mekong Delta. A study conducted by U.S. Army, Vietnam, and Commander, Naval Forces, Vietnam, concluded that additional units of the 9th Infantry Division could be accommodated at Dong Tam without dredging. Further, with a modest addition of naval craft to the already scheduled river assault squadrons, an expanded force could support two brigades afloat and one at Dong Tam. Through judicious use of naval river craft and Army planes and helicopters the entire 9th Division could be effectively employed in the delta; the Vietnam Marine Corps and, eventually, Vietnamese river assault group units could also be drawn into operations. An organization of two Mobile Riverine Force brigades, each with three infantry battalions and supporting artillery, was considered the most desirable. The third brigade was to operate out of Dong Tam, either independently or in conjunction with the Mobile Riverine Force. This arrangement would provide flexibility, reduce reliance on land bases, demand fewer aircraft, and help sustain pressure on the Viet Cong. It would also eliminate regular river assault squadron operations out of Dong Tam, which could develop a pattern easily detected by the enemy. The 3d Brigade with two maneuver battalions was to be sent from the Tan An area to Dong Tam Base to facilitate its transition to the second Mobile Riverine Force. The division headquarters was transferred from Camp Martin Cox at Bearcat to its new base camp at Dong Tam on 25 July.

As of July 1968 no definite date had been established for embarking the long-awaited third infantry battalion of the 2d Brigade aboard ships of the Mobile Riverine Force. The availability of the third infantry battalion was contingent upon readjustments in 9th Infantry Division base security missions.

While general organization changes to the Mobile Riverine Force were being formulated, a major change was made in its mission. On 16 July the 2d Brigade was assigned the province of Kien Hoa as a primary area of operations, with the added mission of conducting pacification activities of a more permanent nature than those previously undertaken by the Mobile Riverine Force. The Accelerated Pacification Program guided from Headquarters, U.S. Military Assistance Command, Vietnam, prompted this assignment. After six months of operations that concentrated on the area north of the My Tho River, including Long An Province and the Rung Sat Special Zone, and after an additional six months of operations ranging more widely afield and deeper into the delta, the Mobile Riverine Force returned to concentrate on Kien Hoa. At this time Major General Harris W. Hollis, commanding the 9th Division, decided to provide the force with its third maneuver battalion and to require all three battalions to conduct airmobile and riverine operations in Kien Hoa Province. One of the battalions was based ashore in the vicinity of Ben Tre and two battalions remained afloat. The concentration on Kien Hoa Province was directed shortly after formal approval of the riverine modified tables of organization and equipment for the 2d Brigade and shortly before the arrival of the U.S. Navy craft required to lift the maneuver elements of an additional brigade.

The operational rotation of one infantry battalion from the Mobile Riverine Force to the Ben Tre base was quite different from the rotation of a battalion to Dong Tam. The May 1967 preparations of the 2d Brigade for Mobile Riverine Force operations had provided for each infantry battalion to leave at Dong Tam equipment not required when it was based afloat. Semipermanent facilities at Dong Tam reduced the need of each battalion for organic equipment to operate a nearly independent battalion base. The first battalion sent to the Ben Tre base, therefore, required equipment that Mobile Riverine Force battalions had not needed since before June 1967. The addition of the third infantry battalion as a land-based unit consequently brought a new organization and a logistics problem that the Mobile Riverine Force had not anticipated in its plan for employing three infantry battalions in continuing strike operations from a base entirely afloat.

Concentration by the Mobile Riverine force on Kien Hoa Province presented special considerations for operational flexibility. Previous operations in Kien Hoa had revealed the limited waterway network off the major rivers. Helicopters had proved necessary both to deploy blocking forces inland in those areas lacking navigable waterways and to assist in waterway reconnaissance. Previous operations had also demonstrated that effective anchorages for the Mobile Riverine Base to support operations in Kien Hoa were limited to four: the vicinity of Dong Tam; east of My Tho; east of Vinh Long; and east of Mocay District on the Co Chien River. Although use of each of these anchorages could facilitate operations into different districts of Kien Hoa Province, changing from one anchorage to another would not be likely to deceive the enemy.

In the past bold changes in the location of the Mobile Riverine Base had achieved surprise against Viet Cong base areas that had not been recently or frequently attacked. This major asset of the Mobile Riverine Force—the mobility of the entire force, including its logistics base—could not be fully used in the concentration of Kien Hoa Province.

Beginning in early September in Kien Hoa Province under operation HOMESTEAD, the 2d Brigade conducted operations throughout the month to find and destroy the enemy in his home territory. The enemy attacked the river craft from ambush with rockets, recoilless rifles, and small arms. According to intelligence reports, the enemy had formed special five-man teams in Kien Hoa to ambush the boats of the Mobile Riverine Force. The main ambush weapon of these teams was usually the RPG2 or RPG7 rocket launcher.

In September an additional river assault squadron and two barracks ships arrived in Vietnam to support the 3d Brigade, 9th Infantry Division. At the same time the 9th Infantry Division completed reorganization of the headquarters of 3d Brigade and one battalion into the riverine modified tables of organization and equipment in anticipation of the establishment of the second Mobile Riverine Force. By the end of 1968 three additional battalions were reorganized, making a total of two brigade headquarters and seven infantry battalions configured for riverine operations.

During October Mobile Riverine Group Alpha supported pacification operations in Kien Hoa Province with the 3d and 4th Battalions, 47th Infantry, the 3d Battalion, 60th Infantry, elements of the 3d Battalion, 34th Artillery, and the 3d Battalion, Vietnam Marine Corps. Mobile Riverine Group Bravo operated with other 9th Infantry and Vietnam ground forces in Vinh Binh, Vinh Long, Long An, Dinh Tuong, and Phong Dinh Provinces in carrying troops and blocking Viet Cong use of waterways.

In order to make the greatest possible use of its resources during the extended period of pacification in Kien Hoa, Dinh Tuong, and Long An Provinces, the Mobile Riverine Force was reorganized on 15 October. Mobile Riverine Group Alpha, supporting the 9th Infantry Division pacification operations, was assigned USS *Benewah,* USS *Askari,* USS *Sphinx,* USS *Westchester County, APL-26,* and *YLLC-4*. Mobile Riverine Group Bravo, carrying out more mobile operations ranging throughout the western delta region, was assigned USS *Mercer,* USS *Nueces,* USS *Vernon County,* and USS *Caroline County*. Five river assault divisions were assigned to Mobile Riverine Group Alpha, three to Mobile Riverine Group Bravo.

By the end of October Task Force 117 had conducted liaison and training with the 21st Vietnam Army Division and had joined the 4th Vietnam Marine Corps Battalion in Navy operations known as SEA LORDS (Southeast Asia Lake Ocean River Delta Strategy). An extensive survey of the western delta canals was also made in anticipation of future operations in that area.

In November the Mobile Riverine Force continued the pattern of operations which had begun after the reorganization in October, with Mobile Riverine Group Alpha operating in the eastern delta and Mobile Riverine Group Bravo operating to the west. Of the five river assault divisions assigned to Mobile Riverine Group Alpha, River Assault Division 91 supported the 3d Vietnam Marine Corps Battalion in operations in Kien Hoa Province; River Assault Division 92 was assigned base defense duties; River Assault Division 111 supported the 3d Battalion, 34th Artillery; River Assault Division 112 operated with the 3d Battalion, 60th Infantry, in Kien Hoa Province; and River Assault Division 151 worked with the 3d Battalion, 39th Infantry, in eastern Long An Province. Of the three river assault divisions assigned to Mobile Riverine Group Bravo, River Assault Division 121 provided for Dong Tam base defense, River Assault Division 132 supported the SEA LORDS interdiction operations, and River Assault Division 152 supported the 4th Vietnam Marine Corps Battalion. River assault craft also supported other troop units in particular operations during the month. (*Table 2*)

TABLE 2—SEA LORDS OPERATIONS, NOVEMBER 1968–JANUARY 1969

Operations	Fire-fights	Munitions Caches Uncovered	Other Caches Uncovered	Con-firmed Enemy Killed	Enemy Captured
SEARCH TURN (began 2 November 1968)	200	14 (11.0 tons)	1 (1.0 tons)	219	27
TRAN HUNG DAO (began 16 November 1968)	276	3 (11.4 tons)	0	470	26
GIANT SLINGSHOT (began 6 December 1968)	1,044	244 (137.0 tons)	22 (384.9 tons)	1,910	232
BARRIER REEF (began 2 January 1969)	77	1 (0.4 tons)	0	189	46

A significant incident occurred in November when USS *Westchester County* was mined as she lay at anchor with the other ships of Mobile Riverine Group Alpha on the My Tho River. At 0323 on 1 November, two explosions ripped separate holes on the starboard side of the LST. Three of the assault craft that were tied up alongside and two helicopters that were on board were damaged. Although the LST was not in danger of sinking, several compartments were flooded and internal blast damage was extensive. There was no damage to the ship's main engines or other machinery and she sailed to Dong Tam for emergency repairs before proceeding to a repair facility. The mining was apparently the work of enemy swimmers or sappers who penetrated, undetected, the base security forces. American casualties were 25 killed, 27 wounded, and 4 missing.

Enemy swimmers or sappers again struck the Mobile Riverine Force on the night of 15 November when the *YLLC-4* (salvage lift craft, light) was mined and sunk while at anchor on the Ham Luong River. Casualties in this instance were two killed and thirteen wounded. Because damage was extensive and the location hazardous, it was determined that salvage would be uneconomical; and the craft was destroyed to eliminate it as a navigational hazard.

On 13 November 1968 the 1st Brigade replaced the 3d Brigade at Dong Tam and the 3d Brigade returned to operate in Long An Province. This deployment moved the riverine-organized 3d Brigade away from the area that the Mobile Afloat Force concept had designated for follow-up riverine operations—the area south of the My Tho River. Part of Mobile Riverine Group Alpha continued to support the 3d Brigade in Long An Province and other U.S. forces in III Corps Tactical Zone.

Riverine warfare in December again involved interdiction, escort, patrol, base area search, and pacification. Small unit Navy actions were conducted over wide areas in Kien Hoa, Kien Giang. Chuong Thien, and An Xuyen Provinces. Mobile Riverine Group Alpha operations were confined for the most part to activity in Kien Hoa Province and support of the 2d Brigade, 9th Infantry Division. Mobile Riverine Group Bravo continued to carry out a variety of special operations in the southern delta in co-ordination with units of the 2d, 3d, and 4th Battalions of the Vietnam Marine Corps.

The 2d Brigade, supported by Mobile Riverine Group Alpha, engaged in a series of operations in December designed to keep constant pressure on the Viet Cong. With frequent insertions of troops in the Ham Long, Mo Cay, and Truc Giang Districts of Kien Hoa Province, 2d Brigade ground forces continued to seek out the enemy, especially members of the Viet Cong political organization. Of the many people detained for questioning, about 20 percent were subsequently classified as Viet Cong and the rest as innocent civilians.

Throughout January of 1969 the Mobile Riverine Force conducted operations in the provinces of Dinh Tuong, Vinh Long, Long An, and Kien Hoa as the Mobile Riverine Force again moved farther afield. On 7 January two battalions were landed in the Don Nhan district of western Kien Hoa Province, an area not previously penetrated by U.S. forces. Two platoons of enemy guerrillas were engaged by Army troops while assault craft established several water blocks to prevent the escape of the guerrillas. This strategy was intended to break up the enemy underground organization, disrupt enemy plans, demoralize enemy forces, and aid pacification. The Mobile Riverine Force used helicopters extensively in the operation, especially in January and February when the greatest number became available.

The activities of Mobile Riverine Group Alpha became more

Province in support of the 2d Brigade. Constant pressure was applied to enemy forces there in support of the allied program to commit more troops and time to the pacification effort. Mobile Riverine Group Bravo, operating with the 3d and 4th Battalions, Vietnam Marine Corps, advanced into Chuong Thien, Kien Giang, Phong Dinh, and northern Ba Xuyen Provinces.

In early January 1969 Mobile Riverine Group Alpha initiated a cordon and search operation on Thoi Son Island, in the My Tho River south of Dong Tam. Twenty-four river assault craft of River Assault Divisions 92 and 111, two infantry battalions, eight river patrol boats, and Vietnam Navy units participated in this operation which was directed against Viet Cong guerrillas and swimmer and sapper units based on the eastern end of the island. The island people were moved temporarily to three collection points, screened by the National Police and issued new identification cards. River craft assumed blocking stations and the island was swept by infantry units seeking Viet Cong. A total of 1,353 people voluntarily assembled at the three collection points or were apprehended in the sweep. Seventy Viet Cong were apprehended by the end of the operation on 7 January 1969.

On 12 January boats of River Assault Division 91 were withdrawn from operations preliminary to the planned turnover of 25 river assault craft to the Vietnam Navy on 1 February. Vietnamese naval crews had undergone on-the-job training with River Assault Division 91 units since early December 1968. River Assault Squadron 13 joined Mobile Riverine Group Alpha and River Assault Division 132 was relieved by River Assault Division 92 in Operation SEA LORDS. River Assault Division 132 returned to the Mobile Riverine Base in Kien Hoa and supported the 4th Battalion, 47th Infantry. River Assault Division 131 supported the 3d Battalion, 34th Artillery; River Assault Division 112 assumed support duties for the 3d Battalion, 60th Infantry, and River Assault Division 111 assumed base defense duties.

River Assault Squadron 15 had begun reconnaissance operations in an enemy base area in southern Kien Giang Province in late December 1968 and had continued these operations into January. Eighteen river assault craft, working in co-ordination with the 2d and 3d Battalions, Vietnam Marine Corps, conducted patrols and landed troops along the Can Cao Canal. Ground fighting with enemy forces was sporadic throughout the campaign, which lasted until 7 January. Despite intelligence reports of significant enemy forces in the area, U.S. and Vietnamese troops encountered only small groups of the enemy that employed hit-and-run tactics.

This same river assault squadron, with the 2d Vietnam Marine Corps Battalion, began operations along the Song Cai Tu and Song Cai Lon Rivers in Kien Giong Province on 11 January to round up enemy forces suspected of being in the region. The enemy had used the territory before for storage and for offensive operations in Chuong Tien, Kien Giang, and Phong Dinh Provinces. U.S. and Vietnamese troops were landed at a number of beaches but found only enemy ground forces of squad size or smaller. After troop landings, river assault craft established blocking stations and checked a total of 189 sampans throughout the operation, which lasted until 18 January. The enemy attacked assault craft of the riverine force eight times. Of the total of twenty-six U.S. sailors wounded, five were injured when an ATC was sunk by a water mine on the Song Cai Tu. Two sailors and one Vietnam marine died when the mined craft sank almost immediately.

On 1 February the twenty-five river assault craft of Division 91 were transferred by the U.S. Navy to the Vietnam Navy. Combining these craft with eight assault support patrol boats received directly under the military assistance program, the Vietnam Navy formed two river assault and interdiction divisions, which conducted operations in conjunction with the U.S. Navy. Coincident with the turnover, River Assault Division 91 was dissolved.

Standard infantry operations by water and air continued in February as the Mobile Riverine Force operated in several districts of Kien Hoa Province in support of the 2d Brigade. On two occasions river assault craft came under particularly heavy and well-aimed enemy fire from the river banks. On 24 February, units of River Assault Division 131 received combined rocket and automatic weapons fire from both banks of the Song Ba Lai at a position three miles northeast of Ben Tre. Six craft were hit and slightly damaged; eleven U.S. sailors were wounded. Again, on 27 February, units of River Assault Division 112 came under heavy rocket, recoilless rifle, and automatic weapons fire from both banks of the Song Ba Lai at a position four miles northeast of Ben Tre. In this attack there were twelve U.S. Navy sailors wounded and five of the river assault craft received hits causing minor damage.

Enemy swimmers with SCUBA gear were sighted in close to the USS *Vernon County* (LST-1161) at Mobile Riverine Base Alpha at Dong Tam on two successive days—25 and 26 February. In both cases concussion grenades were dropped into the water, and subsequent hull inspections turned up no damage.

During the same period Mobile Riverine Force elements ambushed a Viet Cong water convoy. Elements of the 3d Battalion, 60th Infantry, in night positions along the Rach An Binh, three miles southeast of Mo Cay, detected three large motorized sampans moving northward along the waterway, firing into the banks. The soldiers quickly set up an ambush and took the sampans under fire. Twenty-one of the enemy were killed and the three sampans were captured with no American casualties.

Water blockades along the Song Can Tho and Kinh Xa Mo in Phong Dinh Province, begun on 30 January by Mobile Riverine Group Bravo, continued into February. The 21st Vietnam Army Infantry Division had been conducting reconnaissance in force to prevent massing of Viet Cong in the area. The river assault craft, working in conjunction with elements of the 21st Vietnam Army Division, established a water blockade along the Song Can Tho from the Cai Range Bridge in Phong Dinh Province to a point eight miles west of Can Tho, and along the Kinh Xa Mo from Thuan Mon to the junction of the Kinh Xa Mo and Song Can Tho. One company each of the 2d Vietnam Marine Corps Battalion and the 295th Phong Dinh Regional Force were embarked as reserves. During the operation, which lasted until 3 February, over 7,000 sampans were inspected. Ground forces reported only light and sporadic fire. Enemy swimmers were seen by Mobile Riverine Group Bravo on 5, 7, and 9 February, but in each case no swimmers were captured and there was no hull damage to boats.

Operating with 160 river assault craft in March because of the transfer of the twenty-five boats to the Vietnam Navy in February, the Navy elements of the Mobile Riverine Force again ranged the delta in river assault operations in co-ordination with the U.S. Army and Vietnam armed forces. Group Alpha continued operations in Kien Hoa Province with the 2d Brigade. Attacks against river assault craft continued into March and ground units engaged in heavy firefights on several occasions. Group Bravo and the Vietnam marines conducted a successful strike into Chuong Thien Province.

A plan for again combining both task groups of the Mobile Riverine Force took effect on 4 March as the units of Task Group Alpha put in at the My Tho anchorage. The single mobile riverine base allowed for a more efficient utilization of resources and reduced the number of troops needed for base defense from two river assault divisions to one, thereby allowing the extra division to be employed in offensive operations. Tactical flexibility was also maintained should the need arise for two task groups.

During April naval units of the Mobile Riverine Force participated in diversified operations with different missions and in various areas. Reconnaissance in force, patrolling, ambushes, troop transport, inspection, fire support, blocking, escort duties, and psychological warfare were carried out by river assault craft, often in conjunction with U.S. Army or Vietnam armed forces, as they operated from northern Long An Province to the southernmost reaches of the Ca Mau peninsula. The long-term riverine assault operations in Kien Hoa Province continued as the combined Army and Navy units continued to inflict losses on the enemy.

On 22 April River Assault Division 132 was on the Cai Tu River eight and one-half miles southwest of Vi Thanh. During the firefight, a water mine exploded sixty feet off the starboard bow of a command and control boat and caused minor flooding that was brought under control. Potential losses were averted on 24 April when a Viet Cong command-detonated mine was discovered attached to the antiswimmer net of an APL between the bow and ponton. The homemade mine, which was estimated to weight from 150 to 175 pounds, was discovered when an antiswimmer net was being raised as the ship prepared to get under way; inspection by mine disposal experts revealed the mine with its detonator lead severed. The detonator wire was probably cut during a minesweep patrol by a base defense boat. On 29 April an assault support patrol boat was sunk on the Cai Tu River as an enemy mine was detonated beneath its stern during an operation in Chuong Thien Province.

The need for further base and boat defensive measures was apparent in the number of thwarted and successful enemy swimmer attacks against the Mobile Riverine Force. Increased emphasis was placed on use of nets, concussion grenades, and hull inspections by underwater demolition teams.

The main thrust of Mobile Riverine Force operations in May continued against the enemy in Kien Hoa Province. However, three excursions lasting up to a week each were made by detachments of six to eight river assault craft into the Can Giuoc District of Long An Province in support of the 5th Battalion, 60th Infantry, of the 3d Brigade.

During June the U.S. Navy turned over to the Vietnam Navy sixty-four additional river assault craft valued at $18.5 million. (*Table 3*) Sailors of the Vietnam Navy had already trained on the job with U.S. Navy river assault craft crews with whom they had been integrated during the preceding months. River Assault

Squadrons 9 and 11 were decommissioned on 10 and 27 June, respectively.

TABLE 3—U.S. RIVER CRAFT TRANSFERRED TO VIETNAM NAVY IN JUNE 1969

Craft	10 June	15 June	21 June	Total
ATC	12	12	11	35
ASPB	8	8		16
Monitor	2	3	3	8
CCB	2	1	1	4
Refueler	1			1
Total	25	24	15	64

Mobile Riverine Force activities were concentrated in Kien Hoa Province during June and consisted primarily of assault landings, troop sweeps and ambushes, and blocking, escorting, and defoliation missions, although some psychological warfare and medical civic action programs were conducted as well. Operations of limited duration also took the force into Go Cong, Long An, and Vinh Binh Provinces. The total of 554 of the enemy killed by the Mobile Riverine Force in June, although substantial, was the lowest figure since January 1969, indicating a reduced tempo of operations.

Mobile Riverine Force operations were even more limited in July. On 12 June 1969 the 9th Infantry Division had been notified of its impending departure from Vietnam. The 2d Brigade was the first to be inactivated, probably because the 1st and 3d Brigades had had more experience in the area just south of Saigon where there was still a need for at least one brigade. The division was inactivated in phases. The 3d Battalion, 60th Infantry, left the country in early July. The river force divisions supporting the 9th Division were used chiefly in defense of Dong Tam Base, but they also supported Vietnam Army, Regional Forces, and Popular Forces units. River Assault Flotilla One at the end of July consisted of 113 craft in five divisions, two divisions assigned to River Assault Squadron 13 and three to Squadron 15. Sixty-three of the enemy were killed in July operations.

When the departure of the 9th Infantry Division was announced, there appeared in the press considerable conjecture on the fate of the Mekong Delta. Most articles were openly pessimistic about the ability of Republic of Vietnam forces to hold onto the gains made in the Mekong Delta after two and a half years of U.S.

operations there. A feature article of 28 July 1969, "Where the Reds Are Stopped in Vietnam" in *U.S. News & World Report,* was guardedly optimistic, and summed up the results of riverine warfare in the delta. Viet Cong defections, it declared, had increased to 300 per month from a pre- 1969 rate of 50, and the enemy was no longer able to mass forces as he had in the past. Roads and canals that had been closed for years were now open to public use. The Vietnam government appeared to be ruling more effectively in the rural areas and refugees were moving back to their land in larger numbers.

When asked "What happens once the 9th Division leaves?" Major General Harris W. Hollis, the division commander, was quoted in a *New York Times* article as saying: "The mission for which this division was sent to the Mekong Delta has been largely discharged—that of dealing with the Viet Cong and the North Vietnamese until such time as Republic of Vietnam Armed Forces can take over this function. These forces, whom we have assisted, are now ready to do this."

The Navy meanwhile was well on its way toward creating a U.S. and Vietnamese force to keep the Viet Cong from using the vital rivers and canals. With the realization that no additional U.S. Army forces would be placed afloat the Navy had begun in late 1968 to search for other ways to use its great number of river craft.

Operation SEA LORDS

As early as December 1968 the U.S. Navy, in co-ordination with the Vietnam Army and province forces, had begun a limited program to keep the enemy away from the rivers and canals in western Long An and Kien Tuong Provinces. In July and August 1969 as more river craft became available, the Navy initiated Operation SEA LORDS under the control of the newly formed Task Force 194 located at Can Tho. With the formal disestablishment of River Assault Flotilla One on 25 August 1969 all but one of the barracks ships were returned to the continental United States and decommissioned. The repair ships were taken over by the Naval Support Activity and dispersed throughout the delta to support SEA LORDS. The boats of two river assault squadrons were turned over to the Vietnam Navy and the remainder were absorbed by SEA LORDS.

A study conducted in preparation for SEA LORDS determined that the principal water route to exploit for the purpose of stopping the Communist flow of supplies entering the IV Corps Tactical Area from Cambodia was the canal route linking Ha Tien on the Gulf of Thailand with Chau Doc on the upper Mekong River. This route, however, closely parallels the border and the risk of real or contrived border incidents dictated against placing a SEA LORDS barrier there until the plan had been tested in a less sensitive area. It was decided, therefore, that two parallel canals some thirty-five and forty miles southeast of the border would be used to form a double barrier and to inaugurate the SEA LORDS campaign. "Interdiction in depth had its attactiveness from an operations analysis point of view, and, at the same time, two waterways would be opened for friendly traffic. In conjunction with this barrier, river patrols would be strengthened from Long Xuyen through the Vam Nao Crossover to the Mekong."

The second objective of SEA LORDS—control of vital trans-delta inland waterways—would be accomplished by the removal of obstructions to navigation in the Cho Gao Canal linking the Vam Co and My Tho Rivers; by strike operations along the Mang Thit-Nicolai Canal, which joins the Co Chien and Bassac Rivers; and by reopening of the Bassac-Bac Lieu rice route in the lower delta. Penetration of rivers in the Cau Mau peninsula, the third objective, actually began before formal proposals were made to the senior adviser of IV Corps Tactical Zone, Major General George S. Eckhardt. A patrol boat incursion of the Cua Long River on 18 October 1968 is usually considered the first of the SEA LORDS operations, although a few earlier such operations were conducted by MARKET TIME.

General Eckhardt endorsed the Navy's proposals, and organization for SEA LORDS proceeded rapidly. Captain Robert S. Salzer, U.S. Navy, previously commander of the Navy component of the Mobile Riverine Force, was designated First Sea Lord and assigned a staff of nine officers and six enlisted men at General Eckhardt's headquarters in Can Tho. The Commander of Naval Forces, Vietnam, was given the task force number 194. Captain Salzer became commander of Task Group 194.0 and exercised operational control commencing 15 October 1968 of three other task groups: 194.5, Coastal Raiding and Blocking Group; 194.6, Riverine Raiding and Blocking Group; and 194.7, Riverine Strike Group. He was directed to designate one of the three task force commanders to command each specific SEA LORDS operation, with the commander of Task Force 115 usually expected to direct SEA LORDS invasions from the sea and the commander of Task

Force 116 the riverine strikes involving large commitments of ground forces.

On 2 November the first of the barrier campaigns, later given the name SEARCH TURN, was launched. Heavy craft of the Mobile Riverine Force and supporting ground troops succeeded in securing the waterways in a five-day operation that resulted in twenty-one Viet Cong killed and the capture of sizable quantities of arms and ammunition. A permanent naval patrol was then established, its main purpose to keep secure the western ends of the barrier and the network of perpendicular canals running north from Rach Gia to Ha Tien. According to intelligence reports, the principal Communist messengers passed through this territory.

While the operation was in progress other SEA LORDS forces were employed in clearing the Cho Gao Canal, which was open to navigation on 6 November. Later in the month Tan Dinh and Dung Island in the Bassac River were sealed off by a naval blockade while ground forces conducted sweep operations. MARKET TIME boats moved into areas in the Ca Mau peninsula that had long been considered exclusively the domain of the Viet Cong. The second of the interdiction barriers was established on 16 November 1968, and a third on 6 December 1968. Given the code name GIANT SLINGSHOT, this last campaign achieved the most dramatic and telling effects on enemy infiltration of all the interdiction barriers.

Thirty miles west of Saigon a peculiarly drawn border thrusts the Cambodian "Parrot's Beak" deep into Vietnam's III Corps area. The Parrot's Beak had long been known as a Communist base from which supplies moved across the border, and well-documented infiltration routes had been traced. These entered South Vietnam between the Vam Co Tay and Vam Co Dong Rivers; one turned south into the delta, the other east to supply the Viet Cong in the countryside surrounding the capital. The two rivers flow on either side of the Parrot's Beak on converging courses to the southeast. They appear to form a slingshot into which the Parrot's Beak neatly fits, hence the code name GIANT SLINGSHOT. For ground support in the GIANT SLINGSHOT operation, Rear Admiral William H. House, who had assumed the post of First Sea Lord upon Captain Salzer's departure, called on the commanding general of II Field Force, Vietnam, Lieutenant General Frederick C. Weyand, and got his endorsement and promise of help.

Because of the distances involved and because it was impossible to bring large ships up river beyond the low bridges at Tan An and Ben Luc, a new basing and support scheme was devised for GIANT

SLINGSHOT. An advance tactical support base was designed, consisting of three or more 30x90-foot Ammi barges on which berthing and messing facilities, storerooms, and a tactical operations center could be constructed and which would contain water purification equipment, generators, and other assorted machinery.

Advance tactical support bases were established at Tuyen Nhon and Moc Hoa on the Vam Co Tay and at Tra Cu and Hiep Hoa on the Vam Co Dong. The site at Hiep Hoa was later abandoned in favor of one at Go Dau Ha and in July 1969 an additional base was placed at Ben Keo near the important city of Tay Ninh. The USS *Askari* and the berthing and messing barge for underwater repair crews were at Tan An, awaiting the arrival of Mobile Base II, a sophisticated four-Ammi complex, specially constructed in the United States with improved berthing and messing facilities and equipped to make extensive boat repairs. The USS *Harnett County* provided support at Ben Luc for the patrol boats until the completion of a shore support base there.

From its very inception, GIANT SLINGSHOT was characterized by frequent, heavy clashes between patrol boats and enemy forces intent on maintaining the lines of communication to their Cambodian storehouse. Extremely large quantities of arms, munitions, and supplies were uncovered in caches buried along the river banks, proving beyond doubt that vital enemy infiltration lines had been cut.

The fourth and last of the interdiction barriers in the Mekong Delta was established on 2 January 1969 when naval patrols began operations on the La Grange–Ong Lon Canal from Tuyen Nhon on the Vam Co Tay River to An Long on the Mekong. Called BARRIER REEF, this operation joined GIANT SLINGSHOT in the east with the two interdiction barriers in the west, SEARCH TURN and TRAN HUNG DAO. The northern ring was then complete; the enemy was no longer free to move men and supplies with impunity from Cambodia into III and IV Corps areas. A naval "tariff" had been imposed on those shipments, measurable in terms of men and supplies captured or destroyed, but the supplies and men that were prevented from getting through cannot be calculated.

Once the barriers were in place, the boats were used to counter enemy pressures and probes. With relatively little disruption to existing organization and logistics, boats were shifted rapidly from one area of operations to another. For example in Operation DOUBLE SHIFT in July 1969, 105 U.S. Navy and Vietnamese Navy boats were quickly concentrated on the waters of the Vam Co Dong north of Go Dau Ha in response to serious enemy threats to the city of Tay Ninh. This sudden and impressive display of naval power, directed by the commander on the scene, Lieutenant Commander Thomas K. Anderson, U.S. Navy, was credited by the commander of II Field Force, Lieutenant General Julian J. Ewell, with having prevented the enemy attack on Tay Ninh from the southwest.

On two separate occasions the mobility of the boats was increased when giant Army skycrane helicopters were used to lift some of them into new areas of operations. In May 1969 six river patrol boats were skyhooked to the upper Saigon River, and in June six more were lifted to the otherwise inaccessible Cai Cai Canal. Both operations achieved tactical surprise.

As each operation progressed, concerted efforts were made to integrate units of the growing Vietnamese Navy. The military desirability and political necessity to "Vietnamize" the naval war were evident long in advance of SEA LORDS planning. It seemed obvious that the Vietnamese Navy's hope of relieving the U.S. Navy of its operational responsibilities in the war as soon as possible would be considerably enhanced by success of SEA LORDS. SEA LORDS was a remarkable organization which came to mean unity of command and rapid response to changing tactical situations. Relatively junior officers and men were often placed in positions of extraordinary responsibility. Tactics and techniques were developed and tested in the heat of combat, and at times even borrowed from the enemy. improved upon, and used to defeat him. The waterborne guardpost, for instance, was a refinement of the favorite enemy tactic of ambush. Using silent boats and night observation devices, the U.S. and Vietnamese boats stalked the would-be Viet Cong ambusher and trapped him. Imagination and leadership provided the plan and a dedicated collection of sailors, soldiers, and airmen made it work.

In addition to use in SEA LORDS, the United States rivercraft turned over to the Vietnam Navy at Can Tho were used to support Vietnam Marine Corps and Vietnam Army units in the central delta. Operations were conducted in the style of the Mobile Riverine Force, but greater emphasis was placed on leaving security forces in areas that had been cleared so that the Vietnam government could continue to control them. The Army-Navy Mobile Riverine Force, which had operated in the Mekong Delta since February 1967, was disestablished on 25 August 1969 and River Flotilla One and 2d Brigade, 9th Infantry Division, were inactivated. The experience of these units was inherited by SEA LORDS and ultimately by the Vietnam Army and Navy.

Armored Troop Carriers Move Up the My Tho River in the Early Morning

CHAPTER X

Conclusions and Summary

The joint river operations conducted by the U.S. Army and Navy in South Vietnam contributed to the success of the military campaign in the Mekong Delta and added substantially to U.S. knowledge of riverine operations.

The strategic concept embodied in the plan for the Mekong Delta Mobile Afloat Force and approved by General Westmoreland in 1966 proved sound and provided a workable blueprint for a variety of projects carried out by the Mobile Riverine Force in the two years it operated. The concept recognized the importance of the Mekong Delta and its resources to the whole conflict. Although the operations planned for the river force ranged from the vicinity of Saigon south through the delta to Mui Bai Bung (Pointe de Ca Mau or Camau Point) at the southern tip of Vietnam, early priority was given to areas in southern III Corps and northern IV Corps. In executing the plan, the Mobile Riverine Force was faithful to the priority assigned to the northern delta, but never carried out fully the intent of the plan approved by General Westmoreland to extend and sustain river operations south of the Bassac River. The operations remained primarily north of the Bassac River in keeping with the area of responsibility assigned to the 9th Infantry Division in that area; the increasing role of the 2d Brigade in the division's plans; and the decrease in operational control of the force by the senior adviser of the IV Corps Tactical Zone.

Perhaps the most significant organizational aspect of the Mobile Afloat Force concept was the integration of Army and Navy units to provide a force uniquely tailored to the nature of the area of operations. Specifically, the capabilities of the two services were used to the fullest by combining tactical movement of maneuver and fire support units by land, air, and water. To this combination was added the close support of the U.S. Air Force. The Mobile Afloat Force plan stipulated that these mobile resources were not to be dissipated on independent U.S. operations but were to be used in close co-ordination with other U.S. and Free World Military Assistance Forces.

The Mobile Riverine Force, which was the organizational implementation of the Mobile Afloat Force concept, was a fortuitous union of the Navy's River Assault Flotilla One and the Army's 2d Brigade, 9th Infantry Division. Somewhat controlled by circumstances, events,. and time, the alliance depended upon a spirit of co-operation and the initiative of the two component commanders in the Mobile Riverine Force. Guidance for the commanders was largely contained in the Mobile Afloat Force plan itself, and from the outset it was up to the commanders to make the plan work. Although many innovations were made to improve equipment and procedures, they caused little deviation from the basic Mobile Afloat Force plan. The most important innovation was the mounting of artillery on barges to provide the force with the direct support of an artillery battalion that was so urgently needed. Another innovation was the building of helicopter landing platforms on armored troop carriers and the use of a helicopter landing barge as an integral part of the forward brigade tactical command post. The adaptation by the naval commander of placing the Ammi pontons alongside the Mobile Riverine Base ships eliminated the need for cargo nets and enabled an entire company to transfer from a barracks ship to assault craft safely in less than twenty minutes.

The decision of Secretary of Defense McNamara in late 1966 to cut the requested number of self-propelled barracks ships by three eliminated berthing space for two of three infantry battalions. The Navy, however, resourcefully provided space for one of the two battalions by giving the force an APL—a barracks barge—and a larger LST of the 1152 class. The Secretary of Defense's decision could have been disastrous to the execution of the Mobile Afloat Force plan had these innovations by the Navy not been made. Even so, the brigade was forced to operate without the third maneuver battalion; the Army commander was obliged to double his efforts to secure the co-operation of Vietnam Army and other U.S. units in order to make the tactical operations of the Mobile Riverine Force successful. It can be postulated that this effort by the brigade commander to assemble a sufficient force consumed much attention and energy that could have been applied to other problems. It can also be argued that the shortage of men and the necessity to operate in conjunction with the Vietnam Army generated successes that might not otherwise have been achieved if the full maneuver force had been provided and if the force had operated less frequently in co-ordination with Vietnam Army units. Although the original Mobile Afloat Force concept provided for co-operative and co-ordinated efforts with the Vietnam Army, the shortage of troops increased the need for provincial and divisional units of the Vietnam Army throughout the various areas in which the Mobile Riverine Force operated.

It should be noted that the mobile riverine base provided for in the original plan made the force unique. When one considers that this Army and Navy force of approximately 5,000 men, capable of combat and containing within itself combat service support, could be moved from 100 to 200 kilometers in a 24-hour period and could then launch a day or night operation within 30 minutes after anchoring, its true potential is apparent. With such capabilities the force was able to carry out wide-ranging operations into previously inaccessible or remote Viet Cong territory.

The original Mobile Afloat Force concept had drawn heavily on the successful features of French riverine operations and the subsequent experience of the Vietnamese river assault groups. The Mobile Riverine Force was able also to capitalize on the knowledge of shortcomings of these earlier experiences. Both the French and the Vietnamese had used a fixed operational base on land. French units were small, rarely consisting of more than a company and five or six combat assault craft. Vietnam Army ground commanders merely used the river assault groups to transport their forces. Neither the French nor the Vietnamese had joint ground and naval forces. Both lacked the helicopter for command and control, logistic resupply, medical evacuation, and, most important, reconnaissance and troop movement. The river bases of French and Vietnam armed forces proved more vulnerable, especially during darkness, than did the afloat base of the Mobile Riverine Force. Finally, the Mobile Riverine Force, because of its mobility, strength of numbers, and Army-Navy co-operation, was capable of sustained operations along a water line of communications that permitted a concentration of force against widely separated enemy base areas. This was not true of the French or Vietnam Army riverine operations because of the small size of the forces and their dependence on a fixed base.

While the problem of command relationships did not inhibit the operations of the Mobile Riverine Force, it was a tender point in the conduct of all activities. Considering that the Army effort to develop riverine doctrine was not accepted by the Navy component commander at the outset, the Mobile Riverine Force might have been faced with insurmountable co-ordination problems, but such was not the case. Relying on the Mobile Afloat Force plan, each component commander had a guide to follow as to common objectives and procedures until doctrine was refined by combat experience.

No joint training for riverine operations was given in the United States because of lack of time and the wide geographic separation of Mobile Riverine Force units, but early joint training in Vietnam was planned. Fortuitously, this training commenced at the river assault squadron-battalion level under the supervision of the advance staff of River Assault Flotilla One at Vung Tau. Although the training in the Rung Sat Special Zone was under combat conditions, tactics and techniques were developed at the boat and platoon, company and river division, battalion and river assault squadron levels. During the period February–May 1967 the flotilla and brigade staffs were able to arrive at a common understanding as to organizational procedures and operational concepts. By starting at the boat and platoon level, the Mobile Riverine Force procedures were built on the needs of the lowest level units, and brigade and flotilla command and staff procedures were developed to meet these needs. With the 2d Brigade conducting tactical operations in the delta during the dry season of early 1967 and the flotilla staff co-ordinating the Rung Sat operations involving 2d Brigade battalions, both staffs gained valuable riverine experience independently. Later, as part of the transition into the Mobile Riverine Force, the advance staff of the flotilla joined the brigade staff in April at Dong Tam. This also provided a necessary step from the single battalion and river assault squadron level of operations to multibattalion, brigade and flotilla operations in late April and May of 1967.

The Mobile Riverine Force command relationships as published in a planning directive from Headquarters, Military Assistance Command, Vietnam, were a compromise to obtain Navy participation in the Mobile Riverine Force. Recognizing an ambiguous, undefined division of command responsibilities between the Army and Navy commanders, the directive compensated for this in part by instructing the chain of command of both the Army and the Navy at each level within the theater to insure co-operative effort. It also instructed the commanders at the lowest level, preferably at the Army and Navy component level of the Mobile Riverine Force, to resolve any problems that might arise. This planning directive, which incorporated the doctrine of close support and mutual co-operation and co-ordination, successfully established the tenor of what was to follow. The Navy was placed in a close support role that adhered closely to the Army principle of direct support. The Navy's decision in mid-1966 to make command and security of the Mobile Riverine Base an Army responsibility resolved a problem that could have become very difficult. Actually the Navy commander assumed tactical control only while the Mobile Riverine Base was being relocated. In all other instances he was cast in the role of supporting commander as long as Navy doctrine was not violated. The Army commander, acting in response to directives, operational plans, and orders from his higher headquarters, determined the plan of operations, which required the naval commander to support his objective. The major factor influencing the relationship between the Army and Navy commanders was the Navy commander's wish to operate independently of the 9th U.S. Division. This insistence provided the one element of disharmony in planning and conducting operations as an integral part of the land campaign for the delta. While it was never stated, it can be assumed that the Navy commander's position reflected the wishes of his Navy chain of command to have separate operations. In defense of the Navy's total effort, however, it can be said that the Navy commander was quick to accede to the basic concept of employing the Mobile Riverine Force in co-ordination with land operations. The activities of the Mobile Riverine Force, in fact, were directly related to the total land campaign being conducted in both III and IV Corps Tactical Zones. Joint operational orders were published and the relationship of the Army and Navy staffs in all planning and operational functions, including the establishment and manning of a joint operations center, was very close.

Perhaps the only area where a clear delineation of responsibility was not possible was at the boat and river division, river assault squadron, and battalion levels. The Navy river assault squadron organization did not parallel that of the Army battalion. Both the platoon leader and the company commander were dealing with Navy enlisted men, while the battalion commander was dealing with a lieutenant senior grade or a lieutenant commander without a comparable supporting staff equivalent to the staff of the battalion he was supporting. The Navy was thus placed in an awkward position, particularly in the event of enemy attack against an assault craft convoy. During the first six months to a year of operations, and prior to rotation of the initial Navy and Army commanders, it was normal precedure for the Navy element to answer directly to the Army officer in command during assault craft movements. The Navy craft did not use direct fire unless explicitly authorized by the brigade commander. As time passed and commanders rotated, however, the precedures established in the Rung Sat and in the first six months of Mobile Riverine Force operations became vague and ambiguous since they were not committed to written joint standing operating procedures. The difference in staffs below the brigade and river flotilla level fostered a centralization at the flotilla and brigade level in planning, control, and execution. While the Mobile Riverine Force operations gradually adhered more to the principle of decentralized planning and execution, future Mobile Riverine Force organizations should correct the disparity in the command and control organizations between echelons of the two services.

The first year of operations of the Mobile Riverine Force was highly successful because the original Mobile Afloat Force concept was carried out faithfully. The operations of the Mobile Riverine Force were wide-ranging—the force was in combat in nine provinces and the Rung Sat Special Zone. These were essentially strike operations against remote enemy base areas that in some instances had not been penetrated in force for two or three years. From these base areas the main force Viet Cong units and the political underground had influenced the local population whose support was vital to the strategy of the Viet Cong. Because of the bold and frequent movement of the large Mobile Riverine Base from which strike operations could be launched with ease, the element of surprise so important to combat success was achieved. In most cases enemy defenses and tactics were directed toward evasion or resistance to air and land assaults. Early riverine operations often capitalized on these enemy dispositions. Later, when the enemy learned to orient his defenses toward the waterways, the 9th Division commander provided the helicopter support necessary to enable troops to maneuver rapidly from the land side against the enemy. As the first U.S. maneuver unit to conduct sustained operations in the IV Corps Tactical Zone, the Mobile Riverine Force developed good relationships with the commander of the 7th Vietnam Army Division and elements of the 25th Vietnam Army Division. Co-ordinated large-scale operations were conducted in a number of remote areas, contributing to the erosion of Viet Cong strength, which before the advent of the U.S. forces in the area had been equal to that of the Vietnam Army. While the efforts of the Mobile Riverine Force were primarily concentrated against Long An and Dinh Tuong Provinces, key economic provinces for control of the delta, the force also was able to strike in Go Cong and Kien Hoa Provinces. Although only indirectly related to pacification, the limitations imposed on Viet Cong movement and the losses inflicted on Viet Cong units resulted in a reduction in the influence of the Viet Cong on the people in the area.

During the *Tet* offensive of January-February 1968, the Mobile Riverine Force was used in succession against Viet Cong forces in the populous cities of My Tho, Vinh Long, and Can Tho, which were seriously threatened. After the battles for these cities, the Mobile Riverine Force was credited with having "saved the delta" by its direct action against the enemy in these important centers before the Vietnam Army was able to rally its forces. Here again the fact that this large, concentrated force with its own base could be moved so rapidly over such great distances was the key to the Mobile Riverine Force's success against the Viet Cong in the IV Corps Tactical Zone.

During the spring of 1968 when the Mobile Riverine Force was placed under the operational control of the senior adviser of IV Corps, it again successfully penetrated remote areas. The IV Corps, however, had not the aircraft or supplies to sustain Mobile Riverine Force operations, and the force was therefore available only intermittently to the senior adviser of the IV Corps Tactical Zone.

When 9th Division headquarters moved from Bearcat to Dong Tam in August 1968, its mission was concentrated in Long An, Dinh Tuong, and Kien Hoa Provinces. (*Map 16*) With this focusing of the area of responsibility on the Mekong Delta, it can be assumed that the division commander strongly wished to integrate the Mobile Riverine Force into the divisional effort. Further, a renewed emphasis on pacification shifted the strategy away from strike operations, and as a consequence the Mobile Riverine Force largely concentrated on Kien Hoa Province. During the late summer of 1968 helicopters for troop lift were almost eliminated from the support of the force. The 9th U.S. Division decided to provide airlift chiefly for the other two operating brigades and to place almost total reliance on water movement for the 2d Brigade. This decision was a deviation from the initial operational plan of employing the Mobile Riverine Force for strikes utilizing boats and helicopters, a plan that had proved successful in the previous year's operations. Not until October of 1968 was the Mobile Riverine Force again provided with helicopters in keeping with the initial concept.

Restriction to one geographical area had limited the force in mid-1968, especially in respect to attempting surprise, and it was

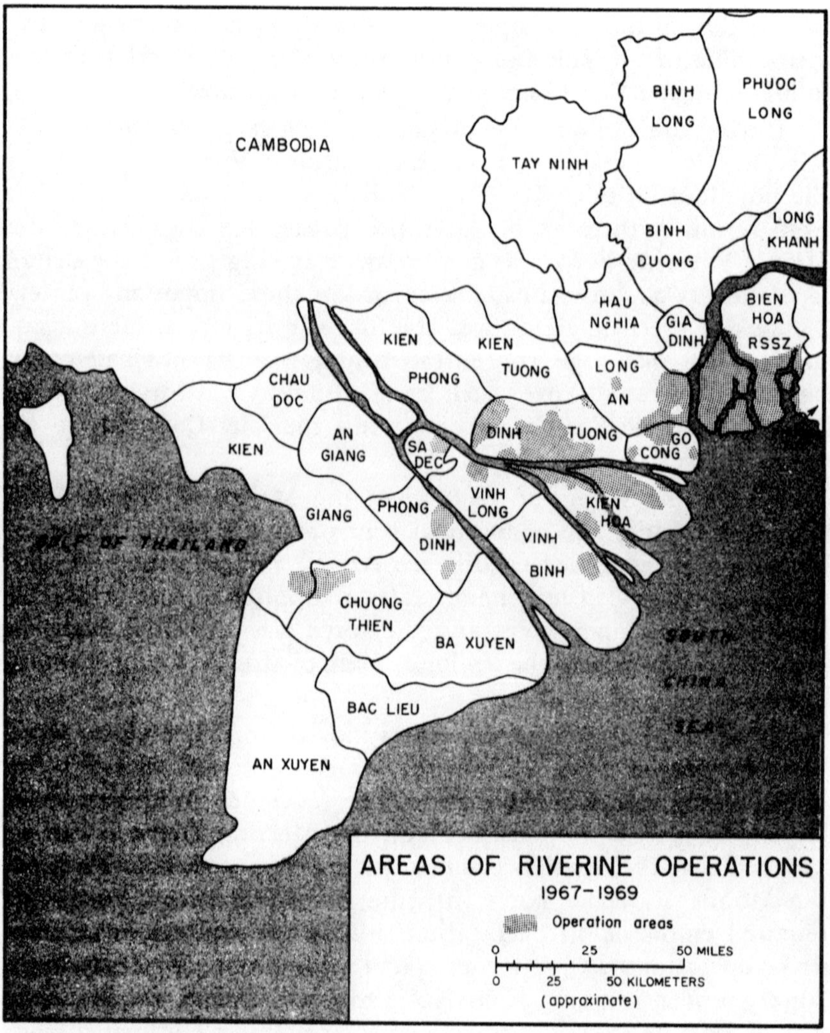

MAP 16

obliged to resort to other means of deception. The Viet Cong were able, however, to analyze and anticipate movements on the waterways, reportedly by using a warning system established along the banks. Because of limited and predictable water routes and a growing enemy knowledge of the Mobile Riverine Force, river ambushes became more common. When aircraft were lacking, the force was unable to retaliate except from the water. Nor was it any longer permitted to make the long moves to new areas as set forth in the Mobile Afloat Force concept. With the full use of helicopters beginning in October, the force produced results comparable with or superior to those of other 9th Division brigades and with the results obtained by the Mobile Riverine Force during its first year in South Vietnam.

The Mobile Riverine Force made significant contributions to the war in Vietnam. Its presence in 1967 and 1968 tipped the balance of power in the northern portion of the Mekong Delta in favor of the U.S. and South Vietnam forces. Dong Tam was developed as a division base without reducing the firm ground available to Vietnamese units in the delta and activities of the base increased the security of the important nearby city of My Tho. The Dong Tam area at one time had been under strong Viet Cong influence, and main force and local enemy units moved virtually at will until U.S. occupation of Dong Tam began in January 1967. As operations by battalions slated to join the Mobile Riverine Force continued, both the 514th and the 263d Viet Cong Battalions were brushed back from the populated area into the more remote Plain of Reeds. Even though the Viet Cong 261st Main Force Battalion was brought as a reinforcement from Kien Hoa into Dinh Tuong Province in June of 1967, the combined operations of the Mobile Riverine Force and 7th Vietnam Army Division kept the Viet Cong from moving freely around Dong Tam. Riverine operations inflicted significant casualties on Viet Cong units and made them less effective. Highway 4, the main ground artery of the delta, which was often closed to traffic in the period 1965 through early 1967, was opened and the farm produce of the delta, both for domestic and export purposes, could reach the markets. With the completion of Dong Tam Base, the 9th Division headquarters and three brigades were finally able to move into Dinh Tuong Province and the security of the northern portion of the delta was vastly improved. When the Navy extended its efforts to the Plain of Reeds and far to the west toward the Cambodian border in late 1968 and 1969, its operations were made easier by the earlier operations of the Mobile Riverine Force during 1967 and 1968. The Navy SEA LORDS operations evolved from the concept that fielded the Mobile Riverine Force and GAME WARDEN operations.

The Mobile Riverine Force wrote a distinct chapter in U.S. military history. The joint contributions made by the Army and Navy resulted in the accumulation of a body of knowledge that has been translated into service publications setting forth joint doctrine on riverine operations. In the event of future riverine operations, the service doctrine recognizes the need for a joint task force commander to provide unity of command. Those involved in the early operations of the Mobile Riverine Force possessed no prior riverine experience and were forced to rely on historic examples, their own judgment, and related Army and Navy doctrine to build a new American force. While basic service differences did arise from time to time, those immediately responsible at all echelons from the soldier and sailor on up found reasonable solutions and carried them out effectively and harmoniously to the credit of both services.

Glossary

AK47	Chinese-made rifle
APA	Attack transport
APB	Self-propelled barracks ship
APC	Armored personnel carrier
APL	Barracks ship, non-self-propelled
ARL	Landing craft repair ship
ASPB	Assault support patrol boat
ATC	Armored troop carrier
B–40	Chinese-made rocket
BARRIER REEF	The fourth and last of the SEA LORDS interdiction barrier operations in the western delta, commencing 2 January 1969
CCB	Command and communications boat
CIDG	Civilian Irregular Defense Group
CORONADO I	A Mobile Riverine Force operation designed to destroy Cho Gao District Company and enhance the security of Cho Gao Canal in Dinh Tuong Province, 1 June–26 July 1967
CORONADO III	A Mobile Riverine Force operation in the Rung Sat Special Zone designed to disrupt possible Viet Cong attacks on shipping in the Long Tau channel, 5–17 August 1967
CORONADO V	A combined airmobile, mechanized, and riverine operation in Cam Son Secret Zone, Dinh Tuong Province, and Ham Long District, Kien Hoa Province, 12 September–8 October 1967
CORONADO VI	An operation in the lower Rung Sat Special Zone, 11–18 October 1967
CORONADO VIII	A Mobile Riverine Force operation in Nhon Trach and the Rung Sat Special Zone, 27–29 October 1967
CORONADO IX	A Mobile Riverine Force operation involving deep riverine penetrations into enemy re-

doubts and sanctuaries to achieve decisive action in Dinh Tuong Province, 1 November 1967–21 January 1968

CORONADO X — An operation in which the Mobile Riverine Force responded to Viet Cong attacks on My Tho and Vinh Long, drove the enemy from those provincial capitals, then operated near Cai Lay on Highway 4, 18 January–13 February 1968

CORONADO XI — A combined riverine and airmobile operation to relieve pressure on Can Tho and locate and destroy Viet Cong units in Phong Dinh and Ba Xuyen provinces, 13 February–6 March 1968

Dinassauts — *Divisions navales d'assaut* (French naval assault divisions)

Duong Cua Dan (People's Road) — An operation by the 1st and later 3d Brigade, 9th Infantry Division, to protect and upgrade Highway 4 northwest of My Tho and to conduct reconnaissance in force operations on both sides of Highway 4 in Dinh Tuong Province, 16 March–30 July 1968

E8 — Expendable launcher. Lightweight and portable, it fires 16 riot-control canisters in each of four volleys, producing a rapid buildup of a large chemical cloud.

G–2 — Assistant chief of staff for military intelligence at an army, corps (field force in Vietnam), or division headquarters

G–3 — Assistant chief of staff for operations at an army, corps (field force in Vietnam), or division headquarters

G–4 — Assistant chief of staff for supply at an army, corps (field force in Vietnam), or division headquarters

GAME WARDEN — U.S. Navy (Task Force 116) operation designated to thwart Viet Cong use of waterways as supply and infiltration routes

GIANT SLINGSHOT — The third SEA LORDS operation, commencing 6 December 1968, in the Parrot's Beak

GREAT BEND	A Mobile Riverine Force operation in the western Rung Sat Special Zone, 13 June–26 July 1967
HOMESTEAD	A Mobile Riverine Force operation in Kien Hoa Province, September 1968
IPW	Prisoner of war interrogation
J–3	Assistant chief of staff for military operations, MACV
JACKSTAY	A U.S. Marine Corps operation in the Rung Sat Special Zone in late 1966
JP–4	A kerosene-based fuel for turbine engines
LCA	Landing craft, assault
LCI	Landing craft, infantry
LCM	Landing craft, mechanized
LCT	Landing craft, tank
LCU	Landing craft, utility, a light lift craft
LCVP	Landing craft, vehicle or personnel
LSIL	Landing ship, infantry, large
LSM	Landing ship, medium
LSSL	Landing ship, support, large
LST	Landing ship, tank
LZ	Landing zone
M16	Current standard American rifle
M43	Soviet-made rifle firing intermediate 7.62–mm. cartridges
M102	American-made 105-mm. howitzer
MACV	U.S. Military Assistant Command, Vietnam
MARKET TIME	U.S. Navy (Task Force 115) operation designed to seal the coast of South Vietnam against infiltration of enemy troops and supplies
MCS	Mine countermeasures support ship
MDMAF	Mekong Delta Mobile Afloat Force
Monitor	An armored gunboat armed with 20- and 40-mm. guns and 81-mm. direct fire mortars
MRB	Mobile Riverine Base
N–1	Navy flotilla officer in charge of administration

N–2	Navy flotilla officer in charge of intelligence
N–3	Navy flotilla officer in charge of operations
N–4	Navy flotilla officer in charge of supply
POL	Petroleum, oils, and lubricants
RIVER RAIDER I	An operation in the upper Long Tau shipping channel and in the southwestern Rung Sat Special Zone, 16 February–20 March 1967, the first joint operation of Army and Navy forces which were to constitute the Mobile Riverine Force
ROAD	Reorganization Objective Army Divisions
RPD	Chinese-made light machine gun
RPG2	Soviet-made antitank rocket
RSSZ	Rung Sat Special Zone
S–1	Adjutant of a brigade or smaller unit
S–2	Officer in charge of the military intelligence section of a brigade or smaller unit
S–3	Officer in charge of the operations and training section of a brigade or smaller unit
S–4	Officer in charge of the supply and evacuation section of a brigade or smaller unit
S–5	Civil affairs officer of a brigade or smaller unit
SEAL	Navy sea-air-land teams
SEA LORDS	The U.S. Navy's Southeast Asia Lake, Ocean, River, Delta Strategy Operations
SEARCH TURN	The first of the SEA LORDS barrier operations in the western delta, commencing 2 November 1968
SKS	Chinese-made carbine
TRAN HUNG DAO	The second of the SEA LORDS barrier operations in the western delta, commencing 16 November 1968
TRUONG CONG DINH	A riverine operation initially designed to drive enemy forces away from My Tho and eliminate enemy interdiction of Highway 4, 7 March–2 April 1968
WATER TRAP	A major cordon and search operation of Thoi Son Island in the My Tho River south of

Dong Tam during the first week of January 1969

YFNB	Large covered lighter
YLLC	Salvage lift craft, light
YTB	Large harbor tug

Index

☆ U.S. GOVERNMENT PRINTING OFFICE : 1985 O - 489-903

NOTES

JOSEPH SMITH *and* *the* RETURN *of* HEAVENLY MANIFESTATIONS

WHEN THE *Lights* CAME ON

Praise for *When the Lights Came On*

"The work that God set in motion through Joseph Smith is what Isaiah called a "marvelous work and a wonder," or more literally, "a miraculous miracle." This book by Trevan Hatch both delineates and celebrates the opening scenes of this religious revolution for what it is—truly a miracle. Through this work, readers will gain access to descriptions of myriads of manifestations and revelatory experiences so fundamental and foundational to the Restoration. It is a book that one will want to keep close at hand, one to which readers will return again and again."

—Robert L. Millet, Professor Emeritus of Ancient Scripture, Brigham Young University

"I absolutely LOVED this book. I could not put it down! The entire premise of the book is powerful and I found the organization and presentation of the evidences to be overwhelming. This is a book you don't just read—you *experience* it. It's a testimony building book. While I'm familiar with some of the stories and quotes referenced in this book, I've never seen so many new ones, nor have I ever seen them presented in such a context as this, nor with such comprehensiveness. Plus, it's very engaging and interesting to read. Trevan Hatch has written a truly insightful and valuable book that sheds new light and understanding on the restoration and the context behind it."

—Stephen M. R. Covey, bestselling author of *The Speed of Trust*

JOSEPH SMITH *and* *the* RETURN *of* HEAVENLY MANIFESTATIONS

WHEN THE *Lights* CAME ON

TREVAN G. HATCH

CFI
An imprint of Cedar Fort, Inc.
Springville, Utah

ISBN 13: 978-1-4621-1881-6

Published by CFI, an imprint of Cedar Fort, Inc.
2373 W. 700 S., Springville, UT 84663
Distributed by Cedar Fort, Inc., www.cedarfort.com

LIBRARY OF CONGRESS CATALOGING-IN-PUBLICATION DATA

Names: Hatch, Trevan G., author.
Title: When the lights came on : Joseph Smith and the return of heavenly manifestations / Trevan G. Hatch.
Description: Springville, Utah : CIF, an imprint of Cedar Fort, Inc., [2016] | Includes bibliographical references and index.
Identifiers: LCCN 2016012967 (print) | LCCN 2016015402 (ebook) | ISBN 9781462118816 (perfect bound : alk. paper) | ISBN 9781462126705 (epub, pdf, mobi)
Subjects: LCSH: Restoration of the gospel (Mormon doctrine) | Visions--United States--History. | Smith, Joseph, Jr., 1805-1844--First Vision.
Classification: LCC BX8638 .H38 2016 (print) | LCC BX8638 (ebook) | DDC 230/.93--dc23
LC record available at https://lccn.loc.gov/2016012967

Cover design by Shawnda T. Craig

Edited and typeset by Deborah Spencer

Printed in the United States of America

10 9 8 7 6 5 4 3 2 1

Printed on acid-free paper